The Promise of the City

The Promise
of the City

*Space, Identity, and Politics
in Contemporary Social Thought*

Kian Tajbakhsh

UNIVERSITY OF CALIFORNIA PRESS
Berkeley · *Los Angeles* · *London*

The author wishes to thank Timmy Azziz for
suggesting the painting that appears on the cover
of the paperback edition.

University of California Press
Berkeley and Los Angeles, California

University of California Press, Ltd.
London, England

Library of Congress Cataloging-in-Publication Data

Tajbakhsh, Kian, 1962–
   The promise of the city : space, identity, and poli-
tics in contemporary social thought / Kian
Tajbakhsh.
     p. cm.
   Includes bibliographical references and index.
   ISBN 0-520-22277-6 (cloth : alk. paper)—
ISBN 0-520-22278-4 (pbk. : alk. paper)
     1. Sociology, Urban. 2. Marxian school of
sociology. I. Title.
HT153 .T27 2001
307.76—dc21   99-056668
                                              CIP

Manufactured in the United States of America

09 08 07 06 05 04 03 02 01 00

10 9 8 7 6 5 4 3 2 1

The paper used in this publication is both acid-free
and totally chlorine-free (TCF). It meets the mini-
mum requirements of ANSI/NISO Z39.48–1992
(R 1997) (Permanence of Paper). ∞

Freud's personal life, a Jew wandering from Galicia to Vienna and London, with stopovers in Paris, Rome, and New York, conditions his concern to face the other's discontent as ill-ease in the continuous presence of the "other scene" within us. My discontent in living with the other—my strangeness, his strangeness—rests on the perturbed logic that governs this strange bundle of drive and language, of nature and symbol, constituted by the unconscious, always already shaped by the other. It is through unraveling transference—the major dynamics of otherness, of love/hatred for the other, of the foreign component of our psyche—that, on the basis of the other, I become reconciled with my own otherness-foreignness, that I play on it and live by it. How could one tolerate a foreigner if one did not know one was a stranger to oneself? And to think it has taken such a long time for that small truth, which runs against religious uniformist tendencies, to enlighten the people of our time!

Julia Kristeva, Strangers to Ourselves

The idea of the self as being (ideally) homogeneous, non-hybrid, "pure"—an utterly fantastic notion!

Salman Rushdie, Satanic Verses

در خلاف آمد عادت بطلب کام که من
کسب جمعیت از آن زلف پریشان کردم

Hafiz-e Shirazi, fourteenth-century Persian poet

Meaning lies counter to narrowed habit bound
For through life's disheveled strands was my meaning found.
Free translation by *Salar Abdoh*

Contents

Acknowledgments

There is an old Hindu saying to the effect that "when the student is ready, the teacher arrives." If true, then I have been fortunate before my time. Among the many friends and colleagues whose names could fill this page, it is only right then that I thank several people in several cities whose support and encouragement were critical in the completion of this long project. I was first stimulated to think about the theoretical dimensions of urbanism by Mr. Ronaldo Ramirez in London. In fact, I sometimes think of this book as the end of one conversation started at University College a long time ago. Professor John Forester in Ithaca and Professor J. B. S. Uberoi in New Delhi provided the opportunities to try out early versions of the ideas here. In New York, Professor Bob Beauregard has been an always reliable and astute critic of the many drafts and ideas I have passed his way. More important, he has shown by example what it means to be a good colleague, scholar, and balanced urbanite. Also in New York, Professor Ira Katznelson has extended to me the confidence and respect that all young scholars should be lucky to have. His willingness to engage graciously in intellectual debate, even if critical of his own work, has more than once brought to my mind Chaucer's Clerk: "Sownynge in moral vertu was his speche, / And gladly wolde he lerne and gladly teche."

Preface

When I arrived in New York over fifteen years ago, I pursued two interests, one intellectual and one professional. A few words about the tensions between these two concerns will help to clarify the context of the book.

The first area of concern was stimulated by a renewed interest in the socialist ideas broadly understood and loosely built around the Marxian tradition, itself a broader development of specifically Marxist thought. This reexamination seemed particularly pressing at a time of increased social problems and inequality resulting from the conservative policies of the 1980s. Many progressive intellectuals and activists in the city turned to Marx and other critical perspectives in response to these conditions. Ultimately, many came to rethink, revise, reassert, or even reject Marxist solutions for social and political problems.

During this time, I was also involved professionally with community-based organizations engaged in community planning and tenant organizing for affordable housing and other neighborhood-related issues. The mid-1980s were a particularly vibrant period for neighborhood and tenant organizing and grassroots initiatives for housing justice. The 1980s, especially in New York and other major cities, were the years when terms like "gentrification," "yuppies," "Donald Trump," "homelessness," and "skyrocketing rents" became for many familiar terms of discourse. By the mid-1980s, community-based organizations, most of which had emerged ten or fifteen years earlier, seemed to have coalesced into a loose, fragmented movement. Dozens of groups in neighborhoods around the city gave institutional coherence to the network of community-based organizations promoting a progressive urban policy agenda.

Yet a tension emerged between these two dimensions that did not seem to mesh very well. The socialist tradition, and especially its Marxian variant, was founded on the centrality of the working class, the labor movement, and labor-market dynamics for its vision and validity. Where and under what circumstances people worked was both the core problem area that held the secret to the "anatomy of civil society" and the "point" at which progressive politics should be based. All discussions in this intellectual sphere implicitly or explicitly revolved around this set of issues: the centrality of the working class to political life and the dynamics and contradictions of the workplace.

In the world of community-based organizations, which were staffed in many cases with Left-oriented activists, however, the issues were clearly *not* about labor relations, labor-market dynamics, class-based organizations, and "workers." The issues concerned, not production, but consumption: affordable housing, clean streets, safety, land-use conflicts, and the enforcement of housing standards, not wages or working conditions. The modes of action were rent strikes, lobbying city hall, voluntary actions such as neighborhood patrols, not industrial action or collective bargaining with employers. Most significantly, the actors were tenants and neighborhood organizations, not workers or unions. The targets and arena of action were primarily local government agencies, housing costs and neighborhoods, not business enterprises and workplaces.

In short, while the socialist tradition guided us to understand the class basis of power and policy and to appeal to class interests as a means of organizing movements for social and economic justice, the community-based issues did not seem to fit easily into this scheme. Why, I asked myself, were the labor organizations absent in the struggle for better housing in the most impoverished parts of the city? Why were community coalitions formed on the basis of common housing interests or common territorial interests such as neighborhood or district, not on the basis of shared class positions? What explained the gap between these two spheres, between an approach that focused on where people worked and another that focused on where people lived? Indeed, neither perspective made satisfactory sense of the other: community-based activity seemed to fall outside of Marxism's focus on the workplace (I finally understood the spatial implications of the notion of the "point of production"), while the urban, community-based focus seemed to screen out the wider political economy creating urban and housing problems. An entire set of issues about the relationship between where people worked and where they lived seemed to be missing.

For me, at the heart of almost all discussions lay the political-theoretical question of the identity of the social actors. As an urbanist, I saw that people's lives, networks, and identities were patterned geographically and discursively: not only was everyday life patterned across different sites of activity (work, home, community), but these different sites were contexts that transformed the meaning of actors' identities. How were we to make sense of the fact that Mrs. X was a "tenant" and a "worker," identifying as one in one context/space, as the other in another context/space? If we were to avoid falling back into methodological individualism and an essentialism of the subject, a theory of multiple personalities (of "schizophrenia"), or just avoiding the problem by adopting a descriptivism that took each separate element as unrelated and sui generis (as in conventional pluralist analysis), then some new approach to the notion of the patterning of identity was required to fully understand the reality of a heterogeneous and shifting, but nevertheless interrelated, terrain of urban political identities.

It was when a friend suggested I take a look at Ira Katznelson's *City Trenches: Urban Politics and the Patterning of Class in the United States* that I first encountered a formulation that put the separation between the workplace and the community at the center of its interpretation of urban politics and represented the most original attempt to make sense of the geographic dislocation of class identity.[1] Nonetheless, Katznelson's neo-Marxist reformulation remained unsatisfying. While it acknowledged the dislocation of identity with one hand, by reinscribing this within the Marxian class scheme, it took it away with the other. At this point, I found the reformulation of the socialist imaginary by Ernesto Laclau and Chantal Mouffe to be most helpful.[2] Here I found the most rigorous working out of the theoretical dilemma posed by the urban question as well as the conceptual tools necessary to clarify some key aspects of the urbanistic challenge to Marxian theory. Laclau's proposal that we trade in a theoretical agenda based on the priority of an essential identity (class, nation, individualism, ethnicity, race, gender, and so on) for the idea of identities and interests as hybrid, overlapping, mixed up from the outset provided a way of understanding the urban in terms of the spaces of the continual displacement and provisional rearticulation of the subject—a feature of modernity, moreover, no longer restricted by the boundaries of the city but characterizing all social spaces.

I had by now wandered into the debates over postmodernity and modernity within which the critique of Marxism was increasingly being conducted, shifting the principal terms of debate from economics to social theory and philosophy. Consider, for example, one controversy emerging from the debates over the foundations of social theory seemed particularly troublesome: if the realist, foundationalist theories of language and knowledge were to be rejected in favor of the historicism, nominalism, and instability of objects, and if the economic determinism of orthodox Marxism had been discredited, what would become of the so-called objectivity of social systems, such as capitalism, that appeared to "work behind our backs"? Given the postmodernist attack on objectivism and foundationalism, it seemed clear that accounting for the power of systems would have to be rethought in fundamental ways. Nonetheless, the sense that aggregations and stabilizations of power still were an important part of contemporary societies seemed hard to relinquish. Labor markets, the urban ghetto, land and housing markets, the power of the state, and the pathologies of normalizing administrative practices ("regulating the poor") still sat side by side with the increasing flux and heterogeneity of identities, the real virtuality (hyperreality) of urban representational practices, and the apparent loss of legitimacy of "grand narratives" of knowledge, progress, and a universal subject.

Here I found Jürgen Habermas's reformulation of Marx's analysis of structure and agency in terms of system and lifeworld useful.[3] Although it is controversial, I found this distinction increasingly useful in thinking about "structure" and constraint without recourse to the economism of the Marxian notion of structure. At the same time, it did not seem to pose too much of a problem to accept this systems-theoretical notion of structure while dropping the corresponding overly rationalistic idea of the lifeworld found in Habermas's work. The political economy of the city showed me that some concept of structure or system is necessary to account for the aggregations of power in the state and the economy, while the shifting mosaic of the everyday worlds in the city equally required the notion of hybridity.

The city is the emblematic space for the encounter with the stranger, the other, the different. There have been two major responses to this plurality. The first has sought to locate an element common to all differences and thus to reassert an element of universality. Faced with the bewildering, unsettling strangers of Paris, Rousseau condemned the public "masks" worn by urban cosmopolites and dreamed of a transparent society in which each person would come face-to-face with the true character of others in the community. The second response has not sought to transcend but rather to retreat from the multiplicity into securer communal enclaves. In Robert Park's famous observation, the city is "a mosaic of little worlds which touch but do not interpenetrate."[4]

Yet the city holds out another possibility, neither transcendence nor retreat, but engagement with the other, the different. But this cannot be simply the recognition of a multiplicity external to the individual or group subject, domesticated and retotalized within multicultural pluralism. This other city is a place where the different (religions, body colors, strange tongues, pleasures, histories) are respected, not "in themselves," but as the unreconcilable alterity internal to the subject. It is the place where one can "make oneself other for oneself," as Julia Kristeva has said.[5] In his remarkable book *The Uses of Disorder: Personal Identity and City Life,* Richard Sennett brought together in provocative ways the close connections linking the form of the city, the experience of diversity and complexity, and a cosmopolitan ethic based on the recognition of the contingency and alterity of the subject. We can only grow out of an adolescent desire for a purified identity freed from dislocation, instability, and pain, Sennett argues, in the diverse disorganization of the dense city, for "the great promise of city life is a new kind of confusion possible within its borders, an anarchy that will not destroy men, but make them richer and more mature." This is because the essence of urban life is "its diversity and possibilities for complex experience." Only in the unstable and shifting communities of urban life can one "attempt to deal with otherness, to become engaged beyond one's own boundaries of self." This idea of cosmopolis is a radical alternative to both social homogeneity and a plurality of suspicious and mutually exclusive enclaves— which in the end are the same.[6]

This book is the result of my attempt to think through these themes and their interconnections. It is also the expression of my conviction that the modern city has something to teach us about an ethic of pragmatic tolerance for the contingency and ambiguity of our identities, about helping us resist the final closing of boundaries around an idea or space.

Introduction

This is a book about ways of thinking about cities and city life. Specifically, it is about the potential of cities to offer men and women the ability to comprehend and master the complex, multicultural realities of the modern world. It is also about the ways in which the city and its components—markets, governments, communities, public spaces, individuals' social networks—can thwart and limit this aspiration. More specifically, it is an analysis and a critique of the idea of the city in that strand of urban social theory that has looked to Marx for its theoretical and philosophical foundations. The book has two primary aims: first, to give an account of the intellectual history of an important discussion within progressive social theory and to place it in relation to wider developments in critical social theory, and, second, to suggest directions for a post-Marxian critical urban social theory that can give better answers to the pressing questions concerning identities, space, and social structure than those currently available.

Marxian urban theory (or Marxian urbanism, terms that will be used interchangeably) is above all a theory of modernity and the urban process in terms of the relationship between capitalist forms of development and the spatial patterning of the institutions of everyday life. This body of work is concerned with understanding the effects of money and power (capitalist investment and bureaucratic planning) on the everyday lives of those who live and work in the capitalist city. Its chief goal is the integration of phenomena of urban spatial relations within Marxian class theory. For example, it seeks to provide a unifying framework that can capture the relationship between the variety of class, community, neighborhood, ethnic, or territorial forms of identity and group belonging that compose both the fabric of everyday life and the patterns of capitalist investment and urban governance in land, housing, and space.

Marxian urbanism's core thesis can be stated as follows: Because the modern city is one component of the larger capitalist social structure, the contradictions and antagonisms that emerge within and across urban space—which at first sight are organized primarily around neither economic classes nor production relations—are best explained in class terms. Conflicts over affordable housing, the fate of neighborhoods facing demolition, the distribution of resources among areas of the city varying by class, race, or ethnicity, and demands for greater community participation in local decision making express the contradiction pitting the interests of real-estate speculators, rentier landlords, and the local state in the greater commodification and valorization of land, housing, and space against the use values embodied in the homes and residential social networks of working people. By showing how the logic of investment and the circulation of capital shape urban political institutions and the spatial organization of everyday life in terms of the reproduction of labor power, and by demonstrating how urban conflicts, issues, and actors are in turn shaped by these urban processes, Marxian urban theory closes the gap between the apparent nonclass actors and issues and the purported class source of conflict.

Although the modern city is viewed as a mosaic of differentiated and overlapping spheres of communities, workplaces, and neighborhoods organized by status, ethnicity, and religion, Marxian urban theory rejects positions that claim that no one sphere has analytical primacy in the determination and explanation of social change, positions that abandon the idea of an objective set of social relations that structure forms of solidarity, consciousness, and identity. To do so would be to abandon the politico-theoretical implications of historical materialism in which the antagonisms that express a structural contradiction are linked to an emancipatory dialectical process of social change. Marxian urbanism thus retains the idea that class structure, identity, and interest formation are the central categories for understanding urban popular struggles and forms of power. As such, it is the perspective most strategically relevant to an emancipatory politics for the contemporary city.

This is the urbanism associated with the Marxian tradition, as well as that adopted by many other sectors of the Left, and it is the urbanism I challenge in this book. Focusing on the question of the identity of urban actors, I will argue against the primacy of class and for the limits of class—and for the limits of Marxian urban theory. It is important to emphasize, however, that the limits I have in mind are primarily theoretical, not empirical. My goal is not to provide empirical evidence of the prevalence of nonclass forms of urban collective action in a given situation. That such forms of action exist would not be very surprising, but it also would not be very illuminating, since it would not engage adequately with the Marxian assumption that nonclass forms of identity should be understood within a totality of displaced or disguised class elements. Rather, I argue that the patterning of social relations across urban space creates a fissure or dislocation—or as I will call it, borrowing a term from Jacques Derrida, "spacing"—within the very process of identification that forms the basis of group and individual identity. Because this spacing is constitutive of identity and is not the deformation of some prior essential identity (e.g., racial differences are not the fragmentation of a prior class unity but are constitutive of class), it thereby precludes the closure of identity around any single boundary or space.[1] The Marxian notion of class identity presupposes such a closure as a potential, if not an accomplished fact (that is, as a telos). The recognition of the constitutive nature of this dislocation undermines the claim for the analytically privileged status of class identity vis-à-vis other ones in the city.

I am not, it should be emphatically stressed, arguing against the relevance of class, if by this we understand a group that shares economic interests. Given the increasing inequality of economic resources and institutions, the organized collective action of subjects as workers pursuing economic justice is one indispensable element of a progressive political agenda. What I argue against is the idea, still retained by some sections of the Left, that class politics represents, or can in principal represent, the unifying category against the particularism and divisiveness of other identities. What I argue for is rethinking, not ignoring, class, rethinking the concept in the light of the social and theoretical developments of the last several decades that have brought the problem of coalitions to the forefront of both theoretical and strategic considerations. Stanley Aronowitz has summarized the concern of many who have realized that "the question for traditional socialism is whether it will be able to *theorize* its relationship to the new social movements" or be condemned to go along belatedly, in an ad hoc way, with the democratic demands of groups organizing outside the traditional working-class organizations.[2]

Weaknesses in the economistic and reductionist assumptions of Marxian theory, including its urban subdiscipline, have become widely recognized and debated.[3] Less clear are the alternative conceptual tools that should replace them. The works of the three authors I consider in the following three chapters, Manuel Castells, David Harvey, and Ira Katznelson, represent the most important attempts to meet the objections discussed above. They have sought to get around the problem of class and workplace reductionism by proposing revisionist models of space and class. This attempt has not succeeded, and one of the primary goals of this book is to explain why this is so. A critical urbanism building on the democratic socialist tradition cannot be rescued from the difficulties associated with a Marxian mapping of urban space and the spaces of the subject. At the same time, as will become apparent, imagining a new perspective cannot abandon some key questions inherited from the Marxian tradition. The chapters that follow examine the inadequacies of the most important responses to the critique of class reductionism and go on to propose alternate ways of seeing identity, structure, and space that avoid these shortcomings.

IDENTITY, STRUCTURE, AND THE SPACES OF THE CITY

People dwell, but not in the way that they choose. This paraphrase of Marx's well-known observation captures well the three key themes that underlie this book.[4] The first concerns the distinct, but related, questions of subjectivity, identity, and agency; the second, the notion of space and its role in the patterning of everyday life; and the third arises from the acknowledgment that there are systematic constraints on action—that we are not free to make ourselves or act in the world just as we would wish. The debates over the interpretation of these three dimensions—identity, space, and structure—are far from settled. Their conceptualization and relations with each other are the subject of widespread controversy and discussion in contemporary social theory. They play such a significant role because they relate to the most significant themes and controversies facing our societies.

THE PROBLEM OF IDENTITIES

Several factors account for the fact that the problematics of identities, subjectivities, and agency are at the center of political and social discourse today. By the end of the twentieth century, the cities of the West, especially of the United States and Western Europe, had become places where vast arrays of strangers were brought together, yet under sociopolitical circumstances significantly different from those characteristic of the last great wave of immigration, at the end of the nineteenth century.[5] These circumstances include the global migration to the cities of the Western countries, creating new patterns of cultural, ethnic, linguistic, and religious heterogeneity that are now challenging the integrative powers of the nation-state to assimilate, within fixed national boundaries, the increasing presence of diasporic, transnational identities structured around noncontiguous spaces. They also include the globalization of capitalist markets, creating new flows of capital and labor while weakening the ability of the nation-state to regulate either, together with the continuing dynamics of identity politics, which in the name of particularity compete with the universalistic basis of national or socialist class political organizations as bases of resistance to the homogenizing tendencies of global markets or bureaucratic defined roles,[6] and the persistence of racial and ethnic segregation and ghettoization of social space throughout the urban areas of the Western countries, which has undermined the idea of a unitary national identity of equal citizens.

This intensification of heterogeneity and difference—ethnic, racial, linguistic, religious—has raised many questions, particularly in the postcolonial context, where Europe is now decentered.[7] As the discourses and institutions of nineteenth-century industrialism and modernity, most notably the nation-state and class-based social movements and organizations, lose their structuring power over the lifeworlds of the inhabitants of neighborhoods, cities, and regions, questions over the integrative force of current institutions to embrace this apparent surplus of difference increasingly shape public discourse and debate. Between fragmentation and pluralization lies the anxiety over the figure of the universal, of the totality, pushing contemporary social thought to reengage with the question of identity.

The central motif in contemporary debates is without doubt the radical questioning of the foundationalist assumptions of philosophical and sociological discourses shared by both conventional and Marxian theoretical perspectives. This critique is by now widespread and well known, but its implications and ramifications for both theory and practice are still hotly debated and yet to be worked out. Nonetheless, several themes stand out. There has developed a greater sense that identities—who we are, personally, collectively—are best seen as self-reflexive projects of creating selves that are not there simply to be discovered or uncovered.[8] In this view, identities are not expressive of a deep "essentialist" core, but are best seen as contingent and articulated through interdependent and overdetermined practices structured by both conscious intention and unconscious desire. Indeed, many of these motifs have by now entered firmly into the social-theoretical consciousness of the age. Flux, fluidity, multiplicity, overlap, alterity, and hybridity, rather than fixity, natural-ness, and ahistorical essence, are the familiar terms in many of the so-called postmodern perspectives on identity. Whether this represents an (objective) illusion symptomatic of a period of capitalist society domi-nated by the commodity spectacle or whether it reflects the unlocking of the "others" of modernity—that is, the diversity suppressed by certain homogenizing tendencies of the modernist project—also is a central theme in the current debates.

The weakening of nation-states in the face of challenges from out-side (the global economy) and from within their borders (identity pol-itics), has put the status of democracy again in question. However, it has not eliminated the moral demand placed on all those who share a common territory and polity to enter into a public realm with some sense of unifying values and beliefs, however tentative and provisional. This democratic requirement sets the current experience of heterogene-ity off from previous historical periods, when although differences did exist, the problems of forging a public sphere and a common destiny and of entering into a mutual conversation over the destiny of the groups involved were absent.[9] This normative imperative continues to influence and structure the problem of a multicultural democracy today. For example, neither the idea of a single, universalist notion of the good nor a fragmented politics of difference is an adequate response to the pressing problems of collective decision making and problem solving in the context of the recognition of the irreducibility of multiple identi-ties.[10] As national governments minimize their regulative and welfare functions, this dilemma becomes increasingly an issue at the subnational levels of the city and the region.

One response to these dilemmas has been to adopt a perspective that takes complexity as the a priori feature of social identity. These approaches typically begin by deconstructing the so-called essentialist presuppositions embedded in political and cultural discourses so as to expose more clearly the fractured, overdetermined nature of identities, and they thus constitute many of the surfaces of emergence of the dis-course around identity.[11] The meaning of home, the crossing of the border, the journey of the migrant, have been added to the issues of security, liberation, and authenticity as the leitmotifs of the problem of identity today.[12]

THE SPACES OF DWELLING

To dwell is to live in relation to one's environment, landscape, and community within a certain space. One dwells in the multiple spaces of one's subjectivity, but also in between them, on the borders, in between these spaces. One dwells in and on one's body. One dwells in the spaces between oneself and the image of the other. To dwell "means to inhabit the traces left by one's own living"[13] in a memory of a time and a place. Although to be modern means to reconcile oneself to a kind of homelessness, nonetheless, to be fully modern means to make oneself at home in the maelstrom and confusions of modern life. As I use it, "the urban" is the name of the locus of the "experience of modernity." It names the everyday spaces of the city, the place of the encounter with diversity, strangers, the overlapping worlds of multiple allegiances, networks, and identities. The spaces of dwelling represent the second dimension examined here.

At the immediate empirical level, the spaces of the everyday are where people experience the world: homes, streets, neighborhoods, workplaces, public parks, "the city." Through and within these spaces, people experience, concretely, the abstractions of capitalist modernity. Recent social history scholarship has shown, for example, the extent to which the solidarity underpinning the labor movement throughout the nineteenth and twentieth centuries was crucially dependent in many cases upon the local communal bonds that tied together workers' experience in both the workplace and the residential community. These studies have shown that early working-class "culture" as a way of life depended on the articulation of the spaces of home, community, family, and workplace into dense social networks—a conclusion that eludes those aspatial perspectives that view the "point of production" as a unique source of identity for a working-class identity. As Marx and Engels saw, the emergence of the labor movement depended on the concentration of workers into factories and neighborhoods in which a sense of solidarity and common culture, beliefs, and interests could be articulated. Conversely, the decline of working-class organization and support (particularly in the United States) is in part due to the decentralization and diffusion of local communal networks by suburbanization and an increasingly differentiated and autonomous cross-class housing market (cross-class in the Marxian, but not Weberian, sense) in which workplace, residential, family, and communal identities are more distinct and separate.[14]

At the same time, recent theorists with sociospatial and philosophical perspectives on the city have argued that conventional ways in which space has been conceptualized are no longer adequate. Most important in this regard is the weakening of the local, bounded, physical space of the neighborhood or locale as the dominant scale for understanding individual and group identity, which the community-studies tradition took as its point of departure. The bounded community remains today as only one of a wider range of spaces that constitute identity and community. Inherited from the sociospatial conditions of nineteenth-century European and North American industrialization and urbanization, in which artisanal and working-class communities (as well as the nation-state) were spatially and socially bounded, this physicalist conception is no longer adequate for capturing the spaces of identity or power today.[15]

For many transnational, diasporic migrant communities, in contrast to those of the nineteenth century, individual and community identities are structured across multiple, sometimes contradictory spaces in complex patterns of imaginary representations and memory that suggest the need for a reconceptualization of identity and consciousness as fully constituted within fixed boundaries. For example, with reference to the Mixtec identity of migrants from Oaxaca, Mexico, to California, one writer has observed that the form that the new migration takes "erodes standard identities . . . and intersperses the self and other in interpenetrating spaces."[16] But physicalist assumptions persist in the face of changing conditions. A recent ethnographic study conducted in the community-studies tradition examined the public interactions of blacks and whites and the factors reproducing racial segregation and identities in American inner cities. It failed to examine the part played by the electronic commercial media, advertising, and other representations in explaining the patterns of behavior, however.[17] This oversight resulted from an exclusive focus on the bounded institutions of the local neighborhood. What eluded its vision was the fact that the ways racialized bodies are represented "outside" the locale, in television, film, and music videos, could in many cases be variables influencing the identity of local residents that were as important as or more important than anything occurring within "the neighborhood." Indeed, empirical studies employing social-network theory offer support for the idea of a loosening of the boundedness of the local community.[18] What is needed is a new imaginary to think the type of space and spatiality in these instances.

Many elements of contemporary social and geographic thought are extremely suggestive in this regard. Most important of these is the far-reaching reconceptualization of the boundary and the border in terms of undecidability, ambivalence, and hegemony. The critique of the conceptual assumptions underlying the dualism of inside/outside, self/other, and so on, provides many new ways to overcome the traditional ideas of nonpermeable spaces. Robert Park's image of the early-twentieth-century city as "a mosaic of little worlds which touch but do not interpenetrate," rooted as it was in assumptions from sociological objectivism, appears less and less relevant to a world characterized by identities whose primary ground is overdetermined, hybrid, and overlapping. This does not mean that identities cannot represent themselves in terms of rigid otherness or exteriority, or that, as in the case of racial or ethnic residential segregation, the promises of hybrid spaces cannot be violated. What it does mean is that such boundedness is not the expression of a preexisting identity constituted outside discourse, representation, or power but, on the contrary, the institution of a hegemonic closure and rejection of precisely those promises. The idea of spacing, rather than space, best captures these new modalities. Derrida has described spacing as "the index of an irreducible exterior, and at the same time of a movement, a displacement that indicates an irreducible alterity."[19] Rethinking the city in terms of the interpenetrating and the undecidable—that is to say, overdetermined—spaces of gendered identities can help lead us to a cosmopolitan ethic, an openness to the other proceeding from the recognition of the stranger within us.

THE PROBLEM OF STRUCTURE

And yet, however more potentially fluid and open the identity choices seem to be, these choices cannot take place in a vacuum of unconstrained possibilities. Marx sought to account for the most important macrostructures that shape the possibilities of individual and collective action, and many observers have followed him in identifying the capitalist economy as the most significant framer of meaning and action. Marx's theory of the role of the capitalist economy in shaping consciousness, action, and the possibilities of social change was considerably more far-reaching than the important recognition that proletarianization was the most important phenomenon in the lives of nineteenth-century European workers.[20] Marx explicitly sought to link two dimensions of modern societies: economic crisis and class-based collective action. The capitalist economy, taking on a seemingly independent life of its own, had broken away from the immediate control of individuals and communities. Its motions and regularities apparently followed an independent, invisible logic, abstracted from the discursive practices of the everyday. It worked (and still works) "behind our backs." At the same time, in linking the rise of the workers' movement to economic crisis, Marx implicitly tackled the more general problem of the relationship between what today we call structure and agency. He showed how the logic of the abstracted structures of the economy, through crises and the need to expand accumulation, disturbs the reproduction of the communal substratum of everyday life, ushering in resistance, protest, and, potentially, transformation.

Of course, the conceptualization of the economy and its relationship with forms of politics, culture, and ideology has been extensively debated over the last thirty years. Today, there is no question of maintaining a reductive topology in which the economy determines, even in a complicated way, a superstructure of social forms of life and institutions. Yet despite many cogent and compelling critiques of economic determinism, we cannot lose sight of the question Marx was attempting to answer. No serious account of obstacles to and possibilities of progressive social change can ignore the fact that there are powerful shaping macrostructures. Huge new agglomerations of capital and labor, finance, and resources are re-creating the cities and spaces within which we all must live. Far-reaching transformations and intensifications of the capitalist economy on a global scale and changing forms of state power are re-arranging settlement patterns, labor flows, and intergroup relations into new forms of urbanism with important implications for political realignment, cultural-political agendas, new forms of inequality, and exclusion, as well as creating new opportunities for change.[21] Symbolic economies of commodified fantasy and desire such as the Disneyfication of New York's Times Square drive many political-economic projects of urban economic development.[22] Saskia Sassen and Susan Fainstein, for example, have demonstrated the way global economic forces have transformed major world urban centers and constrain local policy options.[23] These forces appear to possess an apparent quasi-natural objectivity that is difficult for localities and regions to escape. At the same time, they create conditions in which neighborhoods and localities seek to resist the local effects and contradictions produced by these large-scale changes.[24]

Nonetheless, it is no longer possible to conceive of the economy as the determining structure in the old manner. The disagreement arises over how to describe its contents in a manner consistent with the critique of economism and how to conceptualize the "objectivity" of the structures in a manner consistent with the critique of essentialism. The first remains an area of controversy, especially within the Left. An increasing number of historians, however, are arguing that the social transformations of the modern period, such as the creation of the nation-state, urbanization, industrialization, and the development of a market economy regulated and constituted through law and institutions, are best seen in terms of the mutually reinforcing logic of the economy and state power.[25] Rather than view the state as a reflection of the functional needs of the economy, they view *both* bureaucratization and commodification as structuring forces. Modernity is thus seen through the eyes of both Marx and Weber.[26]

The second and more complex issue is the way that the apparent objectivity of the structure should be conceptualized. Many critics of poststructuralism or postmodernist perspectives, including most Marxian writers, see the thoroughgoing deconstruction of the objectivity or the "real" as leading to the abandonment of structure for agency, in which identity, consciousness, and agency are "free-floating," "unconstrained," and so forth. Many discourse theorists do indeed give the impression of throwing out the structural baby with the objectivistic bathwater. Indeed, it is regrettable that few poststructuralist analysts of social and political institutions (in contrast to philosophers or literary critics) have engaged seriously with the debates in social theory over the links between identity and structure. Yet I do not think that the charge that certain postmodern positions imply a return to idealistic premises is valid. Despite the undertheorization of the nature of structure, especially in relation to political and economic institutions, it is best to read most variants of discourse theory as attempts to rethink the notion of structure and to deconstruct the identity/structure dyad in ways compatible with the critique of objectivism. Nonetheless, this venerable problem of social theory (the problem of linking the macro and the micro, or social/system integration) needs to be taken up by an anti-essentialist critical social theory.

Taken together, these three dimensions, identities, space, and structure, define the project of critical urban theory and give rise to four related sets of questions.[27] First, how are we best to conceptualize social actors and explain the variation of social action and collective identities across time and space? Second, what are the spatial patterns of economic, political, and cultural institutions? What explains the geography and morphology of modern societies? What accounts for their transformations? What are the meanings of space, and how is it represented and used in everyday life? Third, what are the major macrostructures that limit and constrain social action and the spaces of identity? Fourth, how should the three dimensions be related to each other?

This book is an attempt to provide some answers to these questions. To do this, I focus on the Marxian tradition in urban theory because, although inadequate in many respects, it has been the most important response to this problematic. Accordingly, in the next section, I provide a brief overview of the contribution and limitations of this body of writing as a whole so as to provide the broader context within which the more detailed analysis of the work of the three major writers in the field should be read.

IDENTITIES, SPACE, STRUCTURE, AND THE LIMITS OF URBAN THEORY

Mike Savage and Alan Warde have summarized the main contribution of urban sociology and related branches of thought over the last century as the elucidation of the interdependence of the social institutions that form everyday experience in their contextual spatial settings.[28] Marxian urban theory emerged in the late 1960s as the most ambitious and important attempt to reinterpret this tradition of urban theory within a critical, normative framework. (It is not surprising, therefore, that Walter Benjamin's sociospatial readings have recently been taken up with much interest by critical urbanists. Benjamin's work converges with the central concerns of critical urban theory to unmask and rearticulate the meaning and experience of everyday life—in the streets, in the arcades, and in the parks—within the dynamics of capitalist modernity.)

To understand the reasons behind the emergence of Marxian urban theory, it is important to recall the dominant perspectives on conflict and power in urban political life in the 1950s and 1960s in Western Europe and North America, which were largely articulated from within conventional political science and urban sociology.[29] Robert Dahl's *Who Governs?* published in 1961, which provided a powerful argument for the pluralist nature of the local political system (and, by implication, the national political system as well), quickly became the dominant analytical paradigm, both in the United States and in other countries such as the United Kingdom. For the pluralists, the absence of widespread conflict in the postwar period indicated that the political system was competitive and open to new interest groups, that the distribution of power was noncumulative, and that there was a widespread (although not necessarily unanimous) consensus over the goals and values of public policy in local government. Urban sociology also advanced a largely nonconflictual view of urban life based on an ecological paradigm that in turn was based on biological and mechanistic models derived from the natural and physical sciences. In this perspective, the patterns and transformations of urban space (changing configurations of ethnic and class segregation, the spatial distribution of economic and political functions), explained in terms of an evolutionary paradigm of functional adaptation influenced by "natural" demographic and market variables, reflected an equilibrium of social, demographic, and economic forces in space.

The eruption of social protest around a range of issues, from the new social movements to the "ghetto riots" in the cities of the Western world in the 1960s, clearly rendered these frameworks inadequate. As Claus Offe has pointed out, interpretations that viewed all movements occurring outside formal political channels as the irrational and expressive demands of anomic deviants were at odds with the characteristics of most of these movements.[30] For example, the modernist values and goals of racial justice, equality, dignity, respect for environment, greater local autonomy, and community participation in local decision making espoused by largely working-class and middle-class actors did not support the theories of "irrational" collective behavior or of urban life as consensual and nonconflictual. Especially with regard to urban conflict and urban movements, the dominant explanations simply did not expect the emergence of conflict.

Marxist theory seemed to offer a more promising framework for understanding urban conflict, and both political and theoretical interest in it revived in the 1960s. It differed from the prevailing orthodoxy by seeing conflict, antagonism, and contradiction not as a breakdown of the system but as being at the heart of society and social change. Although Marxism expected conflict, it had more trouble with reconciling two distinctive features of urban conflict with the theory of class antagonism. First, the arenas within which the urban crisis manifested itself and around which mobilization occurred have been typically outside the workplace, in the residential community. Second, the social actors involved in urban struggles were not only outside labor organizations such as trade unions, but they could not be described as occupying uniquely working-class positions, being cross-class or multiclass in composition. These two factors represented a challenge to Marxian explanations of the urban crisis, an area of inquiry that up until that time had not been explicitly addressed within the Marxian paradigm.

Throughout Western Europe and North America in the postwar period, the dynamics of urbanization, real-estate investment, and speculation in city land caused the displacement of large numbers of poor and working-class people. It also brought an alliance of local government and real-estate capital, and in some cases local organized labor, into increasing opposition with local residents who mobilized to protect their homes and neighborhoods. Residents joined together to resist redevelopment, more often than not with little success. Although the participants could be classified as "workers," they were acting as cross-class coalitions of residents or as consumers of housing and space. Because these urban conflicts were over consumption items such as the right to housing and over space, the right to inhabit a locale, their relationship to the class organizations such as trade unions (or also, as in France, the Socialist or Communist Parties) was either nonexistent or fraught with tension.[31] All this added up to new actors, new social contradictions, and new challenges for progressive theory and strategy.

Contemporary observers confirmed the sense of important socioeconomic and political transformations. Reflecting on the Paris student rebellions, for example, Alain Touraine spoke of "new class struggles in new areas of social life such as urban life, the management of needs and resources, of education, which nonetheless were not economic conflicts. Today the working class is no longer the protagonist par excellence of historical evolution." Daniel Singer wrote that the French crisis (of May 1968) "does not confirm the extreme theories about the birth of a new revolutionary class taking place traditionally attributed to industrial workers, the proletariat. They suggest new splits, new cleavages, and new alignments reflecting new social contradictions."[32]

As the "city" began to take shape as an object and terrain of political and ideological conflict, Marxian theorists and socialist politicians took up the challenges of interpreting these new historical realities. Henri Lefebvre, one of the grand old men of Marxist philosophy in France, spoke already in 1968 of "the right to the city" and pointed to the transformation of industrial to urban society as the most significant feature of contemporary social experience. The Situationists and Guy Debord (their best-known member) made the spaces of the city the canvas on which a new antipolitics could be imagined.[33] However, the urban challenge for the Left was captured most systematically by the sociologist Manuel Castells, who was associated at the time with the revisionist Marxism of Louis Althusser and Nikos Poulantzas. He observed toward the end of the 1960s:

> We are witnessing increasing political intervention in the urban neighbor-hoods, in public amenities, transport, etc., and at the same time, the charg-ing of the sphere of "consumption" and "everyday life" with political action and ideological confrontation [that require] new tools of intellectual work. We looked for these tools, mainly, in the Marxist tradition. Why there? Because we had to answer questions linked to topics such as social classes, change, struggle, revolt, contradiction, conflict, politics. These terms and themes refer us back to a sociological theory at the heart of which is the analy-sis of society as a structure of the class struggle. But this theoretical prefer-ence (or venture) poses particularly difficult problems for urban analysis. For here the Marxist tradition is practically non-existent and the development of theory must be linked to the historical recognition of the new problems posed by everyday life.[34]

The Marxian urbanists who in the late 1960s and 1970s began to work out a new paradigm at the confluence of Marxian and urban theory sought to meet the challenge by demonstrating the links between the sources of urban social contradictions in the class-contradictory nature of capitalist society and the manifestation of these contradictions in urban conflicts and antagonisms. This was necessary because the new urbanization seemingly had severed the link between capitalist structure and working-class agency that had been most apparent in the industrial city. At the most general level, the task was, first, to show how the dy-namics of capitalist economic development create the institutions of urban governance and the patterns of everyday life, such as the separa-tion between workplaces and community residential spaces,[35] and, sec-ond, to then show how these urban structures shape new patterns of group identity formation and conflict among urban actors. Because urban social movements typically embrace issues of consumption (e.g., affordable housing, transportation), political autonomy and community control, and other quality-of-life issues, and not issues involving pro-duction relations, this argument was necessary to close the gap between the class source of social contradictions and the nonclass effects of the urban crisis.

At the same time, all theorists turning to this problem recognized, in varying degrees to be sure, the need for a solution that did not simply reduce the urban to matters of class. Sensitized to the problems of total-ity and reductionism by Althusser, Marxian urbanists embraced the need to develop a conceptualization of the urban as relatively autonomous of the class structure. The defining issue for Marxian urbanism therefore can be summarized as the problem of how to integrate the field of urbanism (the spatiality of everyday life) into the Marxian class scheme. At the risk of some simplification, we could say that what links all Marxian theorists of the city is the need to specify a nonreductive relation between the structures and practices that take place at the workplace and the community residence. Why is this? It springs directly from the dual concerns of Marxian theory and urbanism: class and space. As I will demonstrate in Chapter 1, there is an implicit spatial assumption built into the Marxian notion of class, despite the fact that it has been neglected in most debates over class. The Marxian class concept implicitly conflates the abstract notion of class and the institutional and discursive space of the workplace as it developed in Western industrial society. This is not a contingent feature of Marxian theory, as Erik Olin Wright has pointed out.[36]

The physical and discursive separation of workplaces and residential communities is the hidden gap or fissure, the "spacing," in the Marxian concept of class. The modalities of this fissure (or "lack") form the subject of the chapters to follow. Here it is sufficient to point out that all three theorists that I examine below, the leading theorists of Marxian urbanism, take this separation between work and home more or less explicitly as the key problem to be solved. For example, David Harvey has described the goal of Marxian urban theory as the need "to illuminate . . . the vexing questions that surround the relationship between community conflict and community organizing on the one hand, and industrial conflict and work-based organizing on the other." Ira Katznelson's argument in *City Trenches* proceeds from the observation that "American urban politics has been governed by boundaries and rules that stress ethnicity, race and territoriality, rather than class and that emphasize the distribution of goods and services, while excluding questions of production or workplace relations. *The centerpiece of these rules has been the radical separation in people's consciousness, speech, and activity of the politics of work from the politics of community.*" And Manuel Castells has observed that "while the forefront of the process of industrialization was occupied by the struggle between capital and labor to share the product and to shape the state, the backyards of the growing cities were the scene of a stubborn, often ignored resistance by residents to keep autonomy in their homes and meaning in their communities." Castells concludes that "neither the assimilation of urban conflicts to class struggle nor the entire independence of both processes of social change can be sustained. . . . Only by focusing on the interaction between the social dynamics of class struggle and the urban dynamics whose content must be redefined in each historical situation, are we able to understand social change in a comprehensible way."[37]

Between the late 1960s and the late 1980s, emerging in several disciplines and in several national contexts, the Marxian approach in urban theory has made important contributions to our understanding of urban processes.[38] Several questions about cities that we would want to ask would seem difficult to answer without at least some Marxian approaches. These questions concern developments such as the historical patterns of urbanization and city growth that correlate well with large-scale epochal changes such as from feudalism to capitalism (at least in Western Europe and North America), the vast increase in global urbanization since the early nineteenth century, transformations in land use and social geography during the period of industrialization, and cycles of urban decay and renewal. Employing the concept of the reproduction of labor power, the Marxian approach has exposed the structural links between the production spaces of the workplace and the consumption spaces of the community and family and home. The classic distinction between use value and exchange value has been applied to local community, neighborhood, and housing struggles to suggest the contradiction that pits local poor, minority, and working-class residents against property developers and land speculators. Marxian analysts have shown how tightly knit, bounded communities, in the workplace and in the residential community, can create the solidarity required for class-based collective action. Marxian analysis has clarified the contradictory functions of the local state in reconciling consumption and quality-of-life issues with the need to encourage accumulation. The focus on the spatial dimension of the circulation of capital has helped urban theory move away from an evolutionary model of urban change to one that recognizes the role of crises in the rhythms of capital accumulation. This has contributed to explanations of phenomena such as gentrification and abandonment in terms of combined and uneven development, that is, as interrelated phenomena.[39] Moreover, understanding the spatial distribution of economic resources and investment illuminates the geography of inequality and justice as one aspect of the contradictory and crisis-prone dynamic of the capitalist economy.[40]

Despite these strengths, today the Marxian paradigm has lost much of its power. Whereas at its inception it set the parameters for critical urban analysis, by the 1990s, the picture had changed so dramatically that several critics could claim that the Marxian tradition had reached an impasse. For example, Savage has argued that much work in this tradition

> appears totally innocent of the issues raised in social theory by the feminist critique of Marxism, by poststructuralism and postmodernism, and politically by the collapse of communism. [We] must surely face up to current intellectual and political challenges, rather than ignore them. It is . . . the collapse of certainty, of the instability of meanings and values, of constant change and flux which have been brought back into focus. Surely a more adequate response . . . would involve relating issues arising from Marxist cultural criticism with the concerns of urban sociology and urban studies, and . . . breaking with historical narrative.[41]

In reviewing new directions in urban analysis Nigel Thrift makes some similar points. For example, of Sharon Zukin's influential work, he writes:

> Strangely, for all the postmodern trappings of *Landscapes of Power,* it seems to me, rather like Harvey's (1989) *The Condition of Postmodernity,* to have taken remarkably little of the substance of postmodernism on board. Of course some might applaud this stance but more emphasis on work concerning issues like power and the self, consumption and subjectivity, and place as an absent presence, derived from poststructuralist tenets of various kinds, might have helped rather than hindered Zukin's case.[42]

While predictably useful in illuminating the economic dynamics that influence the spatial patterning of social life,[43] the Marxian branch of urban theory has had difficulty capturing the overdetermined nature of agency and identity, developing a nonreductive concept of state power and cultural representation, and breaking with an objectivistic notion of interests and social agency. Of course, these problems are not unique to Marxian urbanism, overlapping in considerable degree with the widespread debates within the Left and among social theorists over the last three decades. Yet, in addition to the problem of breaking with an objectivistic notion of geographic space, they remain the key unresolved questions facing Marxian urban theory.

The first problem presents itself typically in terms of relating workplace and community-based identities, for example, in trade unions and neighborhood organizations such as tenant organizations or movements for greater neighborhood autonomy from central and/or local government. The debate over the nature of urban identity vis-à-vis class has revolved around the question of autonomy or primacy. Urban identities are viewed either as a displaced manifestation of class identities or, where an alternative has emerged, as a basis of action analytically distinct from class, although the latter strictly speaking no longer falls within a Marxian framework. Neither of these solutions avoids the problem of essentialism, and an approach that can capture the way in which identities overlap and are overdetermined is necessary to understand the way group identities interrelate within the mosaic of the city.

The critiques of the reductionist views of the state and governmental action as derivative of the needs of capitalist economic relations are well known and do not need rehearsing here. As a variety of writers have pointed out, deriving the state and government policies from the functional needs of capitalist accumulation does not do justice to the interplay of the economy, the state, and the urbanization process. What is important in the present context is to recognize that for the most part, Marxian urban theory has embraced this reductionist conception of the state, and with it the notion that the principal structuring macroelement in social life remains the capitalist economy. Although economic determinism can be rejected, as an analytical point of departure, the problem of theorizing the relative autonomy of the state remains.

As far as the treatment of space is concerned, Marxian urbanism has tended to operate with a notion of bounded space similar to that of the community-studies tradition. However, the notion of absolute space, that is, as a container of social relations—while working well for some localities that are similar to the small, bounded, artisanal and proletarian communities of the nineteenth-century industrial city—is by itself inadequate to capture the dynamics of identification and social networks in contemporary conditions.

Marxian urban theory has thus inherited, however ambivalently, the answers given to the three questions of identity, space, and structure by the classic Marxian scheme: How should the range of collective identities be understood? What is the role of space in social relations? What are the key constraints and structuring conditions in social life? Katznelson has shown how, by building on Engels's early work on Manchester, the tradition of Marxian urbanism has answered the three questions in terms of linking the variations in working-class formation, the changes in the physical space of the city and in the social institutions of everyday life (the pattern of workplaces, homes, public spaces), and transformations in class structure and capitalist development.[44] Engels's account of how the spatial class structure of industrial capitalism and working-class neighborhoods permitted the sharing of ways of life (what we would today call social networks) pioneered a critical urban social theory by

pointing out how space both mediates structure and agency and con-
structs class identity by distributing and separating subjects across the
urban landscape.

The most important part of this legacy remains the three questions
that lie behind the particular answers given by Marxian urban theory.
The answers themselves—the primacy of class identity, a bounded, physicalist conception of space, and the primacy of the capitalist economy as
the structure of modernity—are no longer adequate. What this suggests,
then, is a shift in the terms of analysis and a concomitant transformation of the agenda of critical urban theory. I am proposing a perspective
that can provide three new answers to the three old questions, answers
that can capture identities that are more fluid, multiple, overdetermined,
or "hybrid," rather than reduced to class, provide a conception of space
that can embrace the representational and imagined, as well as the physical dimensions of the urban with ambivalent, undecidable boundaries,
and identify the repressive effects of "normalization," surveillance, and
overadministration of everyday life that result from the logic of bureaucratization, which now acts alongside commodification as an independent source of the dislocation of settled or sedimented social relations,
identities, and cultural traditions. These three dimensions not only provide the architecture and key concerns of the present book, they also constitute the principal themes in current critical urban theory.

EMERGING THEMES IN CRITICAL URBAN THEORY

Since the high point of the influence of Marxian political economy within
critical urban theory in the 1970s and 1980s, attention has shifted to
what is typically viewed as the "cultural" terrain of constructing cities:
symbolism, representations, the role of the electronic and other popular
media in defining the city and its problems, the everyday practices of
marginal and subaltern populations, such as maintaining oppressed
migrants' home-style architecture and neighborhood associations, and
so on. Some observers have interpreted this shift as the emergence of a
new paradigm, resulting from broader developments in social theory,
from which urbanism has usually imported its conceptual resources, that
have given greater attention to the cultural dimension, the persistence of
racial, ethnic, and other forms of identity politics that emphasize cultural goals and social recognition alongside questions of economic redistribution, as well as the waning of the "urban social movements" organized around local public-consumption goods as significant players in

the local politics of the Western countries.[45] The city is viewed less as a given, a scientific object of inquiry amenable to discoverable laws of motion, than as the site of conflicting cultural, aesthetic, political, and economic discourses competing over the meaning of "the city."

Many of the consequences of this shift are positive and illuminating. From cultural studies, for example, urban sociologists, critical human geographers, and, to a lesser extent, urban political analysts have embraced semiotics and other methodologies of textual analysis, seeing the city as text and deconstructing the representations of the city, its contours, contradictions, and inhabitants, within dominant economic and political discourses.[46] Some writers have begun problematizing the role of the interpreter-analyst in representing/constituting the object of "the city."[47] There has been much more explicit attention given to the problematics of space: how it should be conceptualized, what role it should play in our conceptual frameworks, the significance of the metaphorical dimension of spatial terms such as the "border," "margins," "fissures," and "outside/inside" that play a large role in the new cultural politics of difference.[48] An important implication of these new perspectives is the deconstruction (loosely understood) of the city as a unified object: there are as many cities as there are interpreters of the urban text. At the same time, in the best works, questions of economic structure and the material distribution of resources have, appropriately, not been ignored but have been reread through the cultural lens. The economy is viewed as symbolically constructed, as are images and popular understandings of minorities, the poor, and the ghetto. As Christine Boyer suggested in *Dreaming the Rational City,* the city is better seen not only as a place within which power is deployed but also as the object and effect of power.[49]

Sharon Zukin, for example, has shown how the economic development strategies of the "global" city now depend as much on promoting symbolic and cultural institutions, such as museums, Disneyfied public spaces, and recreational park spaces, as on traditional economic institutions.[50] The strength of Zukin's analysis is the way it allows us to see that cultural representations are now part of the economic structure. For example, the urban revitalization strategies of U.S. cities in the face of depopulation and deindustrialization depend not simply on attracting labor, households, and capital but also on developing an attractive image through cultural and representational strategies that reflect inequalities of power defining "whose city" it is. In his most recent work, Castells has offered a new image of the city as a node within a global network or space of flows of information, complete with the "black holes" of the

infoghetto.[51] Fredric Jameson and David Harvey, despite the reductionism of their orthodox Marxian models, have pointed to the close connections between the aesthetics of the contemporary city and current
regimes of capital and power. In his most recent work, Harvey has shown
the close connections between urbanism, capitalism, and problems of
ecology and the environment.[52] Similarly, Mike Davis's provocative, if
disproportionately pessimistic, City of Quartz might be said to have
brought together Marx and Foucault to excavate a Los Angeles of capitalist surveillance.[53] A renewed interest in bringing the political economy approach to bear on the local political institutions of liberal democratic regimes promises new policy and normative insights.[54] From a
different direction, critical human geographers such as Edward Soja and
Derek Gregory have drawn on postmodern theory to open new ways of
reading the city in terms of the multiple historico-geographies that constitute the spaces of the subject, arguing for a nontotalizing view of the
city as an object that cannot be apprehended from one point.[55] The politics of locations and margins, so central to contemporary cultural politics, has entered the city, as well. Feminist urbanists and geographers
have provided ways for us to think about space as irreducibly gendered.[56]
Others have sought to develop perspectives drawing on a wide range of
ideas derived from phenomenology, hermeneutics, semiotics, and
thinkers such as Benjamin, Foucault, Lefebvre, and Michel de Certeau.
Taken together, these new departures provide many important insights
and directions for a post-Marxist critical urban social theory.

They nevertheless come with several limitations, too. One is the poorly
integrated relationship between what is viewed as "material" issues (economic relations, resources, and inequality) and cultural issues (meaning,
ideologies, representations). The danger here is the opposite of the reduction of these two moments into a base/superstructure scheme. Instead,
the sense of totality and determination in these newer writings hovers
between leaving unelaborated and ad hoc the place of the macrostructure
in the theory and falling back into a base/superstructure model, which
after all never implied one should not take superstructural elements seriously, but only told us what these really "represented." Although I cannot do justice here to the rich variety of these emerging perspectives, I
would point to three main limitations of the current literature. First, the
three-tiered agenda of linking agency, space, and structure in social theory is rarely explicitly taken up in the new writing. Indeed, with the rejection of reductionist and essentialist assumptions of past theory, this
broader agenda also has been discarded. To an extent this reflects the

suspicion of all forms of totalizing knowledge, some of which concerns I share. The type of comparative "triangulation" that such a research agenda suggests does indeed harbor certain positivistic tendencies. Nonetheless, no serious account of the systematic and oppressive features of contemporary social structures and possibilities for reform can do without an understanding of the way these three dimensions influence and delimit each other. At any rate, I do not see why a provisional set of answers, subject to revision and falsification (leaving all the difficulties of such a definition of scientificity aside for the moment), need fall into the objectivistic trap.

Second, there is an undertheorizing of bureaucratization as a structuring moment of contemporary urban life. Coherent notions of state power and its relations to the economy and forms of identity, culture, and tradition are inadequately developed. In this respect, much (although by no means all) of the new postmodern urban literature appears to abandon structure for agency. Where structure is accounted for, attention is focused exclusively on the economy, leaving the state as a residual or derivative aspect of the structure. Of course, it has now become widespread to reject the idea of locating a single source of power. Following Foucault, power is seen as dispersed, capillary, rhizomatic. But this should not blind us to the systematic aggregation and concentration of power into institutions that are relatively stable over time. (I return to this problem in more detail in Chapter 2.) The one-sided emphasis on agency results from, first, the absence of a more satisfactory notion of structure to replace the economic determinism derived from the Marxian model and, second, an inadequate deconstruction of the agency/structure dyad. To move from one pole to the other does not escape the framework within which both are constituted.

The third limitation concerns the absence of a vocabulary for the more elusive dimensions of the self, or the unconscious, in almost all recent formulations concerning the spaces of identity of the subject. Slavoj Žižek has pointed out how the postmodern fascination with the surface, in conjunction with a fear of all "depth models" of the subject, results in a neglect of the fact that the surface of a text (social, urban, film, biological) harbors a deficiency and a lack.[57] However, this is not the lack that a signifier would fill (for which the surface text would be the signified, or "stage of representation" to use Derrida's phrase) but a constitutive lack that nonetheless suggests that in the "surface" there is something that always escapes the eye.[58] Thus, in a pure postmodern politics of plurality and difference (as well as in economistic models of rational choice),

subjects are conceived along fully intentional lines. In contrast, the appeal
of Walter Benjamin's work lies especially here, since for him, "reading
the urban text is not a matter of intellectually scrutinizing the landscape;
rather it is a matter of exploring the fantasy, wish-processes and dreams
locked up in our perception of cities."[59] By spatializing and socializing
the Proustian project of desedimenting the determinations of the past on
the subjective meanings of the present, Benjamin presents an approach
to our lived environment that brings together subject, structure, and
space in wholly new and illuminating ways. Bringing in the psychic reg-
ister of the unconscious, moreover, helps modify the postmodern "notion
of the mobile subject, open to an infinitude of contradictory identifications."[60] As we will see, the partial fixity brought about by identifica-
tory alignments—the psychoanalytical mechanism in which an identity
is taken up by the subject—will help us think in new ways about identity, but also about structure.

The recent work of Michael Peter Smith is a good illustration of the
strengths and limitations of the new postmodern urban theory. Writing
in the context of the United States, Smith aims to develop a postmodern
urban social theory with three main objectives. First, the theory should
be able to explain the more complex, fluid, heterogeneous nature of ethnic and racial formation and identity choices in the context of a global-
izing economy and new patterns of international migration. Second, it
should avoid reducing the dimensions of symbolism, meaning, and action
to an effect of an objective context or structure. And third, it should thematize the power and role of the authorial voice of the social scientist in
the representation of subjects' everyday experience.[61]

Smith rejects views that understand the behavior and identity of social
actors solely in terms of the influence of external forces. Rather than locate
the sources of power relations in "big structures" (to echo Charles Tilly's
phrase), in the nation-state, the relations of production, or the global economy, postmodern ethnography focuses attention on power relations in
the microlevels of the symbolic dimensions of everyday life. These power
relations are embodied in representations, in a variety of discourses such
as music, video, and film, in "concrete" practices such as the coping strategies of poor migrant households, and in communal forms of solidarity at
the level of everyday, urban, space-time. These practices (the "weapons
of the weak") potentially can be expressions of opposition and resistance
to capitalist reproduction at the global and local levels—a fact missed by
a Marxism fixated on the organized class struggle. According to Smith,
analysts should focus on the ways actors negotiate within and then mod-

ify the structural constraints within which they find themselves. Understanding these micronegotiations requires close-grained analysis of the localities where the interchanges between structure and agency are played out. In this view, the urban is the metaphor for the locus of the interaction of structure and agency. Although influenced by economic transformations, state restructuring, and demographic migration, identities are constituted within and across multiple, competing, and overlapping "discursive practices" (race, gender, class, ethnicity, sexuality, locality, nation, and so on) concretized at the level of the local community.

For Smith, postmodern ethnography is the appropriate basis of a new urban theory for two principal reasons. First, by operating with a poststructuralist theory of language, it can capture the flexible and multiple identities embraced by postmodern subjects. Second, by asking people to delineate and reveal the opportunities and constraints they face in making meaning of their lives, that is, by taking as its starting point the "constitution of subjectivity," postmodern ethnography resolves the micro/macro, structure/agency problem. Because it assumes that "the context of social life is no less a social construct than the narrative texts of people's everyday life," it permits the analyst to "read" the refracted presence of objective structures (the imperatives of the labor market, the administrative domination of the bureaucracy, the border police) straight out of the subjects' experiences. Smith recognizes that it is important to address the "objectivity" of social systems, but this is best approached through postmodern ethnographic methods, by which "the investigator can intersubjectively experience the lived contradictions of the larger social system as they are 'imploded' into the social relations and everyday life of the ethnographic subject." Following Foucault, Smith maintains that "the distancing of grand theory from its subjects of inquiry objectifies and therefore masters." By this he wants to say that any knowledge developed from the perspective of the observer, rather than that of the participant, reflects an authorial desire to "produce the real" and the power to do so.[62] Nonetheless, Smith insists that his proposal does not abandon the sociocritical power of theoretical discourse, unlike those social constructionists who react to functionalism by embracing voluntarism with no sense of constraints on action. For example, he suggests that we retain the analytical strategy of studying the variation in modes of resistance, accommodation, and agency to similar economic constraints and forms of social control.[63]

There is much to learn from this. Smith's arguments against foundationalist, teleological, and essentialist assumptions are persuasive. They focus close attention to the everyday spaces and institutions through which people live, eat, work, relax, meet with friends, sleep, and so on— arenas of life that are, so to speak, close to consciousness. They show the way the local is globalized (and the global is localized) as a result of immigration and capital flows that transform and create neighborhoods and communities, illuminating the way that the relevant spaces are multiple, fragmented, and overlapping, representational and cultural (imagined in cultural practices such as "border" music). They also show the need for an alternative model of agency and structure.

However, I would point to two main difficulties with Smith's approach. First, despite adopting certain poststructuralist ideas as a way of overcoming the essentialist assumptions of modernist and Marxian approaches, it is unclear how adequately these are integrated into his postmodern social theory. This becomes clear in the way Smith deals with what he sees as the essentialist consequences of viewing the terrain of the constitution of identity in terms of binary oppositions such as are found in race, gender, and Marxian class models.[64] In its place, he suggests we adopt the postmodern perspective that prioritizes the plurality of the different over the duality of the other. But this overlooks the fact that the significance of deconstruction lies precisely in its recognition that dualisms cannot be simply rejected, or left behind, which would amount to a false sublation. As Gayatri Spivak has noted, deconstruction does not eliminate the fundamental inherited categories of social thought but puts them "under erasure" in that we still have to think with these categories, even if it is against them and in a new way.[65] The deconstruction of the duality of the other opens what Derrida calls *différance,* a neologism that captures the way in which the subject, meaning, and experience are constituted by difference and yet by which presence, be it of the subject, meaning, or experience, is deferred.[66] From this point of view, the purely other and the simply different are symptoms or effects of a hegemonic operation that stabilizes the boundary between two entities that are initially overdetermined vis-à-vis each "other." As Patricia Clough has pointed out in her critique of Smith, a "deconstructive criticism will not simply valorize 'the plurality of the different' over the 'duality of the other'; *différance* points to the persistence of 'othering' in the writing and identity, the persistence of the productivity of the unconscious in writing and identity, even in writing the differences of identity."[67] Smith is aware that his emphasis on the simply different risks falling into a pluralist framework. Yet his appeals to ideas such as "hegemony" and "articulation," while welcome and provocative, are left undeveloped and in the end appear to leave his model closer to the pluralist model than he would like.

Moreover, by claiming that (postmodern) subjectivity is *socially* constructed, Smith overlooks the unconscious dimensions, splits, and divisions that invest the "inter-subjective" realm of the lifeworld with ambivalent demarcations and contested boundaries.[68] Central to this problematic is the question of gender, not only as a subject position around which interests and group identity can be woven, but also in the fundamental sense that subjectivity is irreducibly gendered. Perhaps nowhere is this more apparent than in the spaces of the city. The separations between and differential meanings associated with home, community, and workplace; the fact that the "right to the city" has always been differentially inscribed in a space where the "private" male gaze surveys the "public" streets (do women even now have the freedom of streets?); the entire series of connections that Sennett has shown to exist between the eye, the body, and the concrete spaces of the city—all these reflect internal demarcations of subjectivity, undecidable to be sure.

The second reservation I have with Smith's proposal concerns his notion of structure, which remains ad hoc and untheorized. In fact, Smith's attempt to overcome the problems of linking agency and structure by reading the presence of the structure of macro, global constraints from within the subject's articulatable experience comes up against similar problems experienced by phenomenologically based, interpretive sociology and by Althusserian structuralism, two earlier attempts to resolve the problem in this way.[69] Althusser, it will be recalled, proposed that rather than view the structure as an objectivity standing wholly outside the subject (this radical dichotomy forming the basis of essentialist notions of the liberal subject, itself standing wholly, ideally, outside of all social and historical determinations) we should interiorize the structure within subjects' consciousness and interpret the structure as "immanent in its effects."[70] Although these formulations had far-reaching implications later taken up by writers such as Ernesto Laclau and Stuart Hall, they avoided, rather than resolved, the problem. Many critics saw these formulations converging with the notion of normative integration prevalent in sociological theory. The early work of Manuel Castells also attempted to overcome these subject/structure dichotomies by employing concepts derived from Althusser and Poulantzas. As we will see, their inadequacy explains in part his shift away from Marxian theory as a whole.[71]

Smith's notion of the immanence of the structure within language and immediate experience runs the risk of falling into the "hermeneutic idealism" of interpretive sociology. He claims that the presence of the structure can be read out from within the subjects' linguistic articulation of their everyday experience and that these experiences "spring from interpersonal communication."[72] From a methodological point of view, however, this amounts to equating society with the internal perspective of the lifeworld in which "everything that happens in society [possesses] the transparency of something about which we can speak." It assumes that "what binds sociated individuals to one another and secures the integration of society is a web of communicative actions that thrives only in the light of cultural traditions, and not systemic mechanisms that are out of the reach of members' intuitive knowledge."[73] Therefore, Smith's acknowledgment of the need for "structural" analysis alongside postmodern ethnography remains theoretically ad hoc.[74]

Smith's work thus illustrates well several of the key contributions, as well as the limitations, arising from the rethinking of Marxian urban theory. Elements of the answers I wish to give to the three questions posed at the outset about identity, space, and structure should now be clear from the preceding discussion. First, identities, agency, and subjectivity should indeed be seen as plural, but identities are also "hybrid," that is, overdetermined, and structured by the unconscious desires in a relation of alterity to the other and the self. These elements I argue are best analyzed with concepts derived from the deconstructionist theory associated with Jacques Derrida, psychoanalytical theory, especially that of Jacques Lacan, and the political theory built around the concepts of articulation and hegemony most explicitly developed by Ernesto Laclau and Chantal Mouffe. Against Marxian urbanism, I argue that this notion is incompatible with the Marxian assumption of the analytical primacy of class identity. It is equally incompatible with pluralist theories of interest groups, liberal theories of atomism and individualism, and economic models of individual strategic rationality. However, for the most part, the focus of what follows is concerned only with the critique of Marxian formulations.

Second, I follow Michael Peter Smith and others in adopting an expanded and transformed notion of space that includes, in addition to physical geography, the metaphoric and "imaginal" forms that are part of the symbolic "stuff" that form the experiential world of communities and individuals.[75] However, I suggest that the notion of space, which is associated with fixed boundaries even where it is pluralized, as in postmodernism, be replaced by that of "spacing," a notion derived from deconstruction. The concept of spacing is better at expressing not static heterogeneity but the fluidity of boundaries and the instability of objects. It points to a space of becoming, rather than being.

Third, I suggest that the idea of structure as it is found in most Marxian as well as sociological treatments be transformed in two crucial ways. In its form, structure should be viewed not in terms of the exterior of a fully constituted subjectivity, the total, fully constituted context (e.g., the economy), but as a hegemonic totality that is unstable and whose ability to determine all the elements of the social is limited not by an essential kernel of subjectivity that stands outside of it (the existentialist position) but by a built-in lack or incompleteness. (Marx grasped this in terms of the limit placed on the needs of economy by the resistance of workers to exploitation but placed this contradiction within a higher-order totality without an internal limit.) We can further this conception by a selective use of the lifeworld/system distinction derived from the work of Habermas. That is, we can account for the character and content of the system as qualitatively distinct from the linguistically mediated dimension of the lifeworld. This does not however necessitate the adoption of Habermas's own interpretation of the lifeworld, where an ontological primacy is accorded to communicative action among all other forms of speech act. Habermas's theory of the lifeworld by itself appears too rationalistic and intentional. The analysis of language provided by deconstruction and psychoanalysis as a medium for the constitution of identities is in my view more satisfactory. Taken together, this adds up to a modified version of the lifeworld/system distinction combining a poststructuralist understanding of the lifeworld and a model of social structure derived from Habermas's interpretation of systems theory. By embodying both economic and state processes of commodification and bureaucratization, the Habermasian notion of "system" provides the only coherent answer to the question of the sources of reification of consciousness sought by Marx while at the same time breaking with economic reductionism and an essentialism of the subject. The "system" in this view represents the quasi-natural field of social relations that have been abstracted and regulated through the steering media of money and power and that fall outside the immediate intuitive grasp of subjects' consciousness. The historical development of the system is captured in the idea of increased system rationalization, an idea familiar from Weber's discussion of bureaucracy.

These alternative answers to the three questions of identity, space, and structure add up to an agenda for a critical urban social theory distinct from that found in both the Marxian tradition and current postmodern approaches. There has been an insufficient deconstruction of the problems encountered in the Marxian approach, with the result that the set of questions and problems underlying the Marxian problematic has been abandoned rather than transformed. As is often the case, one consequence of this amnesia of Marxism is the implicit retention of many of its formulations.[76] What is required is to reach back behind the answers provided by Marxist theory and recover the important questions it raised, working through the difficulties in a new way so as to develop a more satisfactory urban theory. Where the agenda of Marxian urbanism seeks to link the variations in working-class formation and action, the changes in physical space and urban morphology, and the dynamics of capitalist development, by contrast, I propose that we adopt a framework linking the variations in collective identities, the transformations in the physical and discursive spaces of everyday life, and the dynamics of systemic rationalization.

I am aware of the ambitious nature of this proposed synthesis. Readers may have noticed that I have already used concurrently the language of French poststructuralism, Habermasian critical theory, and comparative social science. I have deliberately employed concepts from these perspectives so as to suggest the intuitive compatibility of many (but of course not all) of the concepts. This may appear at first glance an improbable approach. Has not much of contemporary critical social theory and philosophy centered on a debate between two opposing and seemingly irreconcilable camps, with theorists such as Foucault, Derrida, and Laclau on the one side and Habermas and Offe on the other? Let me not give the impression that the debate can be simply avoided. There are indeed, in my view, many unresolvable differences. My warrant for connecting the system theoretical notion of self-regulating systems (the market economy and the bureaucratic state) with a poststructuralist view of culture, identity, and language is that each contributes an element that up until now appears missing from the other's camp.

Some poststructuralist accounts appeal to the "anonymous" workings of the market as a source of dislocations but lack a correspondingly theorized account of the social institutions that have taken on systemic characteristics. While the economic reductionist notion of structure has been discarded, no alternative notion has emerged that retains the purpose of the Marxian idea of causality and determination while eschewing the specific foundational answer given by Marxism. The result is that poststructuralist accounts of social forms (as opposed to literary criticism, or philosophy) are highly institutionally underdetermined, with little attention paid to the sociological dimensions of organizations, markets, bureaucracies, and so on.[77] I do not take the position that poststructuralist approaches are incapable of such an analysis, as some critics suggest.[78] What is required is to pursue Marx's project by other means to produce a coherent answer to those Marxist critics of poststructuralism who, with some justification, suggest this is an odd time to develop a critique of totality, when the power of capitalism seems to be more total than at any time before. I do not think the two projects—the critique of totality and essentialism and the delineation of those forms that threaten us with their objectivity—need be mutually exclusive. In the following pages I hope to set out the way these might be thought together.

The objective of the book is to make this alternative three-tier framework for critical urban theory plausible. Another objective is to give an account of and evaluate three decades of Marxian urbanism. To achieve both, my procedure will be to provide close readings of the works of the three theorists who have grappled most extensively with the problems introduced above. My aim is to reengage with these writers in a critical dialogue so as to work out the alternative directions that can be read out from their work. One intellectual historian has described the rationale for this type of enterprise well: "We academics think and teach in terms of books. Critical discourse is dialogical in that it attempts to address itself simultaneously to problems and to the words of others addressing those problems. . . . [I]t is an enactment of the humanistic understanding of research as a conversation with the past through the medium of its significant texts." Dominick LaCapra also adds, pertinently to the circumstances of urban social theory, "It is also an especially vital forum in a contested discipline that is undergoing reconceptualization."[79] Thus, the book is Janus-faced: it glances back at the intellectual history of an important body of work to delineate its core themes and limitations, but it also looks forward, taking what can be learned and, where necessary, moving on.

The plan of the rest of the book is as follows. Taking the motif of the separation of workplace and community residence as a heuristic point of entry (an opposition that is then deconstructed), I try to show how the engagement of Marxism with the spatial dimension of cities plagues it with a quandary. Marxian urbanism is based on the Marxian class concept, which in turn is irreducibly tied to the workplace, but Marxian urbanism aims to make sense of urban phenomena that are not restricted to the workplace. The question faced by all Marxian theorists of the city, then, is how to think in a nonreductionist way the relationship between class and the urban, the workplace and the community. I show that the work of the most significant theorists of Marxian urban theory, Castells, Harvey, and Katznelson, are best seen as attempts at overcoming this quandary. Nonetheless, because the class/urban relation is inherently unstable, each attempt remains caught within the impasse that has characterized Marxian urbanism as a whole.

Chapters 1 through 3 each deal with the problem of the unstable class/urban relation from three distinct but related angles. Each respectively focuses on one theoretical weakness that afflicts Marxian urban theory (essentialism, functionalism, and androcentrism), employs a particular perspective of critique (deconstruction, Habermasian systems theory, and feminist labor history), examines the work of one author whose work is most illustrative of each of the three problems (Castells, Harvey, and Katznelson), and finally, proposes an alternative concept (articulation and overdetermination, system/lifeworld, and the gendering of space). It is best to keep this rather complex architectonic framework in mind when reading the somewhat intricate analysis of the individual chapters.[80] As a whole, the argument presents an interpretation of the "history" of Marxian urbanism—that is to say, its intelligibility—in terms of a complex, nonlinear movement built around a central blockage and hinging on the unstable relationship between the concepts "urban" and "class."[81]

Chapter 1 introduces the core problem with an analysis of the work of Manuel Castells.[82] Drawing from the work of Derrida and Laclau, I use Castells's work to show how the essentialist assumptions underlying his interpretation of the class/urban relation creates an instability around which the discourse helplessly oscillates. Chapters 2 and 3 present two "subsequent" moments responding to the impasse created by this oscillation. The essentialist quandary could be solved in two ways: either by reasserting the logical coherence of class determination of urban processes and identities or, alternatively, by embracing the historicity and undecidability of the class/urban interrelationship. The former option is illustrated in the work of Harvey. However, I show that this solution is achieved only at the expense of a second shortcoming, namely, the functionalist reduction of the interpretation of social action to moments within the circuit of capital. Shifting the level of analysis, Chapter 2 examines the problem of functionalism from the perspective of Habermas's distinction between system and lifeworld in a way consistent with the critique of essentialism developed in Chapter 1. Chapter 3 examines the third and most provocative attempt to present an alternative, historically based escape from the aporias of a Marxian analysis of urban identities. This solution, represented most forcefully in the work of Katznelson, is achieved by espousing developmental (teleological) and androcentric assumptions that it had sought to avoid in the first place. Drawing on feminist labor and social history and building on the results of the previous discussions, this chapter employs Lacanian concepts to reread Katznelson's theory of urban identity in terms of a theory of hegemony and spacing. Nonetheless, the radical implications of Katznelson's theory bring us to the edge and limit of the Marxian urban paradigm.

The fourth and concluding chapter has three parts. After providing a brief summary of the main arguments of the preceding chapters, I address several possible objections that could be leveled at the alternative framework. In response, I argue that that rejecting economism does not, and should not, discount the market economy as a crucial shaper of urban space and of urban life. Then I argue that hybridity and spacing have important implications for everyday life, for city planning practice, and for the design of local political institutions. Finally, I illustrate these claims with two examples from the United States. First, I discuss the implications of the fragmentation of municipal or local government for the diversity of citizens' identities and social relationships and critique a form of liberalism that sees the solution to problems of urban diversity in a plurality of homogeneous enclaves. Second, I examine the place of "community" in recent approaches to urban design and city planning such as the New Urbanism.

CHAPTER I

Marxian Class Analysis, Essentialism, and the Problem of Urban Identity

In the Introduction, I showed how our conceptions of identities and the city are related in important ways, proposing that conceiving of the urban in terms of "spacing" is useful in understanding the idea of the hybridity of identities. I suggested that we not define the city in terms of atomistic individuals engaged in a rational strategic game, the way economists and political scientists tend to do, or in terms of an organic community, or as the arena of class antagonism.

Instead, I believe the notion of hybrid identities offers a more compelling, if less developed, non-essentialist (or at least anti-essentialist) alternative to the liberal, communitarian, or Marxian perspectives on the possibilities of the liberating power of identity in the city.[1] My aim in this chapter is to show that the notion of "identity"—our beliefs about who we are, our relations with others, and the basis on which we can act in the world—is best viewed primarily as hybrid, overlapping, and undecidable.[2]

A second goal of this chapter is to begin to tell the intellectual history of Marxian urban theory. The work of Manuel Castells provides both a logical starting point for that story and the best opportunity to engage with the way Marxian urbanism has attempted to come to terms with the elusive problem of identities in modern urban societies. In what follows, I suggest that we see his work as successive attempts to develop a non-essentialist or nonreductive account of urban identity or urban agency—a more technical way of pointing to the way social and indi-

vidual identities in the spaces of everyday life are overlapping with each
other, incomplete, always struggling to define themselves, never fully
fixed within boundaries (of class, race, ethnicity, or territory, and so on).
The story I tell about the transformations in Castells's thinking traces
the effect of essentialist assumptions on his attempt to escape the class
reductive aspects of Marxian theory.

I distinguish between three phases in his work. The first is characterized by the explicit attempt to integrate the new urban realities within
the framework of Marxian class theory. The second represents the
attempt to marry a "relatively" autonomous urban dynamic with a less
deterministic Marxism. In the third phase, Castells abandons Marxian
class theory entirely, positing the autonomous genesis and development
of urban contradictions and the agents that embody them. My argument,
in brief, is that each phase represents the unsuccessful attempt to develop
a conception of urban identity as contingent or hybrid and to overcome
an essentialist reductionism in the urban/class relation. This impasse is
reflected most clearly in the attempt to reconcile the dimensions of class
and the urban within a social theory of urban agency, oscillating between
the primacy and autonomy of each term. Whereas in the first phase, the
urban is reduced to class, in the third phase, the urban is seen as
autonomous—however, both solutions are equally reductive. Only in the
middle phase can the tentative outlines of an alternative model that aims
at the "articulation" of the two dimensions be detected, a model that is
adequate to poststructuralist critiques of essentialism that show how the
nature of an entity is partly determined by its relationships with other
relevant institutions and actors. For reasons set out below, however,
Castells could not make good on these directions, abandoning the project of integrating class and space. As we will see, these two abstract
dimensions are reflected in the empirical distinction between workplace
and community. Indeed, how the separation between workplaces and
residential communities is integrated with the Marxian concept of class
is the central connecting link through all the analyses of this book.

At a first level, this trajectory explains well the "history" of not only
Castells's work, but of Marxian urban discourse itself. At another level,
what this story represents is the recognition and opening up of an alternative urbanism—what might be called, following Richard Rorty and
Marshall Berman, the "ironic" city. This is a city where selves and communities are conscious of their own contingency, where a certain play-
fulness can exist across boundaries, where the myth of a purified iden-

tity can be seen for what it is, where complexity and alterity are permitted to play their part in the drama of everyday life.

THE PROBLEM OF ESSENTIALISM

Before I turn to Castells's work, it might be useful to say a few words about the notion of essentialism and why I have chosen to approach the problem in this way. At the most general level, essentialism is the doctrine that something is that thing by virtue of possessing certain properties and characteristics that thereby distinguish it from things that it is not. More specifically, it is the principle underlying both metaphysical individualism and sociological holism.[3]

Despite the fact that many, if not most, of the fundamental debates in social theory—such as that between liberals, communitarians, and others in political philosophy—still revolve around disagreement over the nature of individualism, groups, and their relation to society, many have grown impatient with much of the debate around essentialism, including theorists otherwise sympathetic to a "post-essentialist" social theory. For others, anti-essentialism has approached becoming the new orthodoxy in academic social theory. For example, Teresa de Lauretis points out how the term is "time and again repeated with its reductive ring, its self-righteous tone of superiority, its contempt for 'them'—those guilty of it." Similarly, Diana Fuss wants to move the discussion away from the seemingly prevalent goal to "seek out, expose, and ultimately discredit closet essentialists" to one that traces the implications and effects of essentialist assumptions on the discourses within which they stubbornly circulate. This has led others, such as Terry Eagleton, to wonder in exasperation how such an apparently straightforward doctrine as essentialism became the most heinous crime in the postmodern book.[4]

There is some justification for these reactions. But the cant characterizing some discussions should not obscure the significance of the issues involved. The history of the problem of essentialism, kicked off in Western philosophy by Aristotle's discussion of the accidental and the contingent, does not concern us here. Nor is my aim to call down a plague on the house of all "closet" essentialists. That would be neither constructive nor enlightening. More significantly, it would miss the point of my reading of Marxian urbanism, since the writings of the authors I discuss are explicit attempts to avoid the problems of essentialism in developing a Marxian urban theory. The interesting question for me is not whether Marxism is or is not essentialist—it is clear that, in fundamental ways, it is—but what effects its essentialism has on attempts to imagine a "heteropolis," a city that is not atomistic or pluralist (defined in terms of individuals, communities, or groups), or holistic, where individual and collective interests are harmonized in a spiritually unified social order, or fundamentally structured by class antagonisms.

My goal rather is to trace the effects of reductionist assumptions on attempts to escape it. Since I argue that this attempt is unsuccessful, I draw lessons from this impasse for an alternative model. My approach is to apply enough analytical pressure on the tensions of dealing with the separation of work and home to pry open another way of seeing the spaces of identity in the city. This flows from my conviction that the city has something to teach us about a cosmopolitan ethic. Because of its unique attempt to link structure, space, and agency, Marxian urbanism is as good a place to start as any other, if not better, for thinking about this alternative city.

It should be borne in mind that for the most part, in this chapter, I bring to bear my criticisms immanently in deconstructing the three phases of Castells's work, leaving my own position until the end of the chapter. Furthermore, as is the case with the other authors I discuss, I do not intend to provide a comprehensive assessment of Castells's work, of which there are already adequate treatments. Nor will readers find a consideration of the most popular empirical themes that have been generated by Castells's fecund and wide-ranging work. The substance of what follows in this chapter and in the rest of the book is defined by my agenda, set out in the last chapter, rather than by the author I am considering. The approach is not primarily exegetical. It is what may be called a critical reconstruction: themes are unpacked, deconstructed, and put back together in new ways. Identity is the first of these themes.

THE POWER OF IDENTITY AND THE PROBLEM OF ALTERITY IN CASTELLS'S WORK

In his most recent and perhaps most ambitious work to date, *The Rise of the Network Society* and *The Power of Identity,* Castells puts forth a bold vision of the main contours and contradictions of the emerging global society of the twenty-first century.[5] This new "network" society differs in several crucial ways from the preceding industrial form that has characterized capitalism for the last several centuries. In the network society, economic functions are organized primarily around the exchange of information and operate on a planetary scale, not based on nationally anchored industrial production. Organizations take the form of a network of boundary-spanning alliances and linkages, rather than of vertically integrated hierarchical bureaucracies. Work is unstable, flexible, and individualized. Culture is hyperreal or virtual (i.e., media-saturated). The nation-state is weakened and in decline. Finally, political and social movements tend to be organized around the defense of identity and specificity in terms of place and history.

The central contradiction of this new network society lies in the conflict between the opposing dynamics of what Castells calls "the Net" and "the Self." The dominance of the Net arises from the emergence of self-organizing structures such as markets and economic actors and organizations, which are instrumental and abstract and whose goal is the management of increasingly complex flows of information and capital at the planetary level.[6] However, these networks threaten and dominate the reproduction of the identities of social groups and individuals. This is because, whereas identity is constructed on the basis of culture and meaning, which are always specific to place and history, the reproduction of the markets, informational loops, and bureaucratic systems operate in a quasi-autonomous fashion, like cybernetic feedback systems, above the heads and behind the backs of social actors. One result of the clash of these antithetical logics is the emergence of social movements that are characteristic of this postindustrial period, such as religious fundamentalism, urban territorial movements, and environmentalism.

Despite significant differences related to whether they are defensive, legitimizing of the status quo, or seek to transform existing power relations, these new forms of agency share the characteristics of being themselves a "networking, decentered form of organization and intervention." For example, environmental and feminist movements in many countries are organized around local, national, and international coalitions and decentralized networks. This form both mirrors and counteracts the dominant logic of the informational society. These "multiform" networks of social agency are different from the "orderly battalions" of former agents of social change—such as the labor movement—thus making their effects and existence more subtle and decentered. Castells follows Alain Touraine and others in observing that this marks a significant break from the central contradiction of industrial capitalism located in the struggle between classes over the economic product. Indeed, he concludes that labor movements today neither reflect the basic social contradiction nor have the capacity to maintain the privileged positions that they had over other movements in the past.

As with all Castells's previous writings, this new theory of the informational network society is provocative and original and touches on some of the most pressing aspects of contemporary social systems. I would however point to two areas that remain inadequately elaborated. The first relates to the theoretical distinction between the Net and the Self or Identity. It is never made clear precisely what differentiates these two processes and what it is about them that is contradictory or conflictual. For example, it is unclear why there should be resistance to the Net, to the growing domination of everyday life by abstract flows of information, money, and power. The answer to this question I leave until the next chapter. There I will argue that a more satisfactory social theory building on Castells's insights should be constructed around the role of language in social processes and on the theoretical distinction between system and lifeworld.

The second area of difficulty concerns the relationship between identity and alterity. It is important to notice that Castells's objective is to describe and affirm the "liberating power" of an identity that is neither individualist nor fundamentalist, which I take to mean certain forms of communitarianism. The environmentalist, feminist, and gay liberation movements illustrate this liberating power, as do to a lesser extent urban territorial movements for local autonomy, as well as certain kinds of nationalism. This idea prompts at least three questions. First, what is identity a liberation *from?* This of course returns us to the former question about the distinction between the Net and the Self, and which I will discuss in Chapter 2. The second question is: What is the alternative model of identity that Castells wishes to propose in contrast to the atomism of individualism and the organicism of communitarianism? This is never made clear, either in the case studies or in the theoretical reflections. Third: What is the relationship between these different (liberating) identities? Are they separate, positive identities? Or alternatively, are they related in some way? Do they overlap? How do they constitute each other? What are the implications of this question for Castells's conception of identity? What implication does it have for the idea of an emancipatory politics of identity?

In this chapter, I focus on the latter two questions, and suggest that the answer to these questions are closely related: that is, that the alternative model Castells is seeking is linked to the questions of alterity and the relationality of identities. His emphasis on the "decentered" and "multiform" character of the new social movements is highly suggestive, but ultimately fails in uncovering what is emancipatory in the new terrain of identities. He is unable to develop these insights to their fullest, chiefly because he retains a positivistic notion of identity and excludes the moment of alterity or overdetermination in the constitution of identities. An emancipatory politics must operate at the level of identity's paradoxical relationship with alterity, with the realization of the contingency and incompleteness, in the face of the Other and others, of one's historicity, one's own provisional identity.

In this chapter, I defend this thesis through a reconstruction and analysis of Castells's work as a whole. Many of the questions I have raised have been central to his writings of the past three decades, where he has struggled, unsuccessfully in my view, to come to grips with these problems. More important, however, reconstructing his work can help us think about identities because, as I will show, some crucial answers to the questions set out above can be found in the earlier phases of his work, promising directions that he chose not to pursue. By contrast, I want to pick up at the point where Castells branched off from the promising theroretical implications of his earliest work and go down another path. In this way, I can develop the outlines of a hybrid urban identity as well as tell the story, reconstructed retrospectively, of one of the central figures of contemporary social and urban theory.

CASTELLS'S EARLY WORK: CONTEXT AND THEMES

Castells's early work, written in France in the late 1960s and early 1970s and collected most notably in *The Urban Question: A Marxist Approach* (1972; trans. 1977),[7] is read most often as the seminal, but flawed, attempt to develop a coherent Marxian theory of the role of space and urbanism in advanced Western capitalist societies.[8] This work was a fresh departure in two important respects. It represented the first sustained attempt to provide a critical alternative to the dominant ecological perspectives in urban sociology and policy thought. It also highlighted social dynamics and contradictions distinct from industrial production and class-based movements. It showed how the state provides mass consumption goods such as subsidized housing and the organization of urban space through urban planning as a way to guarantee the reproduction of labor power, as well as an appropriate geography for capital circulation and accumulation. It also showed how the politicization of these processes could lead to cross-class "urban social movements."

Castells's work was almost entirely assessed within the confines of the new urban political economy where, understandably, the focus was on the changing configuration of state power, the economy, and, to a lesser extent, the changing character of forms of collective action in cities and localities. Castells's attempt to bring Marxism and the city together therefore was read predominantly in terms of what Marxism could contribute to an empirical study of the city. The theoretical infrastructure and dilemmas of this work were either ignored or rejected for their abstractness and formalism.

Missed in this reception was the other side of the coin, namely, the fact that Castells's project also opened up the question of what the city and space could teach us about Marxism, or social theory more generally. It is rarely noted now, even by Castells himself, that *The Urban Question* was also a provocative attempt to deploy the key theoretical insights of Althusserian structuralism. In fact, it is in the theoretical dilemmas and tensions engendered by the attempt to marry certain Althusserian themes with the empirical demands of the new urban realities that the most important and far-reaching aspects of Castells's early project are to be found. The full meaning of *The Urban Question* can be understood only if it is seen as one of several attempts to create a non-essentialist Marxian social theory. This intellectual project, associated with writers such as Stuart Hall, Nikos Poulantzas, Michele Barrett, Ernesto Laclau, Chantal Mouffe, Barry Hindess, and Paul Hirst, was to a significant degree inspired by Althusser's revisionist Marxism, although many of his more fruitful insights have been lost, both because of the discredit he has received for political and personal reasons and as a result of the apparent general amnesia of all Marxian ideas.

THE ALTHUSSERIAN LEGACY

Althusser's work contained a theoretical dimension and a political dimension that many commentators have illegitimately run together. His theoretical project entailed the attempt to overcome the essentialism or economism in Marxist theory, expressed in the dictum that the economy determines all other social forms "in the last instance." Althusser recognized this as one of a piece with models that posit the truth or reality of the diversity of representations in terms of a deep core or essence that expresses itself in phenomenal forms. Thus political institutions and ideologies could be reduced or traced back to their essential constitution in the economy. Althusser introduced the Freudian concept of "overdeter-

minination" as a way to think the mutually constitutive relations of all
social elements and thereby rejected any foundationalist privileging of
the economic instance, since he argued "the final moment never arrives."[9]
This critique of totality was in many respects close to some of the main
concerns of the deconstruction associated with Derrida. On the other
hand, as a member of the French Communist Party, Althusser was committed to a strategic privileging of working-class agency over other social
bases of collective action and identity. It is this second dimension that
led him to embrace, despite all his philosophical arguments to the contrary, a theoreticism that privileged the scientific standpoint of Marxian
theory. Disappointed by his stands in the May 1968 Paris events, and his
defense of Communist Party orthodoxy, Althusser's revisionist support-
ers either saw the entire project as tainted or forged new paths out of
this impasse.

Castells's early work can be fully appreciated only in this theoretical
and political context. The aim of *The Urban Question* is to develop a
non-essentialist Marxian urban theory in which urban spatial dynamics
and the diversity of social bases of action around ethnic, territorial, workplace, or consumption communities and neighborhoods were not reduced
to the conflict between economic classes. Following writers like Touraine,
Castells sought to identify and acknowledge the reality of new social-
movement actors. The strategic commitment of the book, however, re-
affirms working-class unions and parties relative to these specifically
urban forms of identity as the privileged agents of social(ist) transformation. The project is thus caught in a dilemma between recognizing the relative autonomy of the new urban contradictions and antagonisms and
reasserting the primacy of working-class agency. As a result, *The Urban
Question* embodies two competing, and contradictory, themes. There is
a dominant narrative in which, in familiar Marxian terms, the urban is
defined by role and function in a structural totality that in the final
instance is constituted by capitalist class relations. In this story, the urban
instance is merely one internal moment of an albeit more complex class-
structured totality. In this view, the urban expresses the core principle of
class structure, although it does so via mediations. Yet there runs through
the book an alternative, but more tentative, account of the urban-class
relation. This alternative narrative results from the acknowledgment of
the diversity of the bases of social mobilization in cities other than those
organized around the (waged) workplace. It is the effect on the discourse
of *The Urban Question* of a new logic of relationality, the logic of overdetermination. I have referred to this model of relationality as spacing. In

this view, the urban is not the expression of and thus reducible to class processes but the result of the articulation of diverse social spaces such as those of the workplace and the residential community.

THE SEPARATION BETWEEN WORK AND HOME

To grasp this more concretely, it is necessary to consider a central characteristic of modern (Western) urbanization. Since the Industrial Revolution and the demise of the artisanal household economy, urban space and everyday life have been organized around the separation of the realm of capitalist production, that is, wage work and the labor market, from the residential community organized through the housing market. Although the precise configuration and timing of this development has varied by time and place, the fundamental fact of the separation has not.[10] If we start from a recognition of the centrality of this morphology to the organization of social life, then the Marxian notion of class appears in a somewhat different light. This is because from this urbanistic perspective, it becomes apparent that Marx's notion of class embodies within it an implicit spatial dimension and hierarchy that prioritize the workplace over the other spaces of the everyday. When Marx looked out on the landscape of mid-nineteenth-century European industrialization and pointed to the relations in the new factories as the analytical key to the anatomy of civil society and the basis of a working-class identity, he overlooked the fact that everyday life was being constituted in *two* dimensions: in the places of wage work and, simultaneously, in residential neighborhoods that were becoming increasingly homogeneous in terms of income and status. Whereas the workplace did constitute the space of the emergence of the subject as "worker," residential communities sorted populations not on the basis of their relation to the means of production but, depending on the context, on the basis of status, income, occupation, ethnicity, or race. Whereas the social relations of production created a space for the constitution of subjects as workers and capitalists, the residential communities were the space for the constitutions of subjects as consumers of housing and land, as well as subjects of political and administrative bodies delivering services. Individuals thus experienced capitalist modernity not only as wage workers and producers in the workplace but also in their residential communities as subjects of political and bureaucratic agencies and other forms of collective identity. Marx designated one space, the workplace, to express the core, essential contradictions of the newly emerging capitalist society, and there is no need to dispute the empirical significance of proletarianization on the lives of nineteenth-century workers, as Tilly and others have argued.[11] What is important is that Marx made a structural claim about the priority of the relations of production over other social relations in the constitution of class identity. (And of course in the *Grundrisse,* Marx made a philosophical claim about the unveiling of humanity's true nature for the first time in the capitalist wage form.) From an urbanistic perspective, it then follows that Marx also implicitly privileged the space of the workplace. In other words, the link between the Marxian notion of class and the space of the workplace is not contingent, a reading recently confirmed by Erik Olin Wright, the most rigorous contemporary defender of Marxian class theory: "The category 'workplace relations and practices' is analytically parallel to 'exploitation': both are meant to designate an underlying mechanism which generates particular effects—objective material interests and lived experiences—which, in turn, are constitutive of the concept of class."[12]

The implication of this spatially one-sided emphasis is that the relationship between the workplace and the community in the construction of class identity (and by extension, between the workplace and all other spaces of identity) is unidirectional: class identity (in the Marxian sense) is constituted by the relations of production and in the workplace. The other part of a worker's life, at home, in the family, in the neighborhood, is also fundamentally constituted by the relations in the workplace. The subject as worker carries with him (it was almost always a male worker in the nineteenth century) the same identity when he goes home at night. The social space of the family—of housing, the neighborhood, and its institutions—does not affect the basic constitution of class identity at the workplace.

Note that I am not arguing that social relations of communities never take on a working-class character that is an extension of the class solidarities formed around the workplace. This is a well-known feature of company towns, for example. Rather, I am arguing that this homology be read not as an expression of an undifferentiated class identity but as the hegemonization of the separation in terms of class. Clearly, the opposite, where work and community take on ethnic dimensions, for example, is also logically possible.

But if the workplace is not privileged over other spaces of identity, then from the point of view of a subject's lifeworld, to speak of an identity is to speak of some provisional totality in which *all* the dimensions of identity constitute an experiential unity. For example, to act as a worker is, in the moment of action (such as a strike, or joining a trade union), to organize the multiplicity of possible identifications into a hierarchy of determinations with the "worker" identity as the dominant element. But if the workplace is not privileged, then there is no reason to suppose that the class identity is always structurally the dominant and determining moment. The elements can be redescribed and rearranged into new (provisional) totalities such as ethnic or racial or territorial identifications. This second perspective is antithetical to the idea of the privileging of class and the workplace. The first, essentialist perspective relies on a model of expressive determination. This second model, which begins to emerge in *The Urban Question,* is less clear, but it represents the alternative narrative in that text.

To defend this reading of the dual project of *The Urban Question* as a tension between these two accounts of the relation between work and home, I will lay out briefly the main elements of these two narratives and the tension between them.

PHASE ONE: THE URBAN QUESTION

The Urban Question begins with the recognition of the problem of class essentialism in developing a Marxian urban theory. As we saw in the Introduction, Castells was one of the first to recognize the new constellation of urban contradictions (spatially located, state-organized consumption goods) and urban actors (cross-class, territorially organized collectivities). But he was equally aware of the difficulties these new actors posed for a Marxian account of these new social phenomena, observing that Marxism had so far proved incapable of analyzing urban problems in a sufficiently specific way. This was because Marxian analysts invariably fell prey to two complementary dangers. The first entailed "recognizing these new problems but . . . moving away from a Marxist analysis and giving them a theoretical—and political—priority over economic determination and the class struggle." The second trap led, by contrast, to a "left-wing deviation, which denies the emergence of new forms of social contradiction in the capitalist societies . . . while exhausting itself in intellectual acrobatics to reduce the increasing diversity of the forms of class opposition to a direct opposition between capital and labor."[13] Although Castells did not succeed in *The Urban Question* in reconciling the evident relative autonomy of urban agency vis-à-vis economic class actors with the Marxian postulate of determination in the last instance by the economic, examining the tensions involved in simultaneously recognizing the autonomy of urban actors and wishing to provide a Marxian account provide important clues in developing an alternative framework.

In *The Urban Question,* the dominant narrative is constructed through several argumentative moves. First, the "urban" and the everyday are defined not in terms of the process of production but in terms of consumption and the reproduction of labor power:

> An urban unit is not a unit in terms of production. On the other hand, it possesses a certain specificity in terms of residence, in terms of "everydayness." It is in short the everyday space of a delimited fraction of the labor force. . . . But what does this represent from the point of view of segmentation in terms of the mode of production?—Well, it is a question of the process of reproduction of labor-power: that is the precise definition in terms of Marxist economics of what is called "everyday life."[14]

However, since, in the Marxian scheme, the reproduction of labor power is an internal and necessary component of social production, the result is to restrict the definition of the urban as an internal, analytical moment of the labor process. In this way, the urban also is reinscribed as an internal moment of the production process. Castells maintains, for example, that "we can, therefore, retranslate in terms of the collective reproduction (objectively socialized) of labor power most of the realities connoted by the term urban and analyze the urban units and processes linked with them as units of the collective reproduction of labor power in the capitalist mode of production." Although urban issues do not directly concern the relations of production, and the urban excludes the workplace, the urban is nothing more than the spatial and institutional manifestation of the reproduction of labor power: "In the last analysis, the 'city' is a *residential unit of labor power.*"[15] Thus, the series of equivalences that invite the heterogeneity of the everyday into the coherent narrative of historical materialism link metonymically the following elements: everydayness—the urban—not-production—consumption—the reproduction of labor power. Castells attempts to resolve the tension that results from privileging class on the basis of the relations of production embodied in the workplace while according a specificity to processes based outside class and the workplace by "retranslating" these nonclass phenomena into the more abstract scheme within which the concepts of class and class struggle were constituted in the first place.

Second, although Castells recognizes the autonomy of the urban at the outset, he gradually eliminates it from the dominant urban theory that unfolds in *The Urban Question.* This is because there is a measure of violence visited upon the novelty of the urban if at the end of the day it represents only a functionally necessary moment of the capitalist mode of production, which is itself determined in the last instance by the (workplace-centered) economic sphere. In that case, the course between the Scylla of abandoning Marxism and the Charybdis of reasserting the orthodoxy of economic reductionism has been charted in an unconvincing manner. Castells relies on the Althusserian model of totality and the concept of relative autonomy to navigate these narrow straits. But this reliance is ad hoc, and the results are equivocal.

In fact, this impasse reflects an inconsistency in the initial formulation of the goal of Marxian urban theory. Castells sought to go beyond those interpretations that reduced "the increasing diversity of the forms of class opposition to a direct opposition between capital and labor." But by characterizing the "new forms of social contradiction" leading to new types of social movement and contestation as an increasing diversity of class antagonism, he is simultaneously executing two incompatible maneuvers.[16] By empirically recognizing and introducing a nonclass logic of contradiction and social mobilization, he inaugurates a line of inquiry in opposition to the class reductionism of classical Marxism; yet by continuing to characterize the new antagonisms as forms of "class opposition," he perpetuates the theoretical reduction of their autonomy vis-à-vis social class, processes of production, and the latter's spatial embodiment in the workplace.

The model of an expressive totality centered in the economic realm is clear from the dominant argument of *The Urban Question*. The urban possesses a certain specificity, but the urban is defined in terms of the reproduction of the mode of production, and "the [social] product is not a different element, but only a moment of the labor process. It may always be broken down, in effect, into the (re)production of the means of production and (re)production of labor power."[17] But if the urban is the combination of the moments of reproduction of the elements of the labor process, and the sum of these processes of reproduction is only the specification of the total social product (which itself "is the basis of the social organization"), and this product is "only a moment of the labor-process," then it follows that the urban is also an internal moment of the labor process. And if we turn to the empirical realizations of these processes, it must necessarily follow from the structure of the discourse itself that struggles over housing, for example, or the nature of identities structured by relations of community, whatever their apparent empirical characteristics, must be analyzed under the same concepts as are employed for analyzing economic processes. Castells confirms this: "In a society in which the CMP (Capitalist Mode of Production) is dominant, the *economic* system is the dominant system of the social structure, and therefore, the *production* element is the basis of the organization of space. . . . It is at the level of the productive unit (the *industrial plant*) that the fundamental determination of this relation [between production and space] may be grasped."[18] Thus the economic is not the articulation of its three moments—Production, Consumption, and Exchange—but is itself ultimately structured by the moment of production. The workplace is anchored and privileged in the overall structure of *The Urban Question* as the empirical institutional space of production and class.

The third move of the dominant narrative is to claim that urban actors and antagonism are internal aspects of class antagonism. If the social structure is viewed as a product of the economic realm, as we have seen above, then the urban structure and the practices that derive from it must be as well. Castells defines class as "combinations of the contradictory places defined in the ensemble of the instances of the social structure." At the level of the urban, there can be no modification of this basic determination. Class struggle is no longer a specific type of empirical collective action: it is the name of all actions that emerge from within the mode of production. In that case, there can be no articulation of the urban with class struggle. The former is internal to the latter, and both are structural combinations or effects of the structure of the mode of production. Unless we can specify some part of the social (such as wage-labor relations around the workplace) as embodying class relations, the specificity of class vis-à-vis other identities cannot be established. Indeed, we would not be able even to begin to answer the question of their relationship, for every maneuver would circle within a closed space. Because of the force of the dominant narrative, Castells is led hesitantly but inevitably to the conclusion that "the so-called problems of the city are simply the most refined expression of class antagonisms and of class domination."[19] Castells concludes, therefore, that urban movements can contribute to structural change in the trajectory of capitalist development only if they are subordinated to workers' unions and parties, since only the latter fill the space of identity thrown up by the principal contradiction between capital and labor.

COUNTERNARRATIVES

Although not extensive, there are several themes in *The Urban Question* that point to an albeit tentative counternarrative. This counternarrative is the trace within the dominant discourse of the initial acknowledgment of the problems of reductionism. The key elements of this counternarrative are the rejection of an essentialist basis for social identity, such as a universal human nature defined in terms of reason, rationality, interests, or a philosophical anthropology of labor or praxis, and the adoption of the idea of the historicity of all identity; the idea that all identities are defined relationally vis-à-vis other identities; and the idea that social forms and identities are overdetermined.

First, it is not accidental that the conceptual structure of *The Urban Question* was derived from Althusserian structuralism, since the latter itself sought to introduce a counternarrative to oppose the essentialism of orthodox Marxism's insistence on the finality of the moment of class determination. For example, Castells took over Althusser's critique of "theoretical humanism" in his analysis and rejection of Henri Lefebvre's neo-Marxist urban theory. According to Castells, Lefebvre is committed to a theoretical humanism—the belief that all social structures and historical events are determined by an autonomous will—because he believes "that space, like the whole of society, is the ever-original work of that freedom of Man, the spontaneous expression of his desire. This absolute of Lefebvrian humanism . . . would always be dependent on its metaphysical foundation" and, because it is based on the assumption of a universal human nature or essence, is thus an inadequate starting point to grasp the "social determination of space and urban organization."[20] Castells asserts: "The argument according to which space is purely the product of social construction is equivalent to the assertion that culture gives birth to nature."[21] On the contrary, if actors find themselves in situations not entirely of their choosing, then the patterning of social relations cannot be traced back solely to the intentions of acting subjects because of a dislocation between experience and knowledge.[22] Social processes, Castells argues, "are neither 'wills' nor strategies, but necessary social effects."[23] Furthermore, if subjects (individual or collective) are not ahistorical entities, then to an extent, they are constituted by the structures through which they are interpellated as subjects and within which they (desire to) find themselves.

Despite some ambiguity, this critique of essentialism and ahistoricism pushes in the opposite direction from the first element of the dominant narrative in *The Urban Question*. It is possible to interpret this theory of the production of subjects within the limits of economic class determination, which is what Castells eventually does there. Nonetheless, the notion of breaking with a noncontextual foundation of identity so as to open the space for the historicity of identities runs counter to the idea of class identity being determinant in the last instance—since the last instance is nothing other than that moment or cause that is beyond determination itself.

Once the idea of identity as the expression of an essence is abandoned, the notion of identity is transformed. Identity can be seen to be relational, defined vis-à-vis other identities in a field in which the mutual determination of identities is not arrested at a point of final determination. Castells pursues this insight, the second element of the counternarrative in *The Urban Question*, at several points. For example, in a discussion of the relationship between culture and space, he observes: "Society is not the pure expression of cultures as such, but a more or less contradictory articulation of interests and therefore of social agents, which never present themselves simply as themselves but always, at the same time, in relation to something else." The "dislocation between the system of the production of space [i.e., the distribution and patterning of social relations] and the system of the production of values" makes the one-to-one expression or mapping of a group's values (e.g., proletarian, artisanal) onto an area (e.g., a working-class or artisanal neighborhood) not necessarily impossible, but inherently contingent. Any correspondence "is a question . . . of a specific social relation which is not given in the mere internal characteristics of the group, but expresses a social relationship that then must be established."[24] Interpreting residential milieus as the social structures of the community, we should read this as the rejection of an a priori relation of determination between the objective social position of agents (e.g., their places in the class structure) and the identities that may arise within a particular place.

Finally, Castells introduces the notion of overdetermination to help reconcile the Marxian theory of economic determination with certain patterns of spatial organization that fit only uneasily into that explanatory scheme. For example, he argues that despite the Marxian assumption that the "social differentiation of space is determined according to the place occupied in the relations of production," empirical analysis (of the United States, in this case) suggests that "the relative autonomy of the ideological symbols in relation to the places occupied in the relations of production *produces interference in the economic laws of the distribution of the subjects* among the types of housing and space. . . . This [class-specific] spatial distribution is *overdetermined* by the new ideologico-political cleavage of racial discrimination."[25] That is to say, in this case, it is inadequate to decode the social patterning of space by class analysis alone because of the relative autonomy of space from class determinations. There are phenomena not specific to class that cannot be traced back, without remainder, to the relations of production. In this case, the general model of the urban as the matrix of the reproduction of the mode of production becomes untenable.

By "overdetermination," Castells, following Althusser and Freud, means that, first, any given phenomenon is a result of multiple determinations, such that the meaning of the phenomenon cannot be traced back to one cause or factor. An overdetermined totality thus is one in which there is no single or final instance of determination and meaning. Second, given the relationality in the constitution of identities, this implies that any given element or identity is never fully present to itself, that its conditions of existence and meaning are not contained fully within itself or its boundaries. In the case of the identity of social agents, overdetermination implies, contra essentialism, that agents are, paradoxically, dependent on their relationships with others for their essential characteristics. Laclau and Mouffe have characterized the overdetermination of identity as a situation where "all literality appears subverted and exceeded. . . . [T]he presence of some objects in others hinders the suturing of the identity of any of them."[26] Castells's provocative observation that "meaning has meaning only outside of itself" should be read as echoing the Derridian notion of a constitutive outside, the idea that the relations that an identity possesses with another identity outside of it are essential to it being what it is.[27]

One implication for urbanists of this alternative way of looking at things embodied in the counternarrative that I have argued runs through Castells's early work is that it is no longer possible to paint a picture of the relations between two (or more) entities, for instance, those labeled urban (defined by territory or consumption) and class (defined by the workplace or production), in terms of a hierarchy of determinations that are given in advance, or what Althusser called an "expressive totality." This alternative narrative suggests that the relations between these identities (for example, between trade-union organizations and neighborhood-based organizations such as tenant associations or territorially defined ethnic groups) should not be understood in terms of an a priori general model of the relations between the economy and any other empirical sets of organizations or social relations. The specific relation between community and workplace identities is contingent upon the historical, political, and economic circumstances in which these groups find themselves, and, equally importantly, on the discourses with which these groups express and make sense of their relative goals, interests, and understandings of the goals and interests of others.

One consequence of this is that, as Castells is tentatively beginning to indicate, no one identity gives meaning to all the others. We will examine this model in more detail in the next chapter when we consider David Harvey's idea that urban, community-based struggles are merely "displaced class struggles." Although the dominant narrative in *The Urban Question* also interprets urban struggles as displaced class/workplace struggles, the counternarrative provides another way to see the problem. A further consequence is that the precise character of urban identities is determined through a process of political, economic, and discursive construction or articulation without an essential core. As we will see, Castells draws on Gramsci's notion of "hegemony" in the second phase of his writings to capture this dimension of urban political life.

THE REDUCTION OF THE URBAN
TO A SECONDARY CONTRADICTION

We are in a position to draw some provisional conclusions. Despite the promising potential opened up by the submerged narrative of overdetermination, contrary to the project's initial ambitions—to clear an analytical space for the development of a Marxian urbanism that neither rejected the Marxian political imaginary nor explained away the specificity of the urban—the acknowledgment of the autonomy of nonclass phenomena had only a limited effect on the basic structure of the dominant framework of *The Urban Question*. Castells did not find the solution to the dilemma posed for Marxian urbanism by the separation of work and community, a dilemma also faced explicitly by Harvey and Katznelson, and for the most part implicitly by all other Marxian urban theorists. But the tensions in *The Urban Question* help to clarify this central antinomy.

There are two different models of class in *The Urban Question* that, from an urbanistic viewpoint, must clash with each other. $Class_1$ is embedded in and arises from the web of labor, work, the relations of production, the labor movement, the transformation of nature, the material base, the creation of surplus value, and so on. From the perspective of the historical development of urbanization, this involves a spatial "centering" or delimitation. Marx took industrial society and the (spatially) integrated lifeworld of the proletariat with which he was immediately confronted to be the referent of a conceptual and transcendental unity, the proletariat. There was a certain plausibility to Marx's thesis that, because capitalist society structures the lives of "workers" in so total a way, in every aspect, it was possible to infer from this an experiential unity that could in turn translate itself into an active, unified agent. But this conception entailed a spatial bias toward the differentiated space of wage labor from other spaces of everyday life. The conceptual privilege of (wage) labor was silently, and without trace, articulated to a particular understanding of the patterning of social life. This traditional conception is Class$_1$. From this perspective, the perspective of the unity of the lifeworld, the other spaces were assumed to be unproblematic. Vis-à-vis the determination of identity as structured by the relations of production (in the workplace) they entailed no independent effectivity: a worker remained a worker when he went home, thereby conferring upon the community in which he lived and the home in which he dwelled a working-class character.

However, as soon as the assumption of identity (in the phenomenological sense of the same, the identical, repetition) becomes problematic and thematized, the model shifts to Class$_2$. This reflects Castells's recognition of the historically new nonclass differentiations of antagonistic identities. Here, difference is internal and constitutive of all identities, including that of class. Unity is not a characteristic that resides in one element and gives (unidirectionally) meaning to all others. Concretely, the idea of a unified working class that acts as such (leaving aside the problem of collective "wills" for the moment) must bring together into a new unity previously distinct elements. If the capacity to organize and comprehend the totality of (workers') existence as one of exploitation and oppression by capital, the capacity to break out of the fragmentation of life spawned by the fetishistic masking of a dialectical unity is derived from class consciousness, then from a sociological perspective, class consciousness must of necessity encompass all aspects of an individual's life or subjectivity. It is this understanding that underlies the impetus and attraction of the new social history. But more important, it also reflects the desire and need to extend Marxism so as to encompass social relations outside the workplace. If class is the result of a process of hegemonic construction, to use Laclau's phrase, it cannot refer to any one of the prior constituent elements, such as work, home, community, and so forth. The way in which Class$_2$ is conceived therefore conflicts with the primacy given to the workplace and the determinations following from it. This gap or dislocation between Class$_1$ and Class$_2$ is the precise discursive space that Marxist theory has attempted to fill posi-

tively with concepts such as the "urban" and the "everyday" and nega-
tively with concepts such as "fragmentation," "division," "bifurcation,"
and so on.

Although critical of the marginalization of urban issues within the
Marxian discourse in which he nonetheless has chosen to remain, Castells
at this stage still refers to the worker's struggle as the embodiment of the
"principal contradiction." I have tried to show that the ambiguities inherent in the attempt to assimilate urban processes within a Marxian class
scheme forced Castells to adopt a counternarrative that pushed in opposite directions to the essentialist assumptions of the Marxian class scheme.
All subsequent theoretical strategies—reflected in the shifts in Castells's discourse as well as the very different approaches of Harvey and Katznelson—
are best interpreted as attempts to overcome the impasse illustrated by *The
Urban Question*. It is to these responses that I now turn.

TOWARD HEGEMONY AND ARTICULATION
AS THE LOGICS OF IDENTITY

Even a careful reading of *The Urban Question*, drawing out the ambiguities of the text, could not have led one to predict the shift of position
that Castells subsequently considered necessary to advance the study of
the city. Nevertheless, retrospectively and reconstructively, we can see
why the move was at least a possibility and why there were pressures
tending to push the analysis in this direction. As we have seen, the project of *The Urban Question* was premised upon the elucidation of the
specificity of urban processes, but ended up subsuming its object within
a totality conceived in terms of a class structure. The tensions within *The
Urban Question* thus resulted in an ambiguous and unstable foundation
on which to build the structure of Marxian urbanism.

The arguments of *City, Class, and Power* aim to provide a more empirically and theoretically adequate account of the relationship between
urban movements and class structure. As Castells became skeptical of
the approach adopted in *The Urban Question*, and less satisfied with the
political prescriptions advocating the primacy of workers' organizations,
paradoxically, he abandoned many of the Althusserian and deconstructionist themes such as the concept of relationality and the impossibility
of essentialist identities that in fact held out alternatives to the essentialist totality sketched in *The Urban Question*.

Despite a marked withdrawal from the theoretical terrain so explicitly
elucidated by *The Urban Question*, the second phase of Castells's work

collected in *City, Class, and Power* (1978) represents nonetheless the most promising phase of Castells's writings.[28] By moving away from viewing the urban as mediated within a class totality and by analyzing political coalitions in terms of reciprocal determinations of class and urban elements, this work comes closest to developing a non-essentialist concept of articulation between urban and class identities. Two themes that in particular reflect these new possibilities are examined below: the recognition of new forms of social differentiation linked to the consumption of public goods that go beyond the economic class stratification of industrial society and a more explicit concept of mutual determination among different forces, pushing beyond the monocausal model of an essentialist totality.

City, Class, and Power advances the thesis that "apart from . . . levels of income . . . there is a new source of inequality inherent in the very use of these collective goods which have become a fundamental part of the daily consumption pattern."[29] In the context of the European welfare state of the 1970s, Castells identified access to housing as an example of these new realities. The advent of widespread home purchase through credit supported by governmental means has produced social cleavages and interest groupings that do not simply reflect the levels of income and stratification in the labor market. Government intervention in housing provision, for example, produces nonclass inequalities, since the allocation of these resources is subject to bureaucratic, not profit, mechanisms. The criteria of selectivity governing government forms of housing provision structure a field of contradictions and social relations that are not homologous to those structured through market prices and the wage relation. The relation between these two subsystems, the market system and the bureaucratic/administrative system, cannot be assumed a priori, as in the base-superstructure model.[30] The political realm possesses its own logic, and "each intervention, even economic, will be marked by it."[31]

Moreover, state intervention in collective consumption both reinforces class structures and gives rise to new disparities that "do not correspond to the position occupied in class relations but to the position in the consumption process itself. . . . The positions defined in the specific structure of inequality do not correspond in a one-to-one fashion to the structure of class relationships." As a result, "contradictions at the level of collective consumption do not correspond exactly with those springing directly from the relations of production."[32] Castells thus breaks away from a class-centered model of collective identities. What was implicit in *The Urban Question* here becomes explicit: we cannot trace back the causes of specifically urban cleavages and inequalities to the wage-labor relation and the commodity form, and by extension, to the institutionality of the workplace. These observations suggest two important qualifications to the orthodox Marxian scheme of the previous phase. First, the sources of urban politics (inequalities, collective action) do not necessarily arise from labor-capital relations, and second, the effects of the dynamics that result are not class-specific.

In a discussion of local politics in Paris, for example, Castells observes that the demands resulting from the politicization of consumption issues "are expressed on the one hand through the union movement organized at the place of production, and on the other hand by new means of mass organization . . . in the sphere of collective consumption, from associations of tenants to committees of transport users." Urban problems thus articulate problems of more general scope, and "it is at the level of urban problems that one can see most easily how the logic of capital oppresses not only the working class but all the possibilities of human development."[33] Thus, to claim that social pathologies—pollution, inadequate housing, lack of neighborhood services, and so forth—no longer affect only a vertically delimited social group organized around wage labor (as they perhaps did in an earlier phase of industrialization)[34] is to sever the umbilical cord tying the experience of deprivation uniquely to the structuring effects of the labor market.

In this new model, urban problems rebound on and affect all social classes. The patterning of deprivation vis-à-vis these problems must be analyzed anew to reveal their specific forms of stratification—the crucial new variables being the level and form of state intervention into the supply of collective (or "public") goods and the specifically administrative and political logic underlying these policies. They cannot be read back from the class structure or the state of the class struggle, as the theory of *The Urban Question* suggested. The relationship between labor and urban movements can no longer be analyzed exclusively under the rubric of class struggle, in which all forms of urban or new social movements are reduced to a "direct opposition between capital and labor."[35]

POLITICAL CONSEQUENCES

If there are qualitatively novel, nonclass patterns of inequality and contradictions structuring advanced capitalist societies (which does not imply that class effects have disappeared), how should we conceptualize collective identities that coalesce within this new terrain? What is the relationship of these new types of collective identity, these urban or new social movements, with those that have historically been organized around the workplace?

The way Castells answers these questions in *City, Class, and Power,* in contrast with the positions he took in *The Urban Question,* could not be more striking: the Leninist model has been replaced with the politics of the united front.[36] Urban social movements "permit the progressive formation of an anti-capitalist alliance upon a much broader basis than that of the specific interests of the proletariat. . . . In combining social struggles and exemplary democratic management of the cities, [that is,] hegemony at the mass level[,] . . . the Left begins to win the battle for socialism . . . beyond the bastions of the working class." Contrary to the earlier hypothesis that urban political forces must be subordinated to the working-class movement, *City, Class, and Power* now advances a different hypothesis and prescription: an urban social movement "must be kept independent of a [workers'] political struggle in order to obtain positive urban effects on the one hand and positive political effects on the other; but the two types of processes must be developed"—and this is the key methodological threshold—"not only so that they can achieve specific goals but also so that they can mutually reinforce each other."[37]

We are now clearly faced with a new set of problems and questions. What is the theoretical status of this relation of what he calls "mutual effectivity"? What conceptual revision must be undergone before this mutual determination can be conclusively integrated into the overall theory? The base-superstructure model limits the mutuality of determination, and we saw that *The Urban Question* tries more or less rigorously to remain faithful to this topology, the function of which was to delineate in advance the relations between the elements of urban agency, the economy, and the social structure. Without recourse to the essentialist totality espoused by *The Urban Question*—a complex totality of dialectical mediations ultimately determined by the economic instance—Castells is compelled to draw on new concepts to think this new relation of relative autonomy of urban identities from class-based identities and class structures and marks the decisive break from the objectivistic model of identities as the re-presentation of the economic base.[38] For example, Castells asserts that "a specifically political [that is, class] element can only be grafted on to an autonomous, popular movement based on the daily experience of the masses," not "the workers," note, and that as a consequence, we should focus on "the forms of articulation of urban struggle to the historical process of class struggle." Moreover, he now qualifies the base-superstructure model by the claim that "very fruitful and efficient struggles can develop . . . through ideological instigation."[39]

These abstract theoretical formulations were grounded in the changing political fortunes and challenges of the European and particularly French Socialist and Communist Parties in the 1970s, challenges reflected in the emergence of actors and issues that were departures from what the working-class parties, inspired by Marxism, viewed as their "historical tasks." New social movements arising from the urban middle class were advancing new claims around new issues such as environmental protection, peace, and gender equality. Urban social movements and neighborhood mobilizations introduced the criterion of social justice to the design and planning of cities and as a means of criticizing uneven spatial development. Thus, in these essays of his second phase, Castells was offering theoretical means of conceptualizing the expansion of the traditional social bases and defining issues of the Left: the industrial working class, and the nationalization of industry, along with other issues associated with industrial unionism.

Returning to the question of the relationship between class and the urban, the workplace and the community, we are still left with the question of whether these new popular poles of antagonism and identity are simply added on to the original, working-class base. Indeed, to optimize the potential of this innovation, it is necessary to connect the new notions of mutual effectivity and hegemony with the alternative logic of relationality that was hesitantly and unsystematically present in *The Urban Question*.

In this case, the new, expanded tasks and demands should be interpreted as creating a new discursive totality within which labor and consumption, work and community, class and the urban, must rearticulate and find their (new) meaning. In fact, Castells claims that the new urban politics is "expressed on the one hand through the union movement organized at the place of production and on the other by new means of organization . . . in the sphere of collective consumption."[40] Work and community, production and consumption, class and the urban, are now relatively independent moments within a new totality.

One implication of this alternative model is the abandonment of the essentialist conception of an ontological primacy of labor and class, thereby opening the analysis of plural bases, tasks, and identities to a relational and articulatory perspective. This would not mean that labor or class could not possess a practical or strategic primacy; but no identity could possess an a priori ontological (or structural) primacy vis-à-vis all others. Otherwise, this would negate the provocative proposal that urban social movements and other class forces mutually reinforce each other and that social forces are a result of hegemonic processes, and would restrict mutual reinforcement to the idea of coalitions as the simple addition of different forces. But this model of positive identities cannot shed any light on how the identities of the forces in the coalition are transformed as a result of the decomposition and rearrangement of forces. Another way to pose this problem is to ask at what level, structural or conjunctural, is the link or relation between them conceptualized. If it is at the conjunctural level, as was advanced in *The Urban Question*, this contradicts the claim that urban and class movements are capable of mutually reinforcing each other. If, by contrast, the link operates at the structural level so as to permit such a mutuality, then the model of primary and secondary contradictions in a strict hierarchy of determinations breaks down. It cannot be had both ways.

LIMITS

Despite the introduction of significant innovations, the concepts of grafting, hegemony, and articulation play in the end only a limited role within the framework of *City, Class, and Power*, and ultimately Castells does not break from workplace reductionism. This is due principally to the lack of basic concepts. In the end, he views coalitions and hegemonic constructions as the simple addition of preformed identities. In the absence of a new conceptual framework within which to integrate the non-essentialist concepts—a framework tentatively visible in the Althusserianism of *The Urban Question*—the case studies fall back onto Marxian assumptions and reaffirm the foundational nature of the relations of production, rejecting the possibility that a new "principal" contradiction is being proposed and relegating the politicization of urban, socialized consumption to "a secondary structural contradiction." The text tries to square the circle by claiming—in this case no differently than in *The Urban Question*—that a "structurally secondary contradiction can be a conjuncturally principal one." But this operation simply collapses back into the dominant model of structural totality espoused by *The Urban Question*. Nonetheless, we can now understand why this unstable model is necessary: it is the only way that Castells can chart the path between either abandoning Marxism or relegating urban contradictions to a status secondary and subordinate to class processes.

The resources for a more profound shift of paradigm and a resolution to the impasse faced by Marxian urbanism thus can be found both in *The Urban Question* and, more explicitly, in the essays of *City, Class, and Power,* but these are sharply circumscribed and finally repressed. It is not surprising, therefore, that Castells would feel constrained by the contradictions and antinomies of both attempts to find a way out of the impasse. This second phase of his work is thus suspended between the hesitant commitment to Marxian class theory and the recognition that an adequate interpretation of the new historical realities cannot be accommodated within its framework. It would not be surprising, then, if Castells would be led to undertake yet another attempt to understand the specificity of urban struggles and their relationship to other bases of collective identity.

THE URBAN AS AUTONOMOUS SOCIAL PROCESS

With the publication in 1983 of *The City and the Grassroots,* Castells's work on the character of urban or territorial social identities entered a third phase, culminating in *The Power of Identity* (1997).[41] I began by discussing several elements of the latter. Here I turn to the former's more explicit and extended discussion of urban social movements in order to assess the extent to which *The City and the Grassroots* overcomes the problem of class reductionism of urban identities that bedeviled the two previous phases. In particular, I am concerned with the extent to which this new formulation succeeds in conceptualizing the merger of social identities, their overlapping or hybrid nature. Although I will conclude that *The City and the Grassroots* does not succeed in overcoming a reductionist interpretation of social identities, the attempt has much to teach us about the problem of essentialism, identities, and the city.

THE CITY AND THE GRASSROOTS AS A RESPONSE TO CRITICISMS OF CASTELLS'S EARLIER WORK

The City and the Grassroots can be read as an attempt to overcome several criticisms leveled at Castells's earlier work. His urban theory, critics argued, was too tied to the Marxian notion of the primacy of class struggle in social change. It ignored nonclass bases of discontent, such as gender, race, and ethnicity, as elements of collective identity and discontent in most cities. It ignored nonmaterial inequalities and cultural issues as potential sources of political mobilization in favor of a focus on collective consumption. It was ambivalent about the relationship between urban and class-based political contestation. And finally, the theory's prediction of collective mobilization in response to cutbacks in the provision of local public goods (that is, in collective consumption goods) did not transpire on the expected scale. Critics argued that consumption cleavages, for example, between groups obtaining goods on the private market and those receiving them via public authorities, were more likely to lead to fragmentation and polarization than to a unification of social forces. Although informal protests and even riots continue to be a part of urban life, the last two decades have been characterized by the relative absence of self-conscious urban collective movements organized around local government provision of goods and services, even in Europe, where such provision has historically been more extensive and has been seen as more legitimate than in the United States.[42]

The City and the Grassroots sought to address these shortcomings through three interconnected innovations. First, it presented an ambitious cross-cultural theory of urban social movements centered on the autonomy and historical distinctiveness of struggles over urban meaning. Second, it abandoned the previous commitments to Marxian theory as the privileged explanatory framework for understanding social movements and social change, because the theory of class struggle had been unable to accommodate the diversity of actors and issues reflected in urban movements. Third, Castells proposed a conceptual model that explicitly recognized axes of domination other than economic class as autonomous sources of urban meaning and conflict.[43]

THE MAIN GOALS OF *THE CITY AND THE GRASSROOTS*

The chief goal of *The City and the Grassroots* is to develop an account of urban agency that avoids class reductionism but that at the same time avoids the corresponding essentialism of positing social actors outside of their social, economic, and political contexts or in isolation from other bases of identity. "Neither the assimilation of urban conflicts to class struggle nor the entire independence of both processes of social change can be sustained. . . . Only by focusing on the interaction between the social dynamics of class struggle and the urban dynamics whose content must be redefined in each historical situation, are we able to understand social change in a comprehensible way."[44] In contrast to viewing urban struggles as reducible to class dynamics, *The City and the Grassroots* reinterprets urban politics in terms of the conflicts over urban meaning by multiple actors with different interests and values, conflicts that can be understood only in their given historical contexts. Castells thus has two goals in *The City and the Grassroots*. He aims, first, to provide an account of the genesis, dynamics, and variations of urban-based movements that is not derived from Marxian class theory and, second, to develop an analytical perspective on social movements and collective identities that captures the moment of overdetermination or articulation between identities. *The City and the Grassroots* therefore continues the agenda set out at the beginning of *The Urban Question,* although this time without the Marxian scaffolding.[45] The question is, does Castells succeed in meeting the goals he has set for himself in *The City and the Grassroots?*

THE SAN FRANCISCO MISSION CASE STUDY

Castells's analysis of the urban mobilizations in the predominantly poor, Latino, yet also multi-ethnic San Francisco Mission District between 1967 and 1973 presents a particularly explicit opportunity to examine these issues.

The case examines the genesis, organizational dynamics, transformations, and ultimate demise of the largest urban mobilization in San Francisco's history. At its peak, it involved over twelve thousand of the roughly fifty thousand residents of the district. The mobilization emerged primarily in response to two factors: the threat of displacement by the city government's urban-renewal program and by the availability of substantial funds for neighborhood revitalization from the federal government's Model Cities program. As a result of the success of the initial neighborhood coalition that succeeded in stopping the urban-renewal plans, over sixty neighborhood-based organizations came together to form the Mission Coalition Organization (MCO). The MCO was intended to be a long-term, viable neighborhood coalition that would represent the interests of the Mission residents, especially with respect to the control, management, and direction of the Model Cities program. But unity was not easy to come by. The divergent interests of the many groups involved were compounded by the tension between two conflicting understandings of the mission of the MCO, which, in Castells's interpretation, led to "organizational schizophrenia." Most participating organizations viewed the MCO only as a "coalition of existing orga-

nized constituencies, without any capacity for initiative beyond the man-
date of each participating organization."[46] But the leadership, which had
allegiances to the organizing philosophy of Saul Alinsky, envisioned the
MCO as a vehicle to forge a new collective identity, a new movement
displacing former leaders and boundaries and fragmented interests.

In the first years of its operation, the MCO struggled with the mayor's
office over who should run the federal program at the local level. This
was resolved in 1971 when a twenty-one-member public agency was
formed, with fourteen members appointed by the MCO. During this
time, the MCO's activities were focused on several fronts: the problems
of affordable housing and the lack of employment opportunities for Mission residents, as well as the goal of preserving the neighborhood's Latino
culture. Nonetheless, internal disagreements continued between those
advocating community control, who wanted the MCO to run the Model
Cities program, and others who felt that the MCO should remain an
independent advocacy organization pressuring and influencing City Hall
from the outside. Moreover, the deep tensions between the agenda of different MCO members such as Latino radical nationalists, traditional
Latino social service agencies, middle-class white home owners, Alin-
skyite community activists, conservative church-based groups, and so
on, undermined the viability and unity of the MCO. By 1973, the MCO
had become a "complex puzzle" of competing interest groups. The result
was "organizational paralysis and self-destructive in-fighting."[47] The
organization collapsed.

Castells's central concern is to explain the failure of the MCO to "raise
the level of self-definition and organization to the point that would have
created unity" out of the different constituent components, such that
each element would have transcended its immediate self-interest.[48] He
points to several factors. First, the MCO was unable to expand the base
of support for their initiatives beyond the neighborhood-based groups,
thus forcing them to limit their initiatives to the "level of people's immediate interests." These initiatives included social programs responding
to demands for the preservation of Latino cultural identity, redistributive programs addressing the lack of affordable housing such as rent control, and actions urging local businesses to hire unemployed residents.
But the MCO was unable to articulate the discourse of a particular issue
or grievance around a more abstract or structural dimension. The MCO
failed to transform the limited, parochial, and immediate demands of
Mission residents on such issues as urban services and neighborhood
space, poverty, and cultural identity into a broader and linked set of

demands that exposed the structural, global source of the contradictions. By focusing on what it could get for the Mission residents, the MCO thus merely reinforced the spatially fragmented pattern of neighborhoods pitted against each other for development funds, rather than addressing the problem of uneven development and inequality at the level of the city as a whole. Likewise, it could be an advocate only for recognition of "their" Latino cultural identity, rather than a force opposing cultural discrimination against all minorities.

Second, the effect of the successful achievement of some real but discrete and narrow goals was that the MCO benefited the Mission residents only at the expense of reproducing the social fragmentation of different interest groups and identities. The very gains legitimized and institutionalized the MCO as a pluralistic coalition of interest groups operating within the urban rules of the game of redistributive and symbolic politics, rather than making it an agent of the transformation of those rules, an objective expressed by some organization leaders.

Third, the MCO was constrained from pursuing a more global strategy because of the difficulty of forging and sustaining alliances. For example, to have expanded the urban-spatial dimension beyond the neighborhood to the level of the city would have necessitated an alliance with middle-class neighborhoods whose interests in low-density zoning, historic preservation, and environmental quality were at odds with the interests of poor Latinos in the Mission.[49] Similarly, the MCO was unable to relate the problem of neighborhood poverty to the wider class structure determining the dynamics of the labor market because the labor movement in the city supported the city's pro-growth development agenda.[50] (A potential alternative, which Castells describes in the case of the Madrid popular uprisings in the 1970s, was for the MCO to promote a broader agenda of the city around use value and reject the production and management of urban space and services as profitable commodities, an agenda organized around exchange value.)

The fundamental lesson that Castells draws from the experience of the MCO is that interest-group politics is the key obstacle to "the effective *merger* of the different identities into a popular movement."[51] Moreover, the Mission case illustrates particularly well the tension between instrumental social agency and cooperative coalitions. There is the "social logic of interest groups" in which discrete groups interact through the strategic trade-offs and bargaining that results from the instrumental pursuit of the "piecemeal satisfaction" of different demands for each interest group. True forms of coalition emerge when there is a common collective practice that aims at the redefinition of needs, interests, and thereby identities. In this conclusion can be seen the persistent concern with the problem of essentialism that I have argued runs through Castells's corpus.

WEAKNESSES IN CASTELLS'S INTERPRETATION

Many critics have argued that in moving from orthodoxy to skepticism, Castells has abandoned the rigid reductionism of Marxian class theory only to fall into a pluralism lacking structure and an account of determination or causality. Ira Katznelson, for example, has argued that *The City and the Grassroots* describes only movements across space and time without any sense of a hierarchy of determinations, with no social force or structure being more important than any other. A crucial shortcoming of this empiricist and agency-centered framework (derived in large part from a reading of Touraine's work) is that we cannot expect any type of agency to be more likely than another. *The City and the Grassroots* cannot give good explanations of the variations of urban movements in large part because it abandons the agenda of urban social theory, the project of linking structure, space, and agency within a comparative framework.[52]

In addition, there are several weaknesses and ambiguities in Castells's third phase that are pertinent to the critique of essentialism as I have presented it so far.[53] The central weakness that runs throughout both *The City and the Grassroots* and *The Power of Identity* is that the monism of class reductionism evident in *The Urban Question* has been replaced with a pluralism in which the different identities are now presented as fully autonomous and in which any sense of relationality between identities, either in their genesis or in their dynamics and interrelations, has disappeared. The element of overdetermination, so provocatively, if incompletely, introduced during Castells's Althusserian phase, has fallen away in favor of an empiricism that, at worst, reduces simply to a catalogue of different movements.

Consider the model summarized in the figure. Castells uses the figure to make the provocative distinction between categories appropriate to the level of experience and those appropriate to the level of social structure.[54] As we have seen, neighborhood (N), poverty (P), and minority status (M) are the experiential correlates of the "structural" components, the city (C_Y, i.e., the urban), class (C_L), and race (R), respectively. Poverty is an expression of the broader class structure at the level of immediate

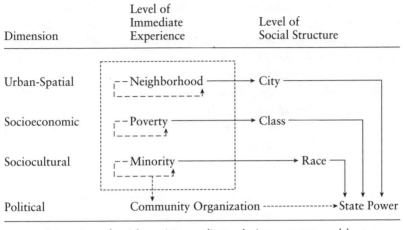

	Level of	
	Immediate	Level of
Dimension	Experience	Social Structure

Urban-Spatial — Neighborhood → City

Socioeconomic — Poverty → Class

Sociocultural — Minority → Race

Political — Community Organization ··············→ State Power

– – – – Connections of social practice according to the interest-group model
———— Connections of social practice according to the social-movement model
········· Connections of social practice according to the community-organization model

experience, neighborhood expresses the broader dynamics of the "city" at the local residential level, and the minority experience expresses the structural relations of race and culture. These constitute the six "basic" elements of the model. Using these elements, Castells proposes a contingent model for the articulation of political identities. "When an organizational operator expresses N, P, and M, separately, we name it an interest group (IG); when they integrate N, C_Y, or P, C_L, or M, R, to challenge SP [state power], we name it a social movement (SM); when they integrate N, P, M, we name it a community organization [CO]."[55] The relationship between organization and base is itself variable: if an organization merely expresses a base, it seals off its boundaries and relates in a monological manner toward all other exterior forces—in other words, as an interest group. If it relates experiential dimensions of cultural oppression, economic inequality, or territorial difference with "structural" institutions of power, it develops a movement along that dimension. If it fails to make this connection beyond a particular lifeworld, and only links together the experiential dimensions of N, P, and R, it remains a community movement.

The model is useful because it captures how the same basic elements can combine to create radically different political forces. Totalities have been deconstructed: any given movement's organization is a complex structure with relatively autonomous elements, none of which in principle is fundamental. The outcomes are a matter of political practice and historical circumstances. As Castells puts it, "The social outcomes of the movement express its articulation and the changing relationships between its elements." A movement thus expresses not an essence derived from its structural base and wholly contained and containable within itself, but is constituted through the relationship it has with other elements: it is paradoxically both itself and outside itself. It *is* the relationship it has with what it *is not*.[56] This contrasts with conventional pluralist theory, in which the interest-group orientation is the only possible mode of action. It also marks a theoretical break with Marxism, in that it does not privilege the class dimension over other possible outcomes.[57]

However, this is also where the limitations of the model and of the framework of Castells's third phase as a whole appear. The key problem can be expressed in terms of the following questions: Does the contingency of the totalities extend to the contingency of the elements themselves? Do the "basic" elements remain unchanged after their combination with other elements? If the meaning or nature of the totalities is contingent upon the articulating practice of the movement's organization, does this not also apply to the "basic" elements themselves? Castells goes on to say that the notion of "basic" elements is in fact something of a fiction ("Neither N, P, nor M were present as pure elements. There was actually a combination of NP and MP, with N and M as elements").[58] Again, is the combination NP qualitatively different from the entity N+P? Although this question may seem excessively nuanced, it will soon become apparent that consideration of it can help shed light on the core of the problem of essentialism.

There are two possible responses to this question, and they reflect the dilemma between autonomy and primacy of the class-urban relation we have traced throughout Castells's work. First, if the answer is "No" in principle, then what we are presented with here is strictly not an articulation but a combination presupposing the closure of the boundaries of the elements, and by extension, therefore, the affirmation of the essentialist assumption of monological action underpinning the interest-group model. The theory would then have ended up affirming what it set out to criticize.

That Castells's model of multiple identities throughout *The City and the Grassroots* and *The Power of Identity* does indeed fall into this trap is reflected in the claim that "the first lesson of our historical journey is the need to analyze separately cities and classes. . . . While the forefront of the process of industrialization was occupied by the struggle between capital and *labor* to share the product and to shape the state, the backyards of the growing cities were the scene of a stubborn, often ignored resistance by residents to keep autonomy in their homes and meaning in their communities." Leaving aside the reification of "cities"—a persistent problem throughout Castells's writings—the juxtaposition of classes and cities obfuscates the process of the historical differentiation between workplace and community as the result of urbanization. In fact, we are faced here with the reverse of the problem in *The Urban Question*: not the marginalization of community-based identities relative to class, but the elimination from the urban of the relational, overdetermined moment between workplace and community identities. As we saw, the elements of work, production, and the economy are one integral component of the urban.[59] Counterposing "residents" to "workers" falls into the naturalistic reduction of attaching identities or physical embodiments to analytical categories. It thus falls short of the central goal of neo-Marxist urban theory, in which "neither the assimilation of urban conflicts to class struggle nor the entire independence of both processes of social change can be sustained. . . . Only by focusing on the interaction between the social dynamics of class struggle and the urban dynamics whose content must be redefined in each historical situation, are we able to understand social change in a comprehensible way."[60]

If the answer is "Yes" to the question of whether the identity of the elements of a coalition potentially change as a result of their interaction, however, this subverts the notion of "basic" elements whose identity is fully present and positive. The implication of this is that there are no basic elements that themselves remain unchanged as a result of their combination with other elements. Another way of saying this is that the boundaries of all and any elements are not fixed but are formed only within a given contingent totality. But to accept this is to enter into a new discursive terrain wherein, as we have seen, identities are paradoxically constituted by their relations with what they are not, that is, where they depend on their relationships with others for their "essential" characteristics. The contingency of the boundaries of elements (be they class, neighborhood, or race) is what I have referred to variously as overdetermination, articulation, and spacing, the contours of which I will lay out more explicitly below.[61]

Despite these implicit deconstructive possibilities, which we have seen run throughout the three phases of Castells's work, his third attempt to conceptualize the class-urban link, and by extension the links between any set of identities in the urban field, again fails to capitalize on the deconstructive moment of spacing. It is ironic that by the time he begins

to isolate the atomistic basis of interest-group politics as the key obstacle to "the effective *merger* of the different identities into a popular movement," he also abandons the theoretical tools with which to surmount
this obstacle. As a consequence, the third-phase theory of multiple identities reduces to the pluralist theory Castells is so at pains to critique and
transcend. Because the elements themselves remain static and ahistorical, we are unable to distinguish between the "combination" of elements
and their "articulation." In the first case, independent collectivities aggre-
gate, leaving the initial entities unchanged. In the latter, the very process
of "merging," "linking," "grafting," and so on, transforms the identities of each element. By taking the first path, Castells's work from the
first to the last phase moves from an essentialism of the totality to an
essentialism of the elements.[62] Both are equally essentialist, because both
pass over the spacing of identities and fail to assimilate fully at a theoretical level the promise of the city.

CONCLUSION: OVERDETERMINATION, SPACING, AND IDENTITIES

In their study of the dynamics of social movement organizations, *Conflict and Consensus: A General Theory of Collective Decisions,* Serge
Moscovici and Willem Doise conclude that in a situation of genuine
compromise, "each person sacrifices fragments of his conviction, facets
of his own reality; he gives up on a degree of individuality in order to
seek an understanding and vision in which all can share."[63] My goal in
this chapter has been to bring to light and demonstrate the usefulness of
this idea as a way to escape the circle within which Castells found himself trapped. I have tried to show the integral connection between the
underlying assumptions of this idea of identity and what I have called
the urban experience, or the promise of the city. I have tried to clarify
and deepen Moscovici and Doise's claim by asking what kind of identity we need to have in order to experience the city as a place where this
genuine kind of compromise is possible. A deconstructive reading of the
provocative, if flawed, pioneering work of one of the founders of Marxian urban theory has helped point to the way to this understanding.

I will elaborate the theoretical model I am proposing here in Chapters 3 and 4, but this much already should be apparent: Identities, I propose, should be seen as overdetermined, that is, where "all literality
appears as constitutively subverted and exceeded . . . the presence of
some objects in the others prevents any of their identities from being

fixed. Objects appear articulated not like pieces in a clockwork mechanism, but because the presence of some in the others hinders the suturing of the identity of any of them."[64] Overdetermination implies that in any given partial fixity around a bloc or coalition, not "all" of what goes to make up a particular entity can be present within that larger unity. There is a moment of each element that escapes and spills over the boundaries that define the bloc as such. Multiculturalism, the politics of difference, and so on, are the current labels for this aspect of modernity.

The city has, if not an exclusive place, then certainly a privileged relationship to this moment of spacing, overdetermination, and alterity. I do not think it is entirely fortuitous that the city has been seen as a risky or dangerous place. In part, this is what connects the city to the politics of difference in its broadest sense, in which we come to find our identities as citizens through the recognition of a part of ourselves in the diverse others that make up the polis. That politics consists of the putting of one's identity at risk. The promise of the city is to suggest a city beyond the twin traps of the enclave, with its forced exclusions, and the commune, with its coerced inclusions, and to provide the possibility of the experience of hybridity, of the experience of the contingency of our spaces.

CHAPTER 2

Beyond the Functionalist Bias in Urban Theory

In the Introduction and the first chapter, I showed how the dilemmas of Marxian urban theory resulted principally from its inability to accommodate the sociological reality of new urban movements within the Marxian bipolar class model. One way to resolve the impasse would be to reassert the power of Marxism to subsume the new realities within the matrix of historical materialism. David Harvey's work adopts this solution through the development of what he calls a "historical-geographical materialism."[1]

The comparison between Castells and Harvey is instructive. As we saw, a certain amount of anxiety over the political and theoretical consequences of the dilemma posed by the separation of workplace and urban identities was a persistent feature of Castells's project. Harvey's key works of the 1970s and 1980s, by contrast, display a marked confidence, a level of conviction that Marxism, suitably attuned to the realities of geography and space, can indeed provide the most compelling interpretation of the diversity of urban-based identities. Someone turning to Castells's *The Urban Question*, subtitled *A Marxist Approach*, might be excused for being surprised at finding virtually no discussion of Marx's own texts or of venerable themes central to the critique of political economy, such as the tendency of the falling rate of profit, the extraction of surplus value, the rate of exploitation, and so forth. Indeed, the labor theory of value plays little overt role in the work. The injunctions in that book to look toward historical materialism and "set out from the processes of production" sit uncomfortably with the absence of explicit treatment of these themes.[2] By contrast, Harvey's Marxian theory of urban social and political dynamics proceeds more or less straightforwardly from the categories of Marx's *Capital*. Since turning to Marxism in the early 1970s with the publication of *Social Justice and the City*, Harvey has been building a modernized historical materialism for the analysis of contemporary urban society drawing directly from Marx's writings of the 1860s. Although his most recent work on justice and the environment reflects a qualified departure from some key assumptions of classical Marxism, his writings from the early 1970s to the present add up to an influential body of work that for many readers represents the most consistently authentic Marxian urban theory. In many ways, Harvey's project in critical human geography and urban theory is analogous to Terry Eagleton's in literary criticism and Alex Callinicos's in the philosophy and theories of history: the defense of historical materialism in the face of contemporary intellectual challenges such as postmodernism, deconstruction, and the like. As we will see, it suffers from similar difficulties.

We will do so, first, by identifying the place that Harvey's reaffirmation of classical Marxism occupies within the discourse of Marxian urbanism, concentrating for the most part on his writings before the publication of *Justice, Nature, and the Geography of Difference* in 1996. Harvey's work is best understood as one option within the constellation of possible reactions to the challenge posed by the complexities of urban spaces (of which the separation between workplace and community is one example and expression) to the viability of a Marxist interpretation of the city and its relation to modern capitalist society. This orthodox or classical position entails unacceptable costs, however, and thus cannot form the basis of a critical urbanism for today's conditions.

How should the constraints on everyday social life in contemporary societies be best understood? The following discussion examines and assesses in some detail Harvey's answer to this question. My argument, echoing several other critics, is that Harvey's position is too functionalist and economistic to be acceptable because it denies the specificity of nonclass phenomena such as community-based movements that form the basis of the urban question and provides no purchase on the problem of the relationality of urban vis-à-vis class movements. At the same time, I claim, his work has more to teach us than most of his critics have allowed. The problems encountered in the functionalist clamping together of system and action perspectives can be remedied through an alternative conceptualization of the distinction between "system" and "lifeworld" in ways fruitful for urban analysis.   .

HARVEY'S ARGUMENT

A central motivation behind Harvey's work is the challenge of illuminating what he calls "the vexing questions that surround the relationship between community conflict and community organizing on the one hand, and industrial conflict and work-based organizing on the other."[3] Harvey's aim is to explain the emergence of conflict and social protest in the city in terms of the encroachment of the imperatives of the economic system on the everyday life of residents and inhabitants of a given sociospatial milieu. It is important to recognize that the general structural principle behind this idea is drawn from the way Marx linked economic crises to the emergence of working-class identity and collective action. For Marx, economic relations and dynamics, by disturbing the communal substructure and the noninstrumental aspects of everyday cosciousness, usher in resistance and organized protest. In the urban context, this is manifested through the contradiction between the use values embedded in space and local territorial social networks and the commodification of space that treats land and space as pure exchange values. Community-based movements are thus by-products of the subordination of the spaces of everyday life to processes of capitalist exchange.

The most extended illustration of this thesis can be found in Harvey's account of the Paris Commune uprising of 1871 in "Paris, 1850–1870," in *Consciousness and the Urban Experience.* Harvey weighs in on the side of those, including Marx himself, who have seen the Paris Commune as a predominantly working-class movement and as an expression of proletarian political aspirations, and against those such as Henri Lefebvre and Castells who have interpreted the uprising as a specifically urban, neighborhood-based, and cross-class phenomenon.

Harvey shows how Baron Haussmann's urban reforms of the 1850s were closely linked to the need of French capitalists and the state to deal with macroeconomic crises, as well as to the growth of the land and housing market in Paris. He argues that one of the consequences of the urban renewal projects was the breakup of cross-class artisanal neighborhoods in the center of Paris and the creation of new class-homogeneous neighborhoods outside central Paris. Since the main areas of militant resistance to the Versailles government were located in these working-class neighborhoods, Harvey concludes that the uprising possessed a predominantly working-class character. To the extent that there were other bases of collective identity present in the movement (populist, nationalist, anarchist, localist, and so on) Harvey reads these as the result of what he calls the "urbanization" of consciousness, by which he means the displacement of class identity onto other axes of identification of the fragmented spaces of the city. This, then, is a story linking the three dimensions of economic structure, space, and working-class and group agency in a distinctively Marxian way.

Critics have responded to Harvey's historical and theoretical work with two types of objection, the first rejecting the economistic treatment of the state and government policy and the second finding the empirical case for the class character of collective action during the Paris Commune unpersuasive. (A third line of argument, drawing on feminist writings, argues that Harvey's approach neglects the dimension of gender.[4] I fully endorse this view. However, I postpone a discussion of the gender critique of urban theory until the next chapter.)

The first criticism holds that Harvey's understanding of the role of the state is reductionist and functionalist. Viewing state policy making as derived from the "needs" of capital accumulation and circulation skews our historical interpretation in three main ways.[5] First, the motivations behind state action in transforming urban space were not solely in response to the "needs" of capital. As Charles Tilly, Theda Skocpol, Ira Katznelson, and others have shown, coercion and capital, power and money, have worked hand in hand throughout the history of European state making and urbanization, without a clear causal hierarchy between the two dimensions.[6] Indeed, in many cases, it was state power that determined the historical development of the capitalist sector. Conversely, the development of modern cities, at least in the cases of Europe and North America, cannot be fully understood without an appreciation of the way space, territory, and cities figured into the development of state power. To infer that spatial patterns and political institutions can be reduced to economic imperatives from the fact that space and political institutions have in many instances been closely imbricated with economic dynamics is to confuse consequence with motivation. Second, the functionalist view cannot fully capture the fact that the emergence of local politics represents an independent patterning of sites of solidarities that is relatively autonomous from the interests emerging from class stratification and the dynamics of the workplace. This is related to the third shortcoming. Viewing the state as an instrument of capital underestimates the fact that politics—the struggle over institutions of liberal, democratic regimes (rights, liberties, citizenship, and so on) was also at stake in the Paris Commune and other urban conflicts.[7]

The second type of objection to Harvey's Marxian urban interpretation is that the historical evidence supports more strongly the alternative reading of the Paris Commune as predominantly a community-based and urban-based, and not a working-class, movement. This position has recently been forcefully advanced by Roger Gould. Drawing on new data on the social networks of the residents of the new neighborhoods that were important locations of mobilization as well as on the discourse of the insurgents, Gould concludes that the Paris Commune was "more a revolt of city dwellers against the French state than of workers against capitalism." Although most of the communards were workers, Gould observes that "it was not as workers that they took up arms against the state, and it was not as a defender of capitalism that the state earned their enmity."[8] This stood in stark contrast to the July Revolutions of 1848, in which the discourse, identity, and demands of the belligerents were organized around clearly economic class issues. For example, in response to high unemployment, a key demand in 1848 was the "right to work." But despite comparable levels of unemployment two decades later, such economic demands were absent from the Paris Commune. Furthermore, whereas the earlier struggle had been centered on the workplace, in the commune it was the neighborhood assemblies and public meetings that formed the focus of popular mobilization. For Gould, these differences reflect the extent to which the participation identities of those involved in the Paris Commune had become detached from the shop floor conflict between capital and labor since 1848. What had brought about this change? A large part of the answer for Gould, as for Harvey, is the spatial and geographic transformations of everyday life through Haussmann's urban reforms, but they arrive at different conclusions. Gould claims that workers in the new neighborhoods were organized on the basis of neighborhood-based, cross-class social networks and thus saw themselves in territorial, rather than class, terms and in conflict (when it arose) principally with the state, and not with the employer class.

Both sets of criticisms—the reduction of the state policy to the needs of the market economy and the misinterpretation of neighborhood-based identities as fundamentally class ones—point to the inadequacy of Harvey's Marxian class interpretation of this historical episode. But they are less successful in articulating an alternative theoretical model into which these two moments—the state and urban identities—could be incorporated. Because these criticisms tend to underestimate and leave untouched the underlying conceptual basis of Marxian thought, they do not reckon with the ability of structural Marxism to reject these empirical criticisms and reassert on a priori grounds both the subordination of the state to the social relations of production and the priority of economic class identities over other forms of individual and group identification, at least for the period of capitalist modernity in the Western world. Gould's empirical refutation of Harvey's analysis of the Paris Commune is suggestive, but it does not challenge the conceptual framework or underlying assumptions of Harvey's analysis. If Harvey sets out with a perspective that sees a priori class conflict as the source of every manifested conflict that takes place within a capitalist society, then no amount of empirical counterexamples can undermine this theoretical commitment.

The philosophical anthropology underlying Marx's thought (his praxis philosophy) appears to be compatible with several different empirical historical patterns of causal hierarchy or determination. Engels, for example, distinguished between determinant and dominant social principles, so that, for example, political power could become contingently dominant (such as during feudal societies) but the determinant principle remained the forms of interchange with and transformations of objective material nature, or the social relations of production. Writers such as Robert Brenner, Perry Anderson, and Maurice Godelier have developed historical explanations along these lines.[9] My point here is not to promote yet another revisionist Marxian position but to suggest that if we want to provide a new conceptual framework at the same level of theoretical elaboration as the Marxian one, it is necessary to engage with these deeper assumptions. It is this task that most critiques of Marxian urbanism fail to take up.

To incorporate the power of the bureaucratic state as a relatively autonomous factor in an account of social structure and to avoid reductionism when confronted by the diversity of urban identities requires a shift in perspective. I have touched upon the question of the polyvalence of identity in the previous chapter and will elaborate on it in the next two chapters. My focus in this chapter is on the problem of a noneconomistic notion of structure. I suggest that we should expand our understanding of the sources that generate conflict from a sole focus on the market and the system of production to a model that includes *both* the market economy and state power as components of a larger systemic principle that is common to both. To explore this expanded notion of structure, the rest of this chapter examines the theoretical presuppositions of Harvey's Marxian urbanism, for it is here that the assumptions derived from Marx are most rigorously employed, where the pitfalls of functionalist reasoning are most apparent, and where the clues to an alternative framework can be found.

In the next section, I examine Harvey's interpretation of urban conflict through his theory of urban-based movements as "displaced class struggles." I argue that by discounting the political and institutional salience of the distinction between workplace and residential community (one dimension of the multiple spaces of the city), Harvey's model has two principal drawbacks. First, by dismissing the historical significance of urban social movements, the model erases the specifically urban dimension of the experience of modernity, which I have referred to as the overdetermination or spacing of identity. Second, to ground an oppositional political agency, Harvey wishes to identify in small-scale urban communities a social logic distinct from and resistant to the functionalist logic of the capitalist market, but his reliance on Marx's production paradigm prevents him from developing such an alternative concept.

But from Harvey's early work it is possible to recover an alternative, nonfunctionalist logic of identity and agency. This alternative requires us to distinguish between what I call (following Habermas) the system and lifeworld dimensions of modern societies, a version of the structure/agency dualism. This distinction can help us avoid the dead ends reached in Harvey's work. The idea of system that emerges from this analysis contributes to answering the second question with which I started, namely, how best to conceive the content of a macrosocial "structure" without narrowing this down to the single dimension of the economy. I conclude the chapter with a consideration of Claus Offe's analysis of the two logics of collective action in the context of the problems of trade-union politics when faced with the expansion and differentiation of their traditional constituencies.

URBANISM AND THE THEORY OF DISPLACED CLASS STRUGGLES

Harvey has examined urban movements in several articles written in the 1970s and 1980s.[10] In contrast with the phases through which we have seen Castells's work mutate, there is no significant change in perspective throughout this period. The consistency results in part from the self-conscious and deliberate desire to build a *Marxist* theory of urban phenomena. Whereas Castells began with the empirical problem of accounting for novel features of the cities of late-twentieth-century capitalism and attempted to use Marxism to shed light on these, Harvey proceeds from the opposite end: He begins with Marxism and attempts to derive the meanings of urban contradiction, conflict, and agency.[11]

To see how this is the case, it is useful to reconstruct schematically the way Harvey "spins a whole web of arguments" concerning community-based or urban social movements "out of an analysis of the contradictions of capitalism."[12] First, Harvey draws directly from Marx's analysis in *Capital* to derive the logically necessary place of urban contradictions and processes within an overall functioning system of capitalist reproduction. The argument proceeds as follows. Capitalist society is founded on the engine of accumulation, and the accumulation of capital is based on the extraction of surplus value from the direct producers, the workers. Thus, "the class character of capitalist society means the domination of labor by capital." Like Castells, Harvey sees the *reproduction* of the capitalist system as a whole and of labor power specifically as the key link between the logic of capitalism and city life. In contrast to Castells, however, Harvey sees "reproduction" as designating not only collective consumption processes, but the more comprehensive level of the circulation of capital.

However, Harvey continues, because of internal contradictions, the continual cycle of accumulation and circulation does not proceed smoothly. The market behavior of individual capitalist enterprises may clash with the long-term interest of the class as a whole. The domination of labor also implies that "accumulation rests upon a certain violence that the capitalist class inflicts upon labor." Invoking the labor theory of value, Harvey writes that we "know . . . the exploitation of labor power is the source of capitalist profit." Thus, the nexus of exploitation, domination, and violence "arises because the laborer must yield . . . surplus value . . . in return for a living wage." The asymmetry of power is such that "the individual laborer is powerless to resist the onslaught. The only solution is for the laborers to constitute themselves as a class and find collective means to resist the depredations of capital." The final and inevitable consequence is that the system creates its own contradictory pressures: "The capitalist form of accumulation consequently calls into being overt and explicit class struggle between labor and capital."[13] We inhabit a capitalist society, and such a society requires surplus value to remain stable and in existence. Surplus value depends on the exploitation and domination of labor by capital, so to survive, labor must resist the violence of the production process, all of which leads to class struggles. The main "actors" of this drama are capital and labor. So far, this is the familiar Marxian story.

The second step in Harvey's argument is to emphasize that a "geo-graphical-historical materialism" is concerned with processes that encompass the entire landscape of capitalist industrialization and must therefore integrate into the overall scheme features of social life that fall outside the workplace. Harvey recognizes the functionally necessary role of community and family structures for the reproduction of the system, that is, for the reproduction of workers to enter the factories or offices day after day. He attributes this necessity to what he refers to as "per-haps the single most important fact," namely, "that industrial capital-ism, through the reorganization of the work process and the advent of the factory system, forces a separation between place of work and place of reproduction and consumption. The need to reproduce labor power is thus translated into a specific set of production and consumption activ-ities in the household," because, Harvey notes, "the system of produc-tion which capital established was founded on a physical separation between a place of work and a place of residence." Furthermore, because "the need to socialize labor to a work process through control in the liv-ing place is endemic to capitalism," the domination of capital over labor can be logically derived not only for the workplaces but also for the com-munities in which the "laborers" live.[14] Thus, the problem of the sepa-ration between work and community is thematized in a particularly lucid way in terms of the relationships among systemic (or functional) repro-duction, symbolic reproduction, and space.

ELIMINATING THE SPACING BETWEEN
WORKPLACE AND COMMUNITY

Recall that one of the reasons Harvey turned his attention to conflicts around the built environment was in order "to illuminate . . . the vex-ing questions that surround the relationship between community con-flict and community organizing on the one hand, and industrial conflict and work-based organizing on the other." He asserts that "we have a poor understanding of the relationship between the two" and that research on this problem can "shed some light on the position and expe-rience of labor with respect to *living* as well as *working*." Does Harvey succeed in shedding any light on this relationship? Despite remarking that "conditions of life in the community . . . can become a focus of struggle which can assume a certain relative autonomy from that waged in the factory," there is no explicit concern with demonstrating the rel-ative autonomy of the two spheres.[15] On the contrary, as a result of the choice of basic concepts, he is led inexorably to center the reality of urban, community, or neighborhood-based struggles elsewhere. Arguing from within the framework of political economy, he argues that domination of labor in the community is a form of domination derived from the basic class struggle anchored in the workplace. If the former domination can be derived in terms of the "need" of capital to subdue labor, and if class struggles in the workplace are inherent to the relations of production, then community-based struggles are but extensions of that primal and original impulse.

This reasoning leads to his well-known conclusion that urban movements are "*displaced* class struggle, by which I mean class struggle that has its origin in the work process but that ramifies and reverberates throughout all aspects of the system of relations. We can trace these reverberations to every corner of the social totality." This conclusion follows logically from the premises of the framework. Capital is "omnipresent" in such struggles, because capital is the essence of the system. It is the way the machine works, to misquote E. P. Thompson. "Capital-in-general" (which appears synonymous with "the state") is the agency through which a global coordination takes place. This totalizing viewpoint is reflected in Harvey's assertion that "there is nothing of significance that lies outside the context . . . of the contradictory logic of accumulation," nothing of significance that is "not embroiled in its implications."[16]

This model posits an original source of contradiction that then ripples throughout the totality and gives form to all the instances within the totality. This type of essentialism and expressive totality has already been criticized in previous chapters. In this respect, Harvey's argument represents a considerable step backward for Marxian urban theory. It is at the same time typical of Marxian-inspired analysis of urban and other types of new social movements. In a similar vein, for example, Raymond Williams has claimed that "all significant social movements of the last thirty years have started outside the organized class interests and institutions. . . . But there is not one of these issues which, followed through, fails to lead us into the central systems of the industrial-capitalist mode of production and . . . into its system of classes."[17]

Despite its weaknesses, this approach does bring to light an important question raised by the differentiation of the spaces and institutions of work and community in the modern city. This concerns the problem of how to relate agency to the functional categories of urban political economy.

SYSTEM, ACTION, AND THE PROBLEM OF FUNCTIONALISM

Harvey presents one of the most systematic and rigorous accounts of the spatial embodiments of the economic subsystem in capitalist societies. He has contributed above all to our understanding of capitalism as a dynamic, spatial process. By focusing on the circulation of capital, he highlights the crucial temporal and spatial components of capitalist reproduction as a whole. More controversially, he has linked the economic contradictions of capitalism to the changing landscape of post-industrial society through a theory of "capital switching." (The hypothesis holds that surplus industrial capital, idled by crises of overproduction or underconsumption, is invested or switched into real estate and the built environment for greater valorization. New crises, such as over-building, lead to a reversal of the process. This helps account for uneven urban development. In general, however, there has been very little empirical support for this theory.) All these are presented in a more or less consistent systems-functional manner of exposition. As such, he is concerned to analyze social processes in terms of their consequences for the maintenance, or to use Marx's terminology, the expanded reproduction, of a self-reproducing (even if self-contradictory) system. In this context, the abstractions of labor, capital, "capital-in-general," and so on, find their potentially appropriate domain of application.

But Harvey also wishes to say something about the action orientations of subjects who are constituted within cultural communities that must confront the quasi-natural environments of economic (market) and administrative (state) subsystems seemingly broken away from any orientation toward discursively articulatable needs. He wants to account for the *motivations* of subjects, individual or collective, acting under given circumstances, and the way in which members of a community come to a shared understanding in order to orient their actions in accordance with either traditional or agreed-upon norms and values. This is where Harvey runs into trouble.

In order to have access to this hermeneutic dimension of social life, social inquiry must elucidate the level of meaning of social phenomena for participants in a culture or "lifeworld," and to the extent that we accept Weber's distinction between social action and mere stimulus-response behavior, we must make a corresponding differentiation in our mode of inquiry depending on the analytical level in question.[18] We can draw from Weber's thesis the conclusion that action is meaningful when it can be related to the norms that structure the evaluative discourses available to members in a community, although this need not be traced back to the subjective intentions of an individual actor. Interpretive understanding of meaningful action aims to reach the level of everyday understanding, whereas causal explanation seeks to achieve knowledge of regularities and their functional interconnections in an "observation language."

Causal explanation and interpretive explanation are not necessarily mutually exclusive strategies. In fact, they can be made serviceable for an empirical critical theory. Rather than a strict dualism, they can represent possibilities along a continuum. The task of a critical theory is then to show the extent to which social *action* is reduced to *behavior*, that is, to show the way in which the social world as a deliberate outcome of freely associating participants is vitiated by behavior that is unreflective, anchored in unthematized traditions, or restricted to strategic orientations, as in corporatist arrangements. The distinction between action and behavior means that we can no longer move directly from the observational categories of a functionalist systems perspective to those revealing the meaning of participants' actions.

The absence of this distinction causes particularly acute problems in Harvey's work. The neo-Kantian distinctions between the natural and the cultural sciences became a central problem of social theory only after Marx. Because Harvey moves directly from Marx's later writings on political economy to the theoretical elaboration of contemporary urban conflicts, he is deprived of the key insights and concepts of the interpretive sciences. He believes that he can "spin out" arguments linking action orientations to the crisis tendencies of economic system maintenance because, like Marx, he assumes that the reification of consciousness (the source and explanation of social conflict) can be organically linked to economic crises of system reproduction in a one-to-one way.

THE CRITIQUE OF FUNCTIONALIST EXPLANATION

Consider the central concept used to analyze the housing process under capitalism within the Marxian paradigm: the reproduction of labor power. The role of housing is physically to reproduce the workforce so as to return it to productive labor the next morning and produce surplus value. It is an indispensable part of the process of the reproduction of capitalism as a whole. Activities and social relations within a house and a residential community have a twofold character. Despite being distinct from wage labor and productive work, they have a definite position vis-à-vis those processes that produce surplus value: they have a definite place within the circulation of capital as a whole. But they exist in a definite, yet subordinate, position to those processes that constitute labor. The circuits of capital as Marx conceived of them can thus be understood on the model of functionally integrated system environments whose relations with each other are regulated by inputs and outputs, the objective of which ("goal state") is proportionality and system maintenance.[19] So, for example, the workplace is characterized by the institutionalization of a wage contract in which the necessary quantities of labor (production) are exchanged for wages, which in turn secure the reproduction of the unit of labor through the consumption of use values. The household unit is the locus of that reproduction, whose inputs, such as goods and services, deliver the output of labor power back into the market. And so the process goes.

Of course, there is for Marx the objective of exposing as fetishistic the reduction of social action to strategic rationality, the reduction of men's and women's many-sided humanity to the one-dimensionality of a seller of labor power. The problem is how to move from the level of systems theory to that of social action, how to mediate the two moments of description and unmasking. For example, the labor movement is understood as a sociological group whose identity is constituted by the relations of production. However, by itself, this operation obscures the distinction between logic and action, between system rationality and the rationality of social action. It does not distinguish between those "objective" social processes that appear not to depend on the concrete agreement of participants and the dimension of experience and meaning from whose resources individuals and groups draw so as to act socially and collectively. The reduction of the latter to the former is the central characteristic of functionalist explanation as I will use it here.

The critical social theory of Jürgen Habermas provides the most important advance toward a solution to this dilemma consistent with the critique of essentialism carried out in the Introduction and the preceding chapter. With regard to the problem of the reduction of the dimension of experience and meaning to that of "objective" social processes, he argues that it is important to distinguish between "mechanisms for coordinating action that harmonize the *action orientations* of participants from mechanisms that stabilize nonintended interconnections of actions by way of functionally intermeshing *action consequences*. In one case, the integration of an action system is established by a normatively secured or communicatively achieved consensus, in the other case, by a nonnormative regulation of individual decisions that extend beyond the actors' consciousness."[20]

Whereas system integration is achieved via delinguistified media such as money, the social integration of action can be achieved only through the medium of ordinary-language communication. This process occurs within the context of the lifeworld of participants, wherein meaningful action is anchored in cultural traditions and social solidarities draw on these resources. (Accepting Habermas's sociological formulation does not require us to accept his strong, philosophical notion of consensus based on universal speech pragmatics. In fact, I suggest we should not, and instead adopt a pragmatic, hegemonic notion of consensus.)

In Castells's original formulation, urban social movements were conceptualized as emerging from the logic of collective consumption. What gave this conception its coherence is the assumption that the model of functionally distinct environments—production and consumption—is an adequate perspective to understand the formation of collective identities. However, to posit the self-formation of a sociological group such as the working-class or a community from the categories of political economy may serve as an ironic indication of reified intersubjectivity, but it cannot serve as a counterlogic to those reifying processes within capitalism itself. If social action is meaningful, involving norms, motives, and experience, an objectivistic analysis that reveals processes that work behind the backs of participants, who confront these processes merely cognitively, is inadequate to theorize the genesis of social movements. Rather, these contexts of meaning must be grasped through a hermeneutic or interpretive approach.[21]

This dilemma poses specific problems for Harvey's Marxian urbanism when it encounters the problem of relating community and workplace movements. His analysis does not so much oscillate between the two levels of system and lifeworld (which is the case with Castells) as it subsumes the latter within the former. In so doing, Harvey evades— illegitimately, as I hope to show—a persistent dilemma encountered in studies of class and community collective action. To the extent that actors whose identities are based in the workplace and those whose identities are based on their community residence are both subsumed under the functional categories of political economy, that is, conceived of as emerging from objective positions in the economy, the level at which these objective structures are experienced eludes analysis. However, to the extent that an objective context of action is sacrificed for an interpretive sociology *tout court,* the necessity of the collectivity that emerges being a class, as opposed to any other type of collective identity, evaporates, and Marxism loses purchase as the theory of class struggle. Harvey attempts to avoid this dilemma by deriving the forms of experience via a systems analysis of the circuits of capital accumulation. But this holism bypasses the hermeneutic dimension of meaning that acts as the medium of interpretation of the structures of everyday life. As several writers have observed, however, it is the mediation of the cultural or symbolic dimension as well as the institutional context that can explain the variation of responses to similar structural features of capitalism.

Harvey's analysis of the different bases of collective action in the workplace and the community attempts to grasp with one set of concepts both the action orientations arising out of the lifeworld of a social group, such as ethnic or neighborhood solidarities, and the systemic functional interconnections that form the context of action, such as the reproduction of labor power or operations of the housing market. However, because it is tied to a one-sided analysis that views social processes only from the external perspective of an observer, that is to say, as a systems analysis that grasps the functional interconnections of processes and actions that are necessary for the reproduction and maintenance of the system, it remains a functionalist solution.

The inability to maintain the distinction between system and lifeworld as a problem is most apparent in the way the distinction between workplace and place of residence is conceptualized. Methodologically, Harvey follows Marx in assuming the viewpoint of the a priori experiential unity of labor. From this perspective, the separation of work and community is viewed as a contingent, surface feature that does not force a reorganization of the basis of working-class identity. Identity is given within the relations of production, a conception largely derived from the nineteenth-century European conditions of an artisanal community.[22] As such, any *différance* or spacing resulting from the discursive institutionalization of a physical separation is only "apparent," a kind of "fetishistic illusion" generated by capitalist urbanization:

> The split between the place of work and the place of residence means that the struggle of *labor* to control social conditions of its own existence splits into two *seemingly* independent struggles. The first located in the work-place, is over the wage rate. . . . The second fought in the place of residence, is against *secondary* forms of exploitation and appropriation. . . . Of course the dichotomy between living and working is itself an artificial division that the capitalist system imposes.[23]

What leads Harvey to reduce the distinction between the two spheres of social life, that is, to relegate one term of this binary opposition to a subordinate and derivative status?[24] He cannot thematize the system/lifeworld distinction or investigate the institutional realities that make the separation a stubborn and consequential aspect of capitalist modernity because from his standpoint, there really is no difference. There is no difference because he assimilates action and function into one framework and reduces that framework to the functional categories of political economy.

Throughout his texts Harvey speaks as if labor, the category derived from the analysis of the circulation of capital, were the flesh-and-bones people who work and sell their labor power.[25] Even if we assume for the moment that "labor" is an adequate characterization of subjects' roles, at least at the workplace, what, then, is the relationship of the separation between workplace and community to "labor's" unity? In other words, from whence springs labor's fragmentation?

If labor is unified by virtue of the relations of production, then the separation between where labor lives and where labor works is only apparent. Harvey does not mean that the separation does not exist, although he comes perilously close to saying this on several occasions. Rather, he means that labor is not constituted at the same level as the processes issuing in the separation between work and community. Labor exists before and above the sociospatial differentiations that appear concretely. In Chapter 1, this procedure was analyzed in terms of the assumption of two distinct levels, one at which the identity of the working class, that is, labor, is constituted and a second one in which it is represented. The subordination of the second term to the first depends on essentialist assumptions regarding the metaphysical nature of labor or praxis as the core of human identity as such. This applies a fortiori in Harvey's case, although the totalization is considerably more thoroughgoing. Harvey asserts that the separation is really an illusion, writing, for example: "It must surely be plain that the separation between working and living is at best a superficial estrangement, an apparent breaking asunder of what can never be kept apart [that is] the underlying unity between work-based and 'community'-based conflicts. They are . . . but distorted representations . . . which mystify and render opaque the fundamental underlying class antagonism."[26]

But this interpretation raises many questions. For whom, it could be asked, are the differences between unions and community groups in terms of their demands, organizations, issues, antagonists, problems, institutional channels of government, legal constraints, and members only apparent? For whom are the distinctions between different problems confronting everyday life, such as employment at a living wage, or safe streets, or adequate public schooling, only a superficial estrangement? The most significant drawback of Harvey's conclusion is that it bypasses exactly what we need to find out: why people act on the basis of different identities in different places and times. Compare, for example, the above quotation with Katznelson's interpretation of the same phenomenon; he claims that "the links between work and community-based conflicts have been unusually tenuous. Each kind of conflict has its own separate vocabulary and set of institutions: work, class, and trade unions; community, ethnicity, local parties, churches, and voluntary associations."[27]

Even if we were to accept Harvey's postulate that the separation of work and life is an illusion, would this help us understand the reasons whereby people act sometimes on the basis of their workplace and sometimes on the basis of their neighborhood and ethnic community? Absolutely not. Even if we shared Harvey's confidence as to the true anatomy of social reality, revealing under all epiphenomenal, superficial, surface phenomena the true, "underlying" unity of all phenomena, this would still only be a unity *for us,* and not for the subjects whose actions we are trying to interpret. Even if we could assume without any feelings of presumption that we knew to be superficial what the actors themselves considered to be significant, and even if we were right, this still would not help us understand why subjects acted in the manner they did.

This problem of interpretation is not the only one posed by Harvey's attempt to view social processes functionally, only from the perspective of an observer. The functionalist bias underlying Harvey's approach determines three further methodological problems: a commitment to epistemological monism as against eclecticism, an inadequate differentiation between the relations of reciprocity and of exchange, and an insufficiently clear distinction between the dialogical and monological or strategic types of collective action.

METHODOLOGICAL MONISM AND
ECLECTICISM: THE RETURN TO MARX

Reviewing a collection of Marxian essays on the nature of the modern state, Gianfranco Poggi took the volume to task for approaching its objective from the wrong end. The vigorous neo-Marxist theorizing inspired by the works of Ralph Milliband and Nikos Poulantzas had reached an impasse, he argued, because the authors were primarily intent not on solving problems posed by the phenomena of state intervention in contemporary society but on developing a specifically *Marxist* approach to the state. This resulted in implausible positions such as the oft-stated claims that *only* Marxism can have anything of value to say about the state and that "bourgeois" sociology (Max Weber being its chief representative) could not be utilized for a "progressive" theory of the state. Instead of starting with Marx and then approaching the phenomena to be explained by means of it, Poggi concluded, we should start with our problem, whatever it may be, "and hit it with everything we've got—including Marx."

Harvey proceeds in precisely the fashion criticized by Poggi and falls into similar pitfalls. Not only does Harvey rely exclusively on Marxist categories, but there is a further reduction within this corpus to the categories of political economy of the late Marx. Concepts such as ideology and alienation, to name just two, are not explored along the paths opened up by Gramsci or Lukács, for example. There are two theoretical complexes passed over by his work. The first is the consequences of ignoring the long-standing debate between functionalist and interpretive strategies in the social sciences we have just explored. The second is the critique of functionalism within Marx's writings themselves.[28]

Harvey's writings are intended to demonstrate the fact that Marxism not only can be made relevant for contemporary conditions, but that it is the *only* perspective fit to do so. This is a bold claim and a highly implausible one, given that the range of phenomena encompassed by "studies in the history and theory of capitalist urbanization" (as the subtitle given to both *Consciousness and the Urban Experience* and *The Urbanization of Capital* puts it) covers virtually all aspects of human society. Beyond even this, there are strong reasons for considering the project of developing or recovering a pure Marxist theory, or any other pure theory, for that matter, as flawed from the outset.

Within the field of urban political economy during the 1980s, there was considerable debate between proponents of different theoretical frameworks, notably the (neo)Marxist and (neo)Weberian.[29] This controversy was criticized by many who view the "paradigm wars" as counterproductive, the creation of mainly Marxian purists eager to construct a seamless and holistic interpretation. As Castells commented, Marxists seemed to be more concerned with proving that they were Marxists than with being right. Harvey notes the problem himself, but in a significantly ambiguous line of reasoning finds his way back to privileging the Marxian paradigm. The "objective" fragmentation of social reality spawned by capitalism, he writes, produces "confusions" not only in people's minds but also, regrettably, in intellectual discourse. "The intellectual fragmentations of academia appear as tragic reflections of the confusions of an urbanized consciousness; they reflect surface appearances, do little to elucidate inner meanings and connections, and do much to sustain the confusions by replicating them in learned terms."[30]

What precisely is the meaning of "fragmentation" in this context? Is it equivalent to simply the variety of perspectives or their embodiment within distinct academic institutions? Even if an "urbanized" consciousness does imply a confused state, does the plurality of theoretical perspectives reflect nothing more than this? Academics, Harvey has written, "exhibit similar confusions. Neoclassical economists *privilege* entrepreneurial and consumer sovereignties based on the individuation of money; Marxists, the productive forces and class relations necessary to the extraction of surplus value; Weberians, class relations constructed out of market behaviors; . . . feminists, patriarchy, family, and women at work; the Chicago School, the ecology of communities in space; and so on. Each particular perspective tells its own particular truth."[31]

This would appear to sanction the validity of several points of view. (One could add, somewhat mischievously, that it does so in a Weberian and Nietzschean, but distinctly un-Marxist, fashion.) In fact, Harvey makes no such methodological move. As Harvey's entire corpus reveals and as he himself explicitly states, the Marxian paradigm ultimately is to be privileged over the others. Despite the cautions quoted above, the passage continues, "Does this mean that we have to abandon Marx for some eclectic mix of theoretical perspectives? Not at all. If capitalism persists as the dominant mode of production, then it is with the analysis of that mode of production that we have to start. . . . [W]e have no option except to put its class relations at the center of analysis." It is not clear how these two passages escape being entirely contradictory and inconsistent. On the one hand, "each perspective tells its truth," and the Marxian perspective is as guilty of privileging class relations as any other. On the other hand, "we have no option" except to privilege class relations. The chief reason given for the lack of options is that "the circulation of capital is fundamental to the ways we gain and use our collective and individual social power."[32]

But Harvey's reasoning is circular. The reason we have to prioritize class relations is because capitalism persists as the mode of production. The reason we "have no option" but to adopt Marxism as the unique starting point is because the circulation of capital structures social life so totally. But it is only from the perspective of Marxism that capitalism is viewed as the dominant characteristic of contemporary society and only from within Marxian discourse that the theoretical object "mode of production" takes on its specific meaning. Furthermore, it is the Marxist theory of the connections between the accumulation and circulation of capital and other aspects of the social structure that produces statements regarding the relations of effectivity between different elements (e.g., the base-superstructure model).

The apparent force of the argument thus rests on reasoning that assumes what it sets out to demonstrate and prejudges the nature of the social system of which urbanization is a feature. This circularity is nowhere clearer than in the following passage: "I turned to the Marxian categories in the early 1970's, and reaffirm my faith in them here, as the only ones suited to the active construction of rigorous, comprehensive, and scientific understandings of something as complex and rich as the historical geography of the urban process under capitalism." The passage clearly exhibits the dogmatic rejection of other perspectives and the elevation of Marxism to *the* explanatory medium, as well as the circularity of claiming that Marxism is the only pertinent perspective for the analysis of capitalist society when the very object of analysis—contemporaneity as capitalism—is a product of Marxist discourse.

It is important to keep the theoretical and empirical claims clearly demarcated here. The circulation of capital and the tyranny of the labor market continue to impose a powerful influence on social life. The concrete expressions of the ways these processes enter into the determinations of institutional and collective action are an indispensable component of any social science worth the name. But this empirical hypothesis in no way entails the theoretical claim postulating a particular type of concrete determination between spheres of social life. When Harvey writes that "there is a sense in which class relations invade and dominate all other loci of consciousness formation," there is both an a priori methodological claim to privilege class relations and an empirical claim that identities structured through institutions of wage labor in particular historical and geographic circumstances exhibit this overwhelming character.[33] The concept of hegemony would be strictly unthinkable if it did not allow for the latter possibility. The concept of articulation would also be unthinkable in the case of an a priori direction of causality.

Harvey's analysis operates at the first theoretical level. He writes, for example, that the invasion and domination of all other loci by capital "does not mean that everything can be reduced to an analysis of class relations." But given his arguments thus far, why not? Not only would this follow from the logic of Harvey's methodological starting point—

the circulation of capital—but it is reflected in his practice. When he undertakes to analyze social processes, he always begins and ends with categories derived from the functional presuppositions of the circuits of capital. To confirm this seemingly severe interpretation, we need look no further than the opening lines of *The Urbanization of Capital:* "It has been my ambition . . . to progress toward a more definitive Marxian interpretation of the history and theory of urbanization under capital-ism."[34] Thus, his primary objective has been not a more cogent inter-pretation of urban phenomena but a more comprehensive Marxian model of the latter.

One possible reply to this criticism would be to assert the scientific character of Marxism and argue that the objectivity of the designation "capitalism" reflects the true inner nature of contemporary social sys-tems. The movement of particular societies then can be derived from dis-coverable "laws" of history. Harvey's procedure relies partly on such a foundation. He assumes the validity of historical materialism and likens Marxism to an already constructed edifice or structure with some "empty boxes" that need to be filled.[35] But are the spaces that require filling already there, simply waiting to be filled up with the right content? Could not the attempt to fill in boxes—which would be better described as solv-ing problems—lead one to question the way the structure has been put together in the first place? Many of the difficulties of reading Harvey flow from this predicament: he assumes most of Marx's results and sees the task of a critical theory today to build on this basis.

Harvey's *The Limits to Capital,* for example, is above all an attempt to incorporate spatiality within Marxian political economy. He has added to our knowledge of the role of the circulation of capital within capitalism as a whole, throwing light on the dynamic, spatial character of capitalism missed by an aspatial and atemporal focus on accumula-tion. But he has also claimed that this knowledge uniquely equips us to understand features of social life not directly linked to economic processes, those that fall loosely under terms such as "culture," "expe-rience," "community," and so on. Echoing the distinction between struc-ture and practice, the two volumes collecting Harvey's most important work are intended to represent these two dimensions: *The Urbanization of Capital* with respect to structure, capital, and economy, and *Con-sciousness and the Urban Experience* with respect to experience, iden-tity, and culture. In terms that should immediately alert us to the prob-lem of privileging and hierarchy discussed in Chapter 1, Harvey writes, "Interior to this general argument [the economic arguments of *The*

Urbanization of Capital] I want to construct another, which will, I hope, help us understand the politics of urban protest, the forms of urban power, and the various modes of urban experience."[36] Does Harvey provide a convincingly Marxian perspective on urban protest and collective identities? Can they be characterized by a relationship of "interiority"? And does the interiorizing of action within the "system" categories of political economy further commit Harvey to a functionalist analysis of community conflict?

The direct parallels between Harvey's monistic view of theoretical frameworks and his assessment of the diversity of urban identities show how Harvey transposes the problem of eclecticism vis-à-vis theoretical discourses to the analysis of political and social identities in terms of fragmentation and holism. A parallel problem appears in his analysis of social forces: it is the underlying opposition between fragmentation and holism that gives sense to the interpretation of social identities as fragmented. Only relative to a concept of holistic identity—which, to use Derridian terms, would imply the essentialism of "presence," excluding a "constitutive outside"—does the idea of fragmentation take on meaning. The emphasis on the well-known "class in and for itself" model also can be understood from this angle. The impulse behind this type of imaginary, which Marx inherited directly from the German Idealist tradition of the early nineteenth century, can be traced to the neoclassical resurgence of the ideal of the whole Man of Greek antiquity. It was this myth that provided much of the emotive and moral foundations of nineteenth-century European Romanticism. The socialist movement, very much a child of that time's sensibility, imbibed deeply this imaginary of holism. Harvey's analysis likewise depends upon the assumption of the already formed, but yet to be realized, character of the antagonistic collective actors within capitalist societies. That is why, when forced to concede that subjects "internalize diverse conceptions and act upon them in a milieu that demands mixed . . . rather than . . . clear-cut identities," he can deal with the indeterminacy of identity only as "confusion."[37]

RECIPROCITY AND EXCHANGE:
THE FORMS OF SOCIAL INTEGRATION

The second problem posed by Harvey's attempt to view social processes functionally is his inadequate differentiation between reciprocity and exchange as distinct action types. In an early article from 1972 entitled "The Nature of Housing," Harvey explored the role of housing under capitalist conditions by means of the Marxian distinction between use value and exchange value. The totality of qualities that housing can provide for a family, household, or individual constitutes the use value of that house for that particular user. The exchange value relates to the pecuniary qualities that the house has for its owner.[38] Housing as a commodity thus has a twofold character.

Harvey explains the distinction as follows. The "use-value [of a house] contains all kinds of features which can be related to *reciprocity as a mode of economic integration* (particularly in the neighborhood setting); so in some respects the individual purchases or rents opportunities to integrate through reciprocity."[39] Because housing and neighborhoods include qualities such as proximity to different social groups, sources of employment, and lifestyles—all aspects of "social capital"—they constitute the material and normative structures of residents' lifeworlds. In other words, housing and neighborhoods are central components and expressions of the context of meaning of subjects' everyday lives. The meaning given to a house therefore can potentially act as a constituent of identity formation and a central component of the building of group solidarities. As an element in the structuring of a community or neighborhood, it can also influence the patterning of traditions, social solidarities, and organizations—the lifeworld out of which collective action and social movements derive their identity.

Two processes are conflated in Harvey's use of the notion of "reciprocity as a mode of economic integration," and it is important to distinguish between them. Reciprocity operates through the medium of ordinary, everyday language communication, whereas economic integration—a concept Harvey borrows from Karl Polanyi—operates through the "delinguistified" medium of money. In fact, it is only by means of this distinction that we can fully make sense of the Marxian critique of capitalist modernity, which holds that the members of the true community of (producing) subjects have become alienated from their true species-being because subjects relate to others only fetishistically as objects and interact only through an alienated medium such as money. But Harvey makes contradictory use of Polanyi's concept of modes of integration, leading him to clamp together the two analytically distinct dimensions of exchange and reciprocity into a single functionalist totality.

We can see this most clearly in Harvey's most interesting book, *Social Justice and the City*, where he draws on the categories advanced by Polanyi for the three ways in which social action can be coordinated: through exchange by means of a generalized market, through redistribution in terms of some political principle of authority, or through reciprocity.[40] These three modes of integration are then mapped onto Morton Fried's typology of three types of social organization: stratified organization, organization by rank, and egalitarian organization, respectively.[41] Harvey employs the concept of modes of integration to capture the way in which a society coheres or maintains its identity in terms of both action orientations and consequences. The concept functions, therefore, as a similar, although less precise, counterpart to the concepts of social integration and system integration introduced above.

For Harvey, reciprocity involves "the transfer of goods, favors and services among individuals in a given group according to certain well-defined social customs." There is an intimate relationship between reciprocity and egalitarian forms of organization in which social coherence is maintained through "voluntary cooperation loosely sustained by social custom." Significantly, Harvey cites anthropological research on "primitive" societies (which are held to approximate most closely reciprocal and egalitarian forms) to show that these formations are, in his words, "permeated by . . . an 'I-Thou' relationship between man and the natural world rather than an 'I-It' relationship in which man views himself as both separate and different from nature." However, with the process of capitalist modernization, Harvey observes, "reciprocity can be found [only] in urban society in . . . the acts of friendly exchange and mutual support among good neighbors in a community."[42]

There are a number of significant aspects of this argument. First, it links reciprocity as a principle of social organization with the intuitive sense of mutuality and egalitarianism today often associated with local, small-scale urban communities and neighborhoods. Second, it points to the intersubjective (I-Thou) linguistic structure of this gemeinschaft social relation. But there also are several difficulties. I would point to two in particular. It fails to distinguish between reciprocity and economic relations as modes of social integration, and it fails to distinguish between strategic action based on interest (that is, class) positions and dialogical forms of identity formation. Let us look at these in turn.

Reciprocity

First, despite the insistence that reciprocity is a form of economic integration, all the examples and definitions clearly point to the overwhelmingly symbolic dimension of reciprocal relations. This implies that, strictly speaking, reciprocity concerns not the exchange of already constituted objects (commodities) among already constituted social units (individual subjects), but rather refers to the specific manner in which a cultural totality or lifeworld is constituted. Harvey's focus on favors, goods and services, and so forth, is not abstract enough to capture this distinction. From the perspective of reciprocity, it is not the objects themselves that are important, but rather the fact that they are constituted *as objects* and take on a specific meaning within a context in which a subject confronts the other as subject and not as object. To refer to reciprocity as a mode of "transfer" of "goods" among productive units is to project back onto earlier forms the capitalist form of commodity exchanges.[43]

Harvey conceives of reciprocity and exchange at a conceptual threshold below that necessary for the immanent critique of bourgeois forms. Marx viewed the exchange between equivalents under a capitalist market regime as a fiction that masks the reifying effects of objectification on self-consciousness. It is therefore not the context in which individuals exchange goods that is decisive but the orientation toward the other. It is not that objects as such, in their objectivity, are given or transferred but rather whether the participants are able (or unable, in the case of reification) to thematize the normative presuppositions of this interaction as such. Reciprocity does not imply that the other be treated as the objective recipient of an object but that the participants—in this modality—struggle within a process of mutual recognition. What classical German philosophers such as Hegel thought under the ideas of reconciliation and freedom forms a central dimension of the moment of reciprocity, defined as "a relation in which the surrender of the one to the example of the other does not mean loss of self but a gain and an enrichment." This is the moment that breaks the circularity of essentialist, subject-centered reason and represents the (albeit impossible) promise of reconciliation as the "intact intersubjectivity that is only established and maintained in the reciprocity of mutual understanding based on free recognition."[44] (I discuss why a strong notion of reconciliation is "impossible" in the next two chapters, especially in the context of Lacan's theory of the subject.) Mutual recognition is indeed connected to egalitarian social forms, as Harvey recognizes, but it is so only as a utopian ideal, for "from the perspective of the participants, coming to an understanding is not an empirical event that causes de facto agreement; it is a process of mutually convincing one another in which the actions of participants are coordinated on the basis of motivation by reasons."[45] We need to be able to grasp this dimension if we are to be able to distinguish, as Marx intended, merely strategic cooperation on the basis of interest positions from a dialogical encounter in which the very identities of participants are put into question.

Reciprocity and egalitarian forms of social organization are founded not in subject-object relations but in subject-subject relations. If this insight is connected to the fact that reciprocity is allegedly associated with equality—a normative, utopian conception—then we are forced to search for the mechanisms in which, beyond the objectification of the other and hence self-alienation and self-estrangement (terms taken from Marx's *Paris Manuscripts*), members of an emancipated community can confront each other as equals. Reciprocity functions as the intuitive approximation for what Habermas calls "undamaged intersubjectivity" and that Derrida has called the "relation to the other as essentially non-instrumental," that is, the uncoerced interactions of speaking and acting subjects.[46] It therefore excludes analytically strategic manipulations in which the other is treated not as a subject but as an object, not as an end but as a means.

Harvey's work, from *Social Justice and the City* to *Justice, Nature, and the Geography of Difference*,[47] has consistently declared the importance of a normative standpoint for the critique of the capitalist city, but the basis for that position is much clearer in the earlier work, where it is anchored in a concept of reciprocity viewed as the "countervailing" force to the "penetration into human activity" of market processes.[48] This is enormously suggestive. But Harvey wrecks his own ship on the shoals of Marxism's metaphysical assumptions and overreliance on political economy. This is because the methodological merging of system and lifeworld perspectives cannot make room for a concept of reciprocity as social integration as distinct from cooperation based on strategic interests. Harvey lacks a concept to capture precisely what is alien or resistant to commodification and objectification. He cannot adequately open out a space of action outside the confines of strategic-rational action and as a result ends in unwittingly confirming, not critiquing, "bourgeois" subjectivity.

It is worth looking briefly at the way this problem is reflected in his discussion of money and the way this is used to interpret the diversity of urban identities as confusions of a true class identity. Harvey has revived an important strand of urbanistic thought initiated by Georg Simmel that connects money, cities, and personal identity. He follows Marx and Simmel in his analysis of the effect of the money form on cultural and social relations. As a result of the penetration of capitalist relations into traditional community structures, Harvey argues, "bonds of personal dependency are thereby broken and replaced by objective dependency relations between individuals who relate to each other through market prices and money and commodity transactions." He quotes Marx as writing that "individuals are now ruled by abstraction whereas earlier they depended on one another." The abstraction of money is linked directly to the increasing division of labor: "the labor process is represented and fetishized as a passive thing—money."[49] Money is the exemplar of a form of life broken away from concrete human interactions that replaces a holistic community with atomized individuals who can relate to each other only as objects.

Simmel also tried to grasp the cultural significance for everyday life of the urbanized money economies, although in contrast to Marx, he sought to analyze in a more systematic way their ambiguous nature.[50] Individualism, for Simmel, is a novel type of sociality linked closely to the division of labor and the commodity form of exchange, but more important, with the multiple spaces and networks of the city to which one can belong. This point has been recently taken up by social-network theorists. They have built on Simmel's seminal argument that the multiple spaces and associations that urban life supports and with which the subject must identify are the condition for the enhancement of a complex, hybrid sense of self. The complexity of the city, to use Ruth Coser's phrase, is "the seedbed of individual autonomy."[51]

Simmel was also concerned to understand how, in the absence of traditional community forms of solidarity, individuals become integrated into a larger collectivity, a problem that the Chicago School of urban sociology would later address. He suggested that the model of market exchange can only partly fulfill that function because money acts as an imperfect substitute for traditional forms of community. Simmel concluded that although money can contribute to human freedom and liberty through material advancement, it "is very inadequate for the particular and the personal. To the discriminating consciousness, the restrictedness of objective dependencies that money provides is but the background that first throws the resulting differentiated personality and its freedom into full relief."[52]

Harvey borrows from Marx the idea that with capitalism, money becomes the real community. He does this so as to be able to put into ironic relief the transformations in social interactions and cultural forms that the dominance of capitalism has brought about. If money has become the real community, replacing traditional forms of intimate, face-to-face, communal sociality, it becomes possible to draw a systematic link between the generalization of the money form to labor power itself and the (de)formations of patterns of consciousness. This move is crucial to the Marxian theory of urban identity and urban conflict. It provides the path to trace back modern cultural forms (atomized and alienated urban cultures) to their determination by the commodity form. The plethora of institutions, norms, and discourses of liberty and equality widespread since the French Revolution can all be understood, according to Harvey, as the concomitant development in the superstructures of the generalization of the money form and commodification.[53]

Money can be linked not only to these institutional and normative aspects of modernity but also to its "pathological" effects, such as economic and social crises, deformations of personality and family life, and social antagonisms. For Harvey, money—or to be precise, its specifically capitalist articulation—is responsible for the reifications that beset an urbanized consciousness. What Max Weber called the "loss of meaning" due to social rationalization Harvey wishes to interpret as the consequence of capitalist commodification of human labor on states of consciousness. He directs our attention to how "capitalism works and how its workings naturally generate certain states of political and social consciousness."[54]

Despite the apparent differentiation of the sources of social power among "money," "space," and "time," in some of his writings, it is really money that is the preeminent and fundamental determinant of all other forms of power: "Money," Harvey asserts, "represents nothing more than abstract social labor." If this is the case, then the effects of commodification and the spread of the market mechanism can be connected to the inherent antagonism built into the relations of production. Again we see how the connection with class conflict follows clearly from this: "The subsumption of places and spaces [of the city] under the uniform judgment of Plutus sparked resistance, often violent opposition, from all kinds of quarters"; "The incoherent pieces of resistance coalesce and well up." Thus, despite conceding the initial heterogeneity of urban social movements that demand to liberate space from domination, Harvey nevertheless concludes that nonclass forms of collective identity are confusions and a result of the displacement of the true class source of social antagonism.[55] But as we saw earlier, this conclusion neither does justice to the variety of empirical forms of urban-based movements nor permits the inclusion of state power and domination as autonomous sources of social power or structuration.

One of the key reasons for this blockage is that, again, Harvey's Marxism embraces the assumptions of the production paradigm underlying Marx's praxis philosophy. As he puts it in *Consciousness and the Urban Experience,* "The relationship to nature [is] the most fundamental relation ordering human affairs. This relationship is itself expressed primarily through the work process that transforms the raw materials of nature into use values. To put it this way is not to engage in a simplistic economic determinism; it merely advances the thesis that the relation to nature is the most fundamental aspect of human affairs."[56] I do not know whether this is a simple or a complicated economism, but it is one of the clearest examples of the productivist paradigm in contemporary Marxian theory. If labor or objectifying praxis is the fundamental characteristic of human action, how are we to understand reciprocity? Indeed, in his most recent work, Harvey appears to have sensed this difficulty and has retreated somewhat, though not fully, from praxis philosophy.[57]

If Marxian urbanism is to connect its analytical and normative moments, it must be able to deliver on a counterlogic to precisely that feature of capitalist commodity relations that is the basis of its critique—that each person treats others only as things, that is, as external nature. Without this counterlogic, which would require the conceptual terrain opened up by language, Harvey is caught in the circularity of positing the negation of capitalism from capitalist categories themselves. Again, in his latest work, Harvey attempts to incorporate language and discourse into Marx's materialism. The results are only ad hoc and fail to follow up the implications of doing so fully.[58] Without recourse to a philosophy of history, moreover, this Marxian solution fails to explain adequately the mechanisms through which collective actors come to an agreement on their identity and their interests. By viewing the lifeworld and reciprocity as residues of a premodern social organization, and not as a fundamental analytical category with which contemporary society should be understood, Harvey unwittingly collapses the communicative, dialogical process in which contemporary individuals come to understand and give meaning to their everyday experiences into the functionalist categories necessary for system reproduction.

Harvey does not distinguish at an appropriately theoretical level between self-regulating systems that abstract from the pragmatic conditions inherent in everyday speech and communicative interactions that reproduce the symbolic infrastructure of lifeworlds through language. The Marxian critique of modernity is totalizing at precisely this point. If this criticism is correct, we can no longer ground a theory of alienation or domination uniquely in the money or commodity form itself, as urban political economy suggests. As Habermas has put it, "a concept of alienation in contemporary social theory would have to be reformulated in a more abstract way. It would lead away from the analysis of the commodity form towards a critique of instrumental and functional rationality."[59]

Strategic Action and Interest Positions

Central to Harvey's project of the "socialist" city is the uncovering and delineation of a"revolutionary" or oppositional type of agency that is distinct from that created in capitalist cities. The capitalist market depends on the strategic and instrumental interactions of atomized individuals. An "urbanized consciousness" is Harvey's term for this reflection in everyday consciousness of a capitalist, commodified identity in which competitive individualism based on interest positions is the norm and class solidarities are masked.[60] The implication is that if an oppositional politics is to be possible in the context of the modern city, this depends upon an equally oppositional form of agency. This in turn requires a social space that provides the "requisite cognitive and moral competencies and institutional structures." Although changes in contemporary social structures (particularly a high degree of geographical and social mobility) have weakened these spaces, pushing exchange and strategic rationality to the fore, Harvey hints that these spaces are to be found in the reciprocal actions based on the use value of space that purportedly typifies small-scale communities and neighborhoods.[61]

Despite the intuitive appeal of linking use value, reciprocity, and communal city spaces, some key questions remain unanswered. The most important is: Does he succeed in demonstrating that countervailing forces are necessarily embodied in class conflict and that community-based movements ("displaced" class struggles) do not embody such a countervailing impulse?[62] Because Harvey derives the motivations and rationality of class-based collective action from the utilitarian logic of the market itself, he cannot do so. Workers in this view act collectively to pursue the objective interests that are given to them by the structure, which is defined in terms of only one subsystem, the economy.

Seen in this way, the logic of action or the form of agency defining workers is not qualitatively different from the instrumental rationality of the market. The drawback of this objectivistic model of collective action is that it fails to capture the two logics of collective action that parallel the system/lifeworld dualism, as Claus Offe explains them: monologically, actors orient themselves toward success on the basis of a given identity, that is to say, by finding the best means toward a given goal, while dialogically, actors transcend a utilitarian rationality and by questioning the goals of the collectivity come to define a new identity.[63] Harvey's functionalist bias prevents him from escaping an objectivistic conception of identity based on interest positions and a model of action restricted to strategic rationality.[64]

Harvey is led to this conclusion because of the way he conceptualizes the link between self-regulating market processes of exchange and subjective dispositions and identities.[65] He writes, for example, that "the market exchange relationship affects the consciousness of the individual. . . . The individual replaces states of *personal* dependence by states of *material* dependence. The individual becomes 'free' yet is controlled by the hidden hand of the market system."[66] There are two parts to this claim. In the first, Harvey emphasizes the distinction between intersubjective communication, on the basis of which "voluntary uncoerced cooperation" oriented toward mutual understanding characteristic of egalitarian societies can be idealized ("today only in neighborhood communities") and a strategic orientation of subjects oriented toward success. The second part of the claim is that, under capitalism, subjects are constituted through and by the structures of economic reproduction: the fiction of sovereign free choosers propounded by neoclassical economics is only the mask that hides the loss of a context in which a true community can find itself. Under the all-embracing power of the self-regulating market, which socializes subjects as personifications of its functional categories, individuals thus are "controlled by the hidden hand of the market system."

Harvey interprets the strategic rationality engendered by capitalist social relations as contradictory. While it is a reflection of the dominant system of action, it also forms the basis of the negation of that system because the proletariat recognizes its objective interest in the abolition of capitalism and struggles against the capitalist class to achieve that goal. Nonetheless, there remains a tension between two sources of opposition to capitalist dynamics: the reciprocal relations that Harvey claims are residues from precapitalist social formations and the inherent contradictoriness of capitalist production relations. Yet because the real, underlying mechanism of capitalist reproduction is economic exploitation, only the knowledge of this mechanism, and not appeal to another type of rationality external to production and market relations, can provide the basis of a scientific socialist position. As a result, the argument negates its own premise that there exists a substratum of sociality that can resist the objectifying logic of capitalism from the outside.

Harvey recognizes that reciprocity is connected to human relationships that resist market penetration into everyday life—"In the American city, ethnic bonds and a close-knit community structure have done much in the past to help resist the penetration of market exchange relationships into the daily life and hence human relationships within the community"—but there is no alternative model of rationality to grasp this because there is a persistent conflation of reciprocity and strategic action.[67] As such, there is no way out of the reifications of bourgeois capitalism as Harvey's Marxism understands it. The reduction of all action to the model of the producing and maximizing subject fails to grasp the way subjects confront each other communicatively—oriented toward mutual understanding—in a way that genuinely stands resilient against the onslaught of the market and the state.

How does Harvey interpret the diversity of previously "incoherent" urban identities? "The other axes do not disappear but take on curiously warped and contorted forms, which in turn undermine the clarity of class struggle and its objectives. Precisely for this reason, urban social movements take on mixed political coloration and can quickly change their spots according to shifting circumstances."[68] The clarity and purity of class is juxtaposed against the impurity and opacity of nonclass actors. But this is nothing more than an arbitrary assertion of primacy.

In sum, then, Harvey's crude use of the adjective "confusion" to designate what appears as a fetishistic understanding results from the absence of adequate concepts to capture the reality that confronts the urban theorist. The bravado of proletarian chiliasm in statements such as "the consciousness of class emerges supreme within the complex rivalries of urban social movements" and in the claim that the internal contradictions of capital circulation and accumulation produce a situation where "class struggle then surges to the fore as the principle axis of revulsion and revolt"—if nothing else obscures the complexity of the issues involved in untangling the web of intricate differentiations and dislocations that beset the terrain of identities in contemporary urban life.[69] For Harvey, class is present within concrete movements in the way the universal is present in the particular. Urban identities reflect the built environment of the modern city, which is in turn the "instantiation" of capitalist social relations. To borrow freely a phrase from Derrida, for Harvey, class is the "Idea in the Kantian sense, that is, the irruption of the infinite into consciousness."[70]

Harvey can proceed in this way because of the manner in which the basic concepts that are supposed to connect action-theoretical and systems-theoretical dimensions are used to read back the conditions necessary for the development of a consciousness that breaks the bonds of an objective fetish as an all-encompassing power in a unified struggle against capital, freeing itself from the autonomous self-reproduction of the economic sub-system regulated through money exchange. Harvey interprets the class-unspecific side effects of modernization in terms of an underlying class conflict. Habermas has exposed and analyzed the roots—and weaknesses—of precisely this strategy in Marx, so that we can apply his critique of Marx directly to Harvey:

> The young Marx conceives of the unity of system and lifeworld as did the young Hegel, on the model of a ruptured ethical totality whose abstractly divided moments are condemned to pass away. Under these premises, an accumulation process that has broken away from orientations to use-value literally amounts to an illusion—the capitalist system is *nothing more* than the ghostly form of class relations that have become perversely anonymous and fetishized. The systemic autonomy of the production process has the character of an enchantment. Marx is convinced a priori that in capital he has before him *nothing more* than the mystified form of a class relation. Marx conceives of capitalist society so strongly as a totality that he fails to recognize . . . that the differentiation of the state apparatus and the economy *also* represents a higher level of system differentiation. . . . The significance of this level of integration goes beyond the institutionalization of a new class relationship.[71]

A practical-political orientation toward action then can be tied to the historical process by which concrete actions are transformed into abstract performances, that is to say, by which activities meaningful within a cultural context become more and more subsumed as anonymous inputs for purposes of valorization. If the ruptured ethical totality is conceived as the objectification of inner powers through praxis, then emancipation can proceed from labor itself. A class struggle could then be justified as the universal moment of negation and transcendence of this abstract system. However, that argument loses its force once we take into account the differentiation of spheres of action (work, community, family, and so on) within the modern city, as well as the autonomization of subsystems (economy and bureaucracy).

CONCLUSION

At the core of Marxian theory is a concept of the directionality of social change and the identification of a universal agent to carry out the task of social transformation. Harvey therefore cannot avoid making explicit reference to the political implications of his theory, locating the "instru-mentalities" for implementing the "socialist alternative" in the "working-class struggle." For this outcome to be secured, however, requires "a rad-ical transition in American urban politics away from fragmented pluralism into a more class-conscious mode of politics." If this is a call for a more explicit orientation toward the reform of the labor market and economic decision making, there is little with which to disagree. But it is the rela-tionship of class-based action to the multiplicity of other struggles that is the crucial aspect of the contemporary political scene and that is most prob-lematic in Harvey's account. For example, he writes, the barriers to a social-ist alternative "are deeply embedded in . . . the individualism of money, the consciousness of family and community [that] *compete* with the expe-rience of class relations on the job and create a *cacophony* of conflicting ideologies."[72]

To be sure, the commodification and monetarization of everyday life has continued unabated, perhaps with even greater intensity than at any time in the past. But this makes it all the more important to be able to distinguish at an analytical level between this and newer and other sources of pathologies. Harvey overextends the imperatives of one subsystem to account for the totality of modern problems. Class cannot be assumed to be the basis on which a fundamental negation of the contemporary social structure reveals itself because, as Offe has noted, postindustrial societies have experienced a "deepening" and "broadening" of forms of domina-tion and deprivation beyond the experience of labor and outside the space of the workplace. In addition to the increased ability to shift and spread conflict around social sectors, this leads Offe to conclude that the "sys-temic interchangeability of the scenes of conflict and the dimensions of conflict resolution makes any idea of a 'primordial' conflict (such as derived from the Marxian 'law of value') obsolete."[73]

The reproduction of labor power is an economic category of political economy. Just as it is problematic to make assumptions about the actions of "workers" as the personifications of labor power, it is equally erro-neous to analyze community-based struggles as being uniquely deter-mined by the "reproduction" of that labor power. The perspective of the lifeworld is not a subjective "filter" of culture that interprets the already constituted facticity of the economy. The lifeworld is the discursive field in which all action scenarios are constituted. To the extent that subjects act and do not act out parts given to them, that is to say, to the extent that social action is meaningful, both strategic and communicative action are constituted within the everyday life of participants. This hermeneutic insight also carries with it the corollary that we cannot infer from an analysis of the motion of systemic processes, let alone from an analysis of one process restricted to the economic subsystem, that the orientations and antagonisms of urban or community-based subjects necessarily will occur along class lines.

It is worth remarking at this point on an interesting aspect of Harvey's position on the relationships between the multiplicity of social actors, urbanism, postmodernism, and the agenda of socialist politics. In 1989, he published a widely acclaimed book, *The Condition of Postmodernity*. It is a curious book in many ways. It is explicitly designed as a Marxist or historical materialist answer to all those postmodern theorists of contemporary culture who consign Marx to the dustbin of history, along with other Enlightenment thinkers. As I noted at the outset, a central motif of so-called postmodern perspectives is the celebration of the fragment, the local, the irreducibility of difference, and the instability of any fixed meaning or identity. (It is of secondary importance that all these motifs can as readily be associated with modernism.)[74] From our discussion of Harvey's argument it would not be hard to see why he would inveigh against such a perspective. Clearly and correctly, he sees this new sensibility as highly antagonistic to the Marxian political and theoretical project. But his response in this book is disappointing, since one would have hoped that an encounter of an urbanist with the positions that have questioned the holistic aspirations of Marxism would have produced an interesting dialogue. This unfortunately is not the case.

First, as far as defending Marxism is concerned, Harvey's strategy is not to respond to the charges of its critics but simply to reassert a materialist, economistic, and reductive analysis of cultural forms. The chapter entitled "The Crisis of Historical Materialism" is less than three pages long, implying, of course, that there really is no crisis. Considering that Laclau and Mouffe's *Hegemony and Socialist Strategy* (1985), the most important challenge to Marxism to appear so far from a poststructuralist perspective, is not even cited in the book, his intervention into the debate must be considered something of a nonstarter. Nor is there serious discussion of any of the so-called new social movements. Furthermore, because the issues of difference, fragmentation, and so on (in our case involving labor and community-based movements), go to the heart of my critique of the Marxian political imaginary, it would be worth simply noting the key difference between a Marxist and a so-called postmodern politics. Whereas a Marxist conception of revolutionary politics involves the simplification of the social field into two homogeneous camps, a radical democratic politics involves by contrast the proliferation of sites of antagonisms and identities. It is this difference that brings most clearly to light the post-Marxist political challenge.

Harvey, like Castells, did not continue the project of developing a Marxian urban theory after the major publications of the mid-1980s, leaving direct engagement with its issues to take up instead ecological concerns and for an ambiguous relationship with the Marxian socialist tradition. Significantly, Harvey's most recent work, *Justice, Nature, and the Geography of Difference* (1996), acknowledges the limits of Marxian class politics and theory. By acknowledging multiple bases of oppression in addition to economic class exploitation, by conceding that state power and the market economy are two independent sources of alienation and domination, and by rejecting the material base/ideological superstructure model, Harvey, like Castells, has also drawn the conclusion that the impasse of Marxian urban theory is in part internal to Marxian discourse itself.[75] The shortcomings of the Marxian tradition cannot be attributed, as some interpreters have done, solely to the weakness of the working class and the failure to realize the project of a class-based politics in practice.[76]

THE TWO LOGICS OF COLLECTIVE ACTION AND THE CONSEQUENCES FOR THE ANALYSIS OF URBAN SOCIAL MOVEMENTS

The foregoing critique has important implications for the study of class and urban social movements. The foreshortening of the critique of modernity to an economistic critique of instrumental reason modeled on market exchange on which Harvey builds his theory fails to question the model of strategically interacting subjects. As such, such a foundation does not provide an alternative to, and thus cannot escape, the monological orientation of actors that Harvey himself claimed is the negative or pathological effect of the commodification of everyday life. As a consequence, Harvey's analysis affirms the model of action that he wishes to critique, the only difference being that the role of actor is shifted from individuals onto classes. It thus remains within the underlying framework of the interest-group model of politics, that is, as a zero-sum game between (class) actors.

The move away from strategically oriented action requires a perspective wide enough to allow for both monological and dialogical forms of interaction. The debate between methodological individualism and holistic approaches[77] requires an empirical hypothesis as to the concrete institutional embodiment of both logics of collective action, monological and dialogical. The perspective must be sufficiently broad to permit both action types as possibilities along a spectrum of forms of orientations.

Offe has used the framework of the two logics to analyze the dilemmas of trade-union politics in ways relevant to the present discussion. His primary aim is to contest the liberal-bourgeois theory and practice of treating all associational organizations—in particular, business and employers' organizations and labor unions—as subcases of the interest-group model. The plausibility of this reductive approach is based on certain formal similarities shared by both types of organization.[78] Offe contests this view by showing that the class structure of contemporary society provides capital and labor with distinct sets of problems with which their organizations must contend and that there is an inequality built into their respective positions affecting their ability to solve these problems. This relationship of power is connected with the type of reflexivity and action that a class employs vis-à-vis its "interests." He concludes that whereas the business class seeks the means of satisfying ends that are by and large fixed and given and that can be unambiguously calculated (that is, profit), this is not true for the class of wage earners. Whereas business organizations, due to their superior resources and ability to satisfy their ends, can afford to remain within a utilitarian mode of action, the inferior position of workers forces them to shift from a search for adequate means to attempting to redefine the ends or values of the collectivity as such. "Those in the inferior power position can increase their potential for change only by overcoming the comparatively higher costs of collective action by changing the standards according to which these costs are subjectively evaluated within the group." This means that for the relatively powerless, there is a paradoxical condition built into the dynamics of collective action such that "interests can only be met to the extent they are partly redefined."[79] This paradox is connected with the fact that working-class organizations "simultaneously express and define" the interests of their members. In contrast to the merely monological orientation of business and employers' groups, working-class organizations are faced with the dilemma of needing to rely on both a monological and a dialogical relationship with action, the first to succeed in achieving their goals, the second to survive over time.

This argument relies implicitly on the system/lifeworld distinction. Workers must reassess the costs/benefits of action, as defined by the initial situation in which business is in a greater position of power, if they are going to overcome the Olsonian dilemma of collective action. This dilemma arises especially in the case of public goods such as wage regulation or clean air in which benefits are dispersed widely, regardless of individual contributions. If an individual's decision to enter into collective action is based solely upon selfish and instrumental motives, this can result in the "free rider" problem because it can appear rational not to contribute to the group effort. In contrast, "The purpose of [a dialogical orientation in] conflict is, not to 'get something,' but to put ourselves in a position from which we can see better what it really is that we want to get."[80]

Nonetheless, Offe's model cannot by itself justify the assumption that class is always the primary identity adopted by workers. To put into doubt and therefore thematize what one wants and why is the same thing as asking "Who are we?" But by virtue of what feature of social life can we predict that the outcome of such a deliberation should necessarily be the subjective recognition of the collectivity as a class defined in Marxian ways? Even if we grant with Harvey and Offe that there is an inherent antagonism between capital and wage labor and thus that the antagonism is an objective one—that is to say, there is an isomorphism between the contradiction of logical categories and the antagonism between flesh-and-blood actors—this must still contend with the problem that a collective identity depends in part on the recognition of common interests by a group of individuals.[81] As Barry Hindess and Paul Hirst have argued, this "is to admit that there may be other, non-class, forms of communal action." However, they continue, to ground the necessity of class outcomes on the "shared experience of collective struggle is equally problematic . . . since it presupposes what has to be established, namely, that it is class interests that form the basis for communal action."[82]

Allowing for this contingency does not deny the possibility of systematic constraints and pressures or a differential access to the modes of discourse (the basis of power). What it does deny is that the analysis can be restricted to a narrative of class formation. Once plurality is the starting point of analysis, the force of the argument by which unions could represent all wage workers is weakened. When Adam Przeworski writes that "struggle is a struggle *about* class before it is struggle *among* classes," if classes are the "effects of struggles," then who are the initial collectivities in struggle?[83]

This surplus of meaning that escapes the ability of any one institutional embodiment to represent all its constituents reflects not an empirical deficiency on the part of any group, for example, a trade union. It reflects the fact that if identity is relational and unstable, then any boundary that defines an inside, a "we" (in our case that which would constitute class as labor), necessarily depends on an outside with which it stands contrasted. This "outside" is as necessary to the identity of what is enclosed as what appears to be self-contained, inside. Building on these Derridian insights, we should be sensitive to the unstable boundaries of identities, to their "ambivalent demarcations." This continual spilling over is clearly illustrated in another essay by Offe, "Interest Diversity and Trade Union Unity." The essay demonstrates the limits of a discourse that retains the (Marxian) assumption that class identity could potentially unify the heterogeneous reality of its "members."

Acknowledging the hegemonic basis of trade-union organization, Offe observes that "the crucial problem for union policy is whether and how the unity of interests of all 'employees' (a unity that can no longer be taken for granted in developed, capitalist countries) can possibly be restored, or at least prevented from further disintegration, by trade-union organization."[84] The discursive nature of trade-union hegemony implies that labor movements must articulate a diversity of elements—be they economic, political, cultural, or personal—into a totality, or what I have referred to as an experiential unity: "The fundamental assumption of the labor movement is that, compared with the common interests that are held to arise from this socio-economic situation, special interests—such as those arising from the occupation, economic sector, gender, or nationality of the individual employee—play only a subordinate role."[85]

The implications of these observations are that we should shift our analytical perspective from the point of view of one organization organizing one identity (e.g., from trade unions organizing the working class) to a conception of organizations as arenas in which overdetermined identities are hegemonized, which means that no one identity can be fully represented by a unique, finite organization. This is not because the means of representation are inefficient, as might be claimed if false consciousness or trade-union corruption were the type of explanation being advanced. It is because an "outside" is necessary to the constitution of the inside. Offe, like Harvey, by contrast, retains the notion that a full identity is possible under certain empirical conditions. The problem of the surplus of meaning within any local heterogeneity—which he identifies as the chief organizing obstacle encountered by unions—can be overcome, he writes, "under the somewhat paradoxical condition that trade union organization does not limit its political activity to the fact that its members are *employees,* but rather concentrates additionally on those living conditions that are not determined directly by wage-labor relations and have, therefore, traditionally been included under the jurisdiction of the state rather than union policy."[86] We are thus back to precisely the problem confronted by a Marxian urban theory and that forms the theme of our inquiry: how to understand the splitting off of identities that are not "directly" determined by wage labor or within the workplace.

Several problems raised by Offe's work thus are similar to those found in Harvey's. First, what would a trade union be if it accorded equal weight to the identity of racial or sexual minorities that it did to their identity as employees? Offe employs the term "paradoxical" to express the tension inherent in this impossible situation. Second, we are again faced with the unstated axiom that employees or workers are such a priori, even outside the institutional matrix with(in) which we identity them in the first place, the wage labor relation. This sits uncomfortably with the previous acknowledgment—perhaps unwitting—of the hegemonic and not expressive character of unions vis-à-vis working-class identity. Third, the above passage hints at the fact that the "lumpiness" or structuration of collective identities should in part be sought in the institutional patterning of power and everyday life. The fact that the state has taken over institutions that relate to subjects as consumers of urban space, for example, or as clients of municipal bureaucracies, implies that the capacity of unions to hegemonize collective identities structured through these networks—such as community-based movements for better housing, to take one example—is inherently problematic. If there is an asymmetry between the identity as employee and any other identity from the perspective of union organization, this is a constituent feature of trade unions as such: it is not a contingent characteristic.

It might be objected that consumers and occupiers of housing are also wage earners. This is true, but it misses the point: subjects are none of these, not all of them. To adopt the latter position would lead directly to a merely empiricist version of pluralism. It would presuppose, furthermore, that the empirically detectable diversity of institutions, such as the increasing complexity of the labor market, is nothing more than a subjective illusion generated by bourgeois social relations. Indeed, we saw Harvey present the case in precisely these terms. The former alternative would lead, by contrast, beyond the paradigm of objective identity and toward the conception of all collective identities as so-called failed objectivities. Offe admits that trade unions must hegemonize the concrete forms of difference (arising out of gender differences, racial or ethnic divisions, or distinct occupational roles in the economy, and so on) but still retains the idea that the role of unions is to "restore" the class unity defined through an objective analysis of the relations of production. If the assumption of this goal is dropped, we must reaffirm that there is no justification for considering the outcome of union organization as a restoration. It should be considered as an articulation of diverse elements into a new unity, remembering all the while the dependent relation of the new unity, through power, to the system of exclusions on which it is based.

Trade unions cannot represent the totality of differences with which they are faced, and this accounts for their paradoxical situation. If they could do so, as envisaged by Marxism, they would eliminate in an apolitical utopia the very basis on which social identities are based, their reciprocal relation with nonidentity, that is, difference. The agenda of a Marxian socialist labor movement and its theoretical basis in the work considered here live to pursue this dream. But in practice, unions have always been particular institutions, defining as well as representing what it means to be a worker. The limited and finite nature of trade unions (and all other organizations) need not be interpreted as marking the loss of a progressive potential for progressive reform, however. In fact, it implies that a socialist agenda can be built only through the linking of surplus identities across a network of organizations, demands, and identities within an overall framework of democracy, freedom, and equality.

CHAPTER 3

Toward the Historicity and Contingency of Identity

In the previous two chapters, I critiqued two different attempts to develop a foundation for Marxian urban theory. As with all intellectual work, Castells's and Harvey's projects each were influenced (although not determined in any simple way) by the national, historical, and disciplinary contexts within which they were undertaken. Castells's initial formulation, developed within the sociological tradition and linking processes of collective consumption, space, and urban conflict to what he argued was a new phase of state-led capitalist development, was very clearly marked by the specificities of the French political economy, which was characterized by strong state capacity and its prominent role in land-use planning and social policy. Similarly, Harvey's framework, developed within the discourse of critical human geography, reflects to a significant extent the British Left's intellectual milieu, within which his earliest work was written. His guiding assumption of the basic unity of urban working-class identity is no doubt derived not just by deduction from axioms of Marxian theory but from the historical experience of a strong and holistic English working-class culture captured in E. P. Thompson's well-known work.[1]

In this chapter, I consider a third effort to develop a framework for Marxian urban theory, one that takes the specificity of the U.S. sociopolitical structure as a crucial ingredient for avoiding the pitfalls found in the work of Castells and Harvey. In several books and essays published since the early 1980s, most notably *Marxism and the City* and

City Trenches, Ira Katznelson, working from within the disciplines of political science and history, has advanced the most systematic and nuanced attempt to link class and space within the Marxian framework. Katznelson's model shifts its focus away from both the sociological empiricism we saw in Castells and the structural determinism of Harvey's work, emphasizing instead historical and political variables to help account for the contingency of class structure and class experience in the modern capitalist city. What is distinctive about Katznelson's approach is the idea that collective identities—class and community—should be understood as prima facie spatially and institutionally patterned and differentiated. In contrast to Castells, who treats class and the urban as two distinct dimensions, and in contrast to Harvey, who sees community as derivative from class antagonism, Katznelson argues that the historical, cultural, and political specificity of the separation of workplaces and residential communities should be seen as an integral and constitutive part of the development of working-class identities and modes of collective action. Central to this view is the idea that the differentiations of urban space (into workplaces, residential communities, public spaces, and so on) and the relations between them in the context set by local political institutions are the terrain of the formation, rather than the masking, of working-class identities. Of course, Katznelson wants to develop a perspective on the diversity of urban identities that is flexible enough to accommodate historical contingency, yet robust enough to retain the privileged place of Marxian class politics and class analysis. Although I will argue that this dual commitment gives rise to the principal tensions and shortcomings of his project, it is because this approach takes the plurality of urban spaces as the starting point for analyzing the diverse identities in the modern city, and not as something to be explained away, that it contributes to the understanding of the hybridity of identities that we began sketching in the Introduction and Chapter 1. My task in this chapter is to evaluate this third, historical approach to the Marxian framework for the problems of identity, space, and structure.

Before turning to Katznelson's Marxian urban theory, it would be useful to discuss briefly two related themes that form the context of Katznelson's work and of the discussion of it that follows. The first concerns the history and place of Marxist and socialist discourse in American political culture. The second pertains to the debates over the peculiarly limited nature of urban policy making in U.S. cities and the relative absence of working-class–based urban movements and agendas.

MARXISM AND SOCIALISM IN THE UNITED STATES

The United States has had an unusual significance for the study of working-class politics and for Marxian theory. The absence of a direct feudal past, the powerful hegemony of the ideology of the market, the privileged role of business in social and political life, the inequalities of income and wealth, and the occasional eruptions of industrial strife have meant that the United States arguably represents the most "pure" form of capitalism. As a result, it has held for some observers particular promise for the growth of Marxian socialist ideologies appealing to working-class individuals and families to support a movement aimed at replacing capitalism with a social order ruled by and for workers. Yet nowhere has this promise gripped the popular imagination less. Socialism, in the Marxian sense, has never been a serious possibility in the United States. The reasons claimed for this absence of socialism, even in the limited form of a working-class national political party—the widespread possibilities of material advancement for most social groups, the high value placed on individual liberty, ethnic heterogeneity resulting from large-scale immigration, the early incorporation of (white, male) workers into the political regime—are well known and need not be rehearsed further here. The problematic of "American exceptionalism," of America's difference from other nation-states, especially those of Western Europe that otherwise resemble it, has nonetheless haunted all Marxian interpretations of the American experience, if only for the simple reason that Marx's original formulations, not developed with the peculiarities of the Americans in view, have persistently faced an uneasy translation to American soil.

By the 1970s, historians of working-class America became tired of pursuing the old question of why socialism never thrived in the United States. As a result, as Michael Kazin has recently put it, they changed the question, and "instead of responding yet again to the dismal negative, they tried to understand what kind of ideology discontented working people *had* expressed."[2] Rather than try to explain what had not occurred—mass working-class mobilizations for a socialist regime—analysts on the Left sought to construct explanations of what had happened, albeit with one eye cocked for what they felt, given the right circumstances, might happen. Katznelson's urban work is in significant part a contribution to this American revisionist labor historiography and is animated by the utopian impulses that inspired the socialist movement.

Paying equal attention to meanings of the concrete everyday lived experiences of working men and women, as well as to the structural contexts within which they forged these meanings, Katznelson was the first to make the concrete spaces of the city a constitutive part of the story of the development of working-class cultural identity in the United States and, by extension, in other national contexts as well.

Katznelson's Marxian urban theory is thus set in a different context from either the post-1968 France of Castells or the academicism of Harvey, although it does share some of the presuppositions of both these positions. Katznelson is in the position of relying on a theoretical and political tradition that has at best been a marginal presence within the United States and thus of appealing, as a social scientist, to the "scientific" aspect of Marxian explanation. On the other hand, the foregrounding of "community" and its local roots is embedded in the tradition of American popular radicalism that writers such as Lawrence Goodwyn, Harry Boyte, and Thomas Bender have identified as an enduring feature of populist political culture in the United States.[3]

THE CITY AND THE LIMITS OF
URBAN POLITICS IN THE UNITED STATES

The second context within which it is important to place Katznelson's work is the debate over the limited nature of urban politics and urban policy making in American cities. Apart from a few short-lived experiments in municipal socialism in the earlier part of this century, and despite the fact that U.S. cities have concentrated the bulk of the industrial working class, very few examples of working-class movements for socialist or radical populist regimes have emerged. American city politics has overwhelmingly been organized around ethnic and religious groups and coalitions, has tended to focus on issues of consumption and distribution of local government services, and has in general marginalized questions about control over economic resources. In many cases, local political regimes have brought together organized labor, local businesses, and other major interest groups around a program of business-led economic growth and have steered clear of class-based agendas that urge significant redistribution of economic resources or regulation of business activity. Despite some examples of union solidarities and class-based activity, urban working classes have responded more often to appeals based on ethnic, racial, or religious ties and on economic self-interest than to appeals for greater redistribution of the wealth and for the increased participation of disadvantaged groups in government and the economy.

There have been several explanations for the constrained nature of urban politics and for the fragmented character of urban working-class identity, or in Marxist terms, for the absence of a unified, militant, working-class identity. Much of the early "community power" debates revolved around the question of the distribution of power within American cities, and I touch on them briefly here only to the extent that they help illuminate the relation between class and the city.

In the dominant pluralist interpretation of urban politics, the political system is characterized as fluid and open enough to challengers to preclude any permanent cleavage along economic lines. To the extent that inequalities do exist, they are not seen as cumulating in elite control in the interests of business. For those who advance this interpretation, class conflict has been absent from city politics because working-class institutions are incorporated into a governing coalition whose members benefit from cooperation, rather than from confrontation, a coalition that represents a compromise of social interests.[4]

This picture of the consensual nature of urban coalitions has been challenged by theorists who advance one of two different types of alternative explanation for the lack of appeal for progressive, Marxian or socialist agendas in American local politics—one centered on the actors involved, the other on structural concerns. The first points to the domination of city politics by local economic and political elites with an interest in enhancing the exchange value of land in opposition to the concerns of poor and working-class residents, whose primary interest is the use value of local neighborhoods and social networks. In this view, class politics is relatively absent in the United States because of the asymmetry of power between these two social groups and because of the ideological hegemony of the market and self-interest over the majority of the population.[5]

The second type of alternative explanation shifts the focus away from the actors engaged in pluralist bargaining or forming elite coalitions and toward the structural context that sets limits to the policy choices available to cities as well as to the forms of politics that can emerge. Drawing from theories of public finance, one type of structuralist explanation sees the functions of local government as falling into three policy domains: growth-oriented economic development, the allocation of urban maintenance and management tasks across the city, and redistributive welfare policies. In the decentralized American federal system, cities must compete for labor and capital, and as a consequence, they are constrained to pursue only those agendas that further economic growth. This has consequences for politics: long-range economic decisions tend to be made behind closed doors by economic elites. Similarly, redistributive welfare policies that would potentially reduce a city's attractiveness to business investment are typically pushed off the agenda or ignored to the extent possible.[6] Both these factors impede open contestation over economic choices by socioeconomically defined groups.

The structural bias in favor of property rights can in fact be traced to the constitutional design of the American federalist structure. Its framers were explicit in their efforts to develop checks and balances against the potential of both state tyranny and threats to property rights. The structure of government authority was designed to exhibit complexity and incoherence, the legacy of which (intended or not) has been the weakening of government's ability to regulate economic institutions, thereby hampering its ability to expand and coordinate its social responsibilities.[7] The fragmented political system, especially marked at the state and local levels, has given business an advantage in policy outcomes. In this view, then, the constrained nature of local politics is shaped by the political and institutional framework, which provides mobile capital with the ability to play regions and cities off one another while impeding coherent policy responses. Working-class collective action to mobilize support against business interests is likewise weakened by jurisdictional fragmentation, which accounts for the fragmented and moderate character of labor organizations at the municipal level.

A related type of structural explanation of why uneven urban economic growth and change has not led to a greater degree of class and group conflict in the United States has focused on the design of the political institutions within the city.[8] In this view, the potential for social conflict is mediated, diffused, and displaced through the structural arrangements of urban government, which segregate the potentially contradictory economic and political functions of local government into different agencies and at different levels of government. For example, the economic and accumulation functions are typically located in agencies at the regional or national levels and are relatively insulated from local political pressure, whereas agencies dealing with the social results of economic policy (those exercising the legitimation function) are located at lower levels of government and are relatively more open to interest groups and popular pressure. (One clear example from the postwar period is the separation between urban-renewal agencies responsible for the displacement of many families and the public-housing authorities who were supposed to deal with the mess.) These arrangements reflect and further the privileged role of business in shaping urban policy. Furthermore, political relations between groups are mediated through the formal organization of political authority. Potential class-based demands that are generated by broader economic changes are thus transformed into escalating demands by fragmented, consumption-oriented groups on the agencies that have the least control over the causes of the problems.

Drawing significantly from Marxian insights, both of these actor-centered and structure-centered models have captured important dimensions of how the American urban political economy channels policy making away from redistributive claims and channels collective action away from class-based coalitions and group mobilizations that would significantly challenge or regulate property rights.

The significance of Katznelson's work lies in the way it addresses three shortcomings of this literature in relation to the problem of cities, space, and class conflict. First, accounts emphasizing the influence of structural contexts or separate policy domains of urban government tend to be inadequately historical, obscuring the contested evolution of the institutions of urban government. Second, structural Marxian theories of urban social movements assume that the passage from contradiction (politicized collective consumption or geographical dislocation) to antagonism, or to put it another way, from grievance to collective action, is too automatic. There is in fact a greater degree of contingency and variation than is allowed for in these approaches. Third, much of the literature on the incorporation of labor into the U.S. political system, even from some writers on the Left, exaggerates the extent to which class-based behavior has been absent from the U.S. experience. The conflation of the *kind* of class ideology and action (divided between, rather than bridging, the workplace and the urban community, for example) and the *degree* of class militancy (reformist, rather than revolutionary) obscures the particularly urban character of class identity in the United States when compared, for example, with class identity in Western Europe. Taken together, these objections amount to a call for the analysis of historical and analytical contingency, and it has been the object of Katznelson's work to revisit both Marxist class theory and urban social theory in ways that can incorporate contingency and complexity into the study of class formation and community-based identities. Katznelson's goal is to construct a conceptual framework that avoids the teleology of Marxist labor historiography that has been rooted in the metanarrative of proletarian coming to consciousness and emancipation—the essentialist narrative of class formation.

Central to Katznelson's revisionist urban theory is the distinction between two dimensions of his work: a methodological reworking of the classical in-itself, for-itself model of class structure and a historical account of the formation of the American working class since the nineteenth century in which urban space plays a key explanatory role. However, these two dimensions work against each other. More specifically, the radical implications of the historical model (which I will call the *City Trenches* thesis, for convenience) are undermined by the developmental assumptions of the revised Marxian class scheme. The revised class model fails to resolve the problems of the classical model, and the historical reinterpretation fails to avoid developmentalist and teleological premises. What is more, gender relations are inadequately incorporated into the explanatory scheme.

The *City Trenches* thesis is ultimately unsuccessful in overcoming teleological assumptions of a class-formation narrative. Nonetheless, the introduction of contingency into the historical account brings us to the very horizon of the Marxian problematic itself. As a consequence, the possibilities opened up by the *City Trenches* thesis indicate a move beyond the categories of historical materialism and the Marxian political imaginary. This is because the logic of contingent (or hybrid) identities undermines the two key assumptions of Marxian (labor) historiography: the unity of a working-class identity and the teleology of a historical narrative. The Marxian scaffolding retained in Katznelson's approach prevents it from fully engaging with these radical possibilities of hybridity and contingency. What things look like when we remove this scaffolding will become more clear as I develop an alternative approach to conceptualizing identities building on the insights we have gleaned earlier from Derridian deconstruction and Laclau's theory of hegemony, as well as on certain elements of Lacanian psychoanalytical theory.

PROBLEMS IN MARXIAN CLASS ANALYSIS

Under what circumstances will individuals and groups map the social geography of capitalist modernity in class terms? To pose the problem of Marxian urban theory in this way is to raise a series of difficult issues that move the themes of structure, agency, contingency, and space to the center of analysis. The question can be properly understood only if it is broken down into its four key components: a claim about the relatively stable and enduring structural contexts within which subjects find themselves and which they then attempt to transform through their actions; an acknowledgment of the diversity and variation of the forms of social and political identities; an analysis of the nature of the urban and spatial forms of a particular society; and the notion of "mapping" as the mechanism through which "objective" structures/contexts are interpreted and given "subjective" meanings.

As is well known, the Marxian theoretical tradition has a long and somewhat tortuous discussion of the base/superstructure metaphor as an answer to the question of how to relate structure and agency. Although Katznelson does not wish to abandon it entirely, nevertheless, he argues that the base/superstructure model in its simple form is an inadequate tool to help answer questions about the historical variability of working-class formation in capitalist cities and is too deterministic to allow for contingency and complexity. According to Katznelson, part of the explanation for the problems encountered in Marxian theory is the conflation of three distinct projects that traditionally constitute it. The first is a philosophy of history that furnishes an abstract model of epochal historical change from one mode of production to another: historical materialism. The second is a logical model of the economy under capitalism, from which are derived the "laws of motion" of the economy, the relations of production in the workplace, and in which classes are the key actors, defined by their economic roles: political economy as developed in *Capital*. The third is a project of concrete, historical explanation developing accounts of given specific social formations treated as a whole, and not just as an economy. At this third level, what is significant is the nature of agency across all social relations and spaces, the variations in concrete outcomes, the causal mechanisms linking the base and superstructure and the three levels, and the explanatory power of Marx's central claim that the logical model of the economy under capitalism identifies the most important factor accounting for the historical development of given specific social formations. The central controversies within Marxian theory then can be viewed in terms of the link between the logical theory of capitalism and a theory of historical capitalist societies as a whole. This is of course a specific manifestation of the more general problem experienced by all the social sciences of managing the field of tension between structure and agency, a field defined by oppositions such as objectivism and subjectivism, structuralism and voluntarism, and so on. As we will see, however, the significance of

Katznelson's methodological discussion goes beyond Marxian theory and is of much broader significance for social explanation.

Katznelson's insight is that most Marxian explanations have attempted to develop accounts of whole societies without making the shift to the third level, where the analyst no longer can depend exclusively upon the categories of the economy at the level of the logical theory of capitalism.[9] This, of course, is a problem for Marxian theory more generally, which has been faced with several options: to continue muddling through with unclear, ad hoc analyses; to reassert orthodoxy and mechanical causality, as Harvey and the early Castells have done; to downplay or ignore the base/superstructure distinction, in the manner of E. P. Thompson or the late Castells; to expand the notion of the base to include culture and ideology, following Raymond Williams; to eliminate the tension between structure and agency theoretically, as Anthony Giddens as well as Ernesto Laclau and Chantal Mouffe have attempted to do; or finally, to restrict the superstructure to only those phenomena that the economy does explain and then to look around for non-Marxist concepts to pick up the analytical slack, the strategy proposed by Eric Hobsbawm. Although recognizing that it results in a Marxism with humbler aspirations, Katznelson follows the last option because he feels that it retains the strengths of classical Marxism and that it can help overcome the impasse reached by Marxian urbanism.

THE FOUR-TIER MODEL OF CLASS

One of Katznelson's objections to approaches such as those of Castells and Harvey is that the linkage assumed to exist between forms of the economy such as proletarianization and the concentration of workers into factories and the types of actors these forms produce has been too mechanical. In this, Castells and Harvey followed Marx and Engels and the Marxist tradition more generally, for whom

> the formation of a class-conscious working class was something of an automatic process. We know, in retrospect, that they were wrong. There is no ineluctable path from the life situations of working people in capitalist cities to their emergence as a group sharing anti-capitalist dispositions with a willingness and capacity to act against the social order. Class formation is not something that occurs as a quantitative matter, more or less. It is a contingent process whose terms and content vary from place to place.[10]

For Katznelson, making sense of this situation requires recognizing four distinct dimensions or levels of class that are related to the three Marxian analytical projects of historical materialism, political economy, and concrete historical explanation introduced above: "the structure of class relations at the macroeconomic level; the lived experience of class in the workplace and in the residence community; groups of people disposed to act in class ways; and class-based collective action."[11] The first level, "class one," refers to the "actors" in terms of the two logical categories of the theory of the mode of production: the buyers and sellers of labor power. Note that this characterization of the key "actors" is not based on an empirical analysis of a given society but is deduced from the abstract model of the social structure. Katznelson refers to this level of class as an "experience-far" concept, by which he means that its valid- ity is dependent on neither the subjective self-understandings of the men and women to which these categories are applied nor the historical- institutional context of a given situation. It is in this sense that we talk about "capitalist" societies in the abstract, equating, for example, the United States, Britain, France, and Germany.

However, the concrete institutions of capitalism such as the organiza- tion of labor and housing markets, geographies of production, and the level and type of urbanization may vary across different cases. Class at the second level then is an "experience-near" category and reflects the entire set of (still "objective") social conditions and institutions within which people live their lives, in and out of the productive economy, in and outside the workplace, across the different spaces of the city, and so on.

The third level of class captures the cultural, symbolic, and linguistic frameworks within which subjects come to "map" or interpret the situ- ations of class two. The distinction between levels two and three allows us to analyze cases where similar social relations give rise to different cultural interpretations. For example, in the nineteenth century, France, Germany, and the United States all experienced capitalist industrializa- tion and transformations in the organization of their labor markets and their patterns of urbanization. But in each case, men and women inter- preted these changes differently on the basis of traditions and cultures that defined their specific situations. Whereas republican, artisanal, and militant syndicalist elements in nineteenth-century French culture sup- plied the interpretive framework employed by the French working class, and Catholic and explicitly Marxist anticapitalist themes led German workers to see solutions in cross-trade unions and political parties, North American workers were characterized by procapitalist, craft-based, and apolitical trade unions.[12] At the same time, organized collective action also varies by place and time, even within a particular country or region.

That is, similarly situated individuals (class two), even when they have come to a shared understanding of the situation (class three), do not automatically organize and act collectively, a result well known at least since Olson's theory of groups. The fourth level of class, the level of collective action *as a class,* reflects this final moment of contingency.

Katznelson employs this four-tier scheme to redefine the notion of class formation as the variable and contingent "process of connection between the four levels of class" in place of both the all-or-nothing character of the classical scheme and the too general conventional structure/agency models of sociological theory.[13] He is thereby able to recast the question I posed at the beginning of this section in more rigorous terms: Under what conditions will class-based interpretations and dispositions (class three) emerge from the experience of social conditions (class two)? What type of class understandings will develop in different circumstances? Katznelson's contribution to urban theory comes here. His answer, in broad strokes, is that the key variable in understanding the history of working-class formation is the way urban space was institutionalized through the political context, represented, interpreted, in short, "mapped," and then acted upon by the working men and women in the cities and new spaces of industrial capitalism. In nineteenth-century Western Europe and North America, in a search for coherence and intelligibility, working people were faced with the task of making sense of a new urban world. Space played a key mediating link between structure and agency. It was a defining element of what it meant to dwell in this new set of often harsh and miserable conditions.[14]

The four-tiered Marxian model of class is clearly an important advance over the more mechanical assumptions operating implicitly in Castells's work and explicitly in Harvey's. Its significance is not simply methodological, however. The four-tier model underlies Katznelson's more important historical arguments about the connections between working-class formation and space in the United States and Western Europe. I do not wish to enter into the comparative historiographical debates taken up in Katznelson's work, especially those that concern the English and U.S. cases. The arguments are too rich and multifaceted to deal with in a brief summary. Instead, I want to focus on one element of the historical interpretation of the case of the United States as a way of returning to our opening set of questions about the limited and "nonclass" nature of urban politics in the United States.

THE *CITY TRENCHES* THESIS

Most cities of the industrializing capitalist countries of the nineteenth century experienced similar forms of urbanization. One common feature of most cities throughout Western Europe and North America (albeit with variations in timing and intensity) was the development of distinct spaces for residential neighborhoods and for separate workplaces in factories and small shops. This new spatial separation between workplace and home or the residential community both followed and stimulated the breakup of the artisanal households of the medieval city. It is difficult from our present vantage point to appreciate how novel this new city space was, given the fact that housing, land, and occupation had been fused for most artisanal households. James Vance's seminal work first put forward the argument that the creation of a distinct workplace and proletariat and the creation of purely residential neighborhoods were two sides of one coin. The creation of a modern labor market was accompanied by the development of an autonomous housing and land market.[15] In the United States, the operations of the new housing market sorted the population into increasingly homogeneous residential neighborhoods distinguished by both class and ethnic, religious, or linguistic attributes, a complex pattern that persists today in cities such as New York.

The new geography of nineteenth-century industrial cities, therefore, in particular the separation between work and home, played a central role in the development of class and group identities. In the United States, the large immigrant population was sorted into ethnically defined residential neighborhoods with their own distinctive institutions and associations. These ethnic enclaves were institutionalized and thus reproduced through the local political system. The political machines of nineteenth-century urban America integrated the newcomers into the polity as voters of territorially and ethnically defined parties and patronage systems. Workplace and residential community, each with its set of institutional affiliations, authority relationships, conflicts, and interests, provided competing bases for working peoples' primary affiliations. As a result, individuals experienced the modern city and modern capitalism in large part through the twin spaces defined by the labor and housing markets. How the new spaces linking working and living were to be mapped thus became a central puzzle of nineteenth-century class formation.

How did urban residents map their cities? Urban historians have found apparently conflicting evidence of cases where ethnic bonds dampened class solidarities, as well as evidence of significant labor organizations and collective activity. In contrast to the workplaces, where employers and workers formed the key actors and where workers could join across ethnic, religious, and linguistic (and more seldom, racial) lines to create sometimes militant trade unions, the ethnic residential communities were cross-class, cross-occupational settings where the social bonds of family, kin, and ethnicity overrode solidarities based on class.[16] For example, in their studies of turn-of-the-century Detroit, where Oliver Zunz found that strong ethnic enclaves produced weak class solidarity, Richard Oestreicher nevertheless found significant labor militancy in the workplace, despite ethnic fragmentations.[17] As Katznelson correctly points out, these are incompatible only if we assume a zero-sum model of collective identity—that more ethnicity means less class. In fact, both capture important aspects of the American experience, the most important of which has been the fact that "class has been lived and fought as a series of partial relationships"[18] mediated by both the spaces of the city and the nature of the political system.

Katznelson suggests that neglect of this fact accounts for a fundamental misreading of American labor history. Because they used the case of England as the benchmark for comparison, observers have tended to see fragmentation in workers' class affiliations the United States, in contrast to the holism of nineteenth-century English working-class identity, which bridged home and work. For Katznelson, however, "what needs to be explained is not the absence of class in American politics but its limitation to the arena of work."[19] The central argument of *City Trenches* builds on this insight to suggest that what is distinctive about the United States is not the absence of class but its limitation to the place of work. The separation between home and work, between the factory and the residence community, a common feature of capitalist industrialization and urbanization in the nineteenth century, has been institutionalized in a distinctive form in the United States.

These new patterns of labor and residence altered the forms of social control and power. In Europe and the United States, as the old system of social order was transformed, the problem of social control was likewise recast in three unprecedented ways: "the attempt to regulate, and proscribe, combinations of workers at the point of production; the use of the franchise to incorporate workers and their leaders into the polity in ways that least threatened social cohesion; and the development of a new nexus of political relationships linking residence communities to government."[20] In the United States, the patterning of power and class related artisans and industrial workers to employers through unions in the workplace and to the state as members of ethnic groups and residents of neighborhood wards through urban political machines in the community.

Unlike in Britain, where a more "holistic" working-class identity bridged home and work, and unlike Belgium, where ethnic identity was predominant in both work and community, in the United States workers identified themselves as workers only in their place of work. According to Katznelson, "the differences in English and American patterns of working-class formation . . . are best accounted for by the impact of the organization and public policies of their respective states." In England and France, the strictly enforced "combination laws" proscribing the right to form unions and to strike pushed workers to organize around community institutions such as pubs, thereby "fusing" both community and workplace cultures in "class" ways. In the United States, by contrast, the early franchise (for men), the relatively diffuse state system in the late nineteenth century, what Stephen Skowronek has called the "system of parties and courts,"[21] and the relatively more tolerant labor laws permitting the organization of grievances around the workplace meant that municipal political institutions were uniquely empowered to organize the growing urban populations not in terms that pitted worker against employer but in terms of the territorial logic of the vote bank, combining chiefly neighborhood and ethnic identities. The differences between English and American constitutional and judicial patterns thus led to significantly different crystallizations of the bifurcation of power between private enterprises and state agencies. In the American context, for example, the strength of labor organizations in the workplace and of urban political machines in the community helps account for the failure "to create a global politics of class or ethnicity, and for the divided character of urban political development and class consciousness."[22]

An important factor in the development of the new urban working class was the reorganization of local associations and clubs such as lodges, benefit associations, parish churches, gangs, athletic clubs, fire companies, and political clubs from cross-class to class-homogeneous institutions. Because "the working class became capable of developing and controlling the institutions of daily neighborhood life," these "provided the possibility for the development of an independent working-class culture" at the moment when artisans were experiencing loss of control over the production process through deskilling, technological change, and the expansion of markets. On the other hand, the political parties that organized public life for workers in the neighborhoods were organized by "artisans who had experienced the world in traditional integrated terms and whose very existence as a class was threatened by industrialization and the separation of work and home."[23]

What Katznelson calls "city trenches," following Antonio Gramsci's remark in the prison notebooks that "the superstructures of civil society are like the trench-systems of modern warfare," the geographically patterned political, economic, and social institutions that came to define urban life in the last quarter of the nineteenth century, had three major elements. First, trade unions developed that "sought to protect the traditional prerogatives of skilled workers" in the workplace. Second, urban political machines developed that "were enmeshed in the organizational life of the neighbor-hoods—their gangs, firehouses, secret societies, saloons." These formed the core of the political community made possible by the extension of the fran-chise to (male, white) workers. Third, local government agencies developed municipal services that were delivered to subjects as members of residen-tial communities. This system of trenches formed an important component securing the hegemony of the emerging political order, since "conflicts about political citizenship were fought on the shared ground of liberal assump-tions." As a result, Katznelson claims, "workers as citizens did not feel they needed to battle the state, for they were included in its embrace." This devel-oping consensus was of such influence that "by the last two decades of the century . . . the uncertainties had been resolved, and . . . the new urban sys-tem dominated the political landscape" in a way that excluded workplace-centered concerns.[24] However representative and defining the local machines were for ethnic working groups, the machines nonetheless also limited the con-tent of those representations in such a way as to mute and displace workplace-centered or class-based identifications. Taken together, this system of trenches constituted the framework within which the "shared assumptions" of urban life operated, creating the context for subsequent conflicts and struggles in the twentieth-century American city:

> American urban politics has been governed by boundaries and rules that stress ethnicity, race and territoriality, rather than class, and that emphasize the dis-tribution of goods and services, while excluding questions of production or workplace relations. The centerpiece of these rules has been the radical sep-aration in people's consciousness, speech and activity of the politics of work from the politics of community. . . . What is distinctive about the [North] American experience is that the linguistic, cultural, and institutional mean-ing given to the differentiation of work and community, a characteristic of all

industrial capitalist societies, has taken a sharply divided form, and that it has done so for a very long time.[25]

There are many strengths in Katznelson's approach, which takes up, at a more sophisticated and nuanced level, to be sure, the same complex of problems that was central to Harvey's and Castells's projects, the problems of urban identity, economic structure, and urban space posed by what Harvey called "the vexing questions that surround the relationship between community conflict and community organizing . . . and industrial conflict and work-based organizing."[26] It offers fresh perspectives on American urban politics. It also offers a historical perspective on urban institutions, addresses the problem of contingency, and provides a systematic account of the partial and spatial character of American working-class and group identity. Katznelson sees the failure of the American working class to live up to its historical tasks as rooted in the specifically urban nature of the American class system and in the specifically class character of the urban system. He finds in these two problems the mutual links accounting for the absence of a more global and radical class consciousness and the explanation for the limited policy choices characterizing U.S. cities.[27] More broadly, the two dimensions of Katznelson's work—the revised class model and the substantive historical account—represent the most sophisticated effort to develop a Marxian urban theory embracing the contingency of identity, a noneconomistic role for state-related variables, and the constitutive function of space in shaping agency and structure.

Nonetheless, whether this uneasy juxtaposition of Marxian theory and its economistic theory of the state with claims for the autonomous influence of the state is theoretically satisfying, and whether the broader framework succeeds in its declared aim of transcending the choices offered by Castells and Harvey, is less clear.[28] It is to that assessment that I now turn.

PROBLEMS

Despite its strengths, there are three ways in which the *City Trenches* thesis remains problematic. Although clearly an advance over the simple in-itself/for-itself model, the revisionist four-tier class model does not succeed in resolving the problems of essentialism, teleology, or developmentalism. Nor does the historical "bifurcation" thesis succeed in transcending the teleological assumptions of Marxian labor historiography. Furthermore, Katznelson's empirical account of the formation of urban working-class culture is lacking a sufficient account of gender relations.

Before turning to these three points, I want to consider briefly an objection often leveled at Katznelson's thesis, an objection coming from the opposite direction from mine: that his revisionist urban theory is not Marxist enough. Echoing Harvey's theory of displaced class struggles, it is a mistake, these critics contend, to view areas of social life as separate and distinct that are in fact unified. To take just one representative example, the editors of a collection of essays on labor history have objected to the *City Trenches* formulation (that class consciousness has been limited to the place of work) by arguing that, in reality, the "divisions between work and other realms of life have not been sharply defined, precisely because such realms are inseparable and are dialectically linked."[29] However, this objection—which is a typical shortcoming of even those social-historical accounts of class formation that do not explicitly rely on Marxist concepts—begs all the questions raised by the separate institutions of the workplace and residential communities in capitalist cities. Invoking "dialectics" muddies, rather than clarifies, the analysis. As Katznelson has observed, the relevant questions concern the fact that (in the United States, at least) "the links between work and community-based conflicts have been unusually tenuous. Each kind of conflict has its own separate vocabulary and set of institutions: work, class, and trade unions; community, ethnicity, local parties, churches, and voluntary associations."[30] The Marxian notion of dialectics is not helpful in elucidating the institutional materiality of these related, yet distinct, realms. This is not to say there is no relationship between them. Rather, as the concepts of overdetermination, articulation, constitutive outside, hegemony, and so on, show, relationality is not dependent upon an antecedent totality from which the terms and their interaction derive their meaning and their ground. The conception of a dialectical totality cannot allow for the logic of spacing through which identities are constituted and patterned. The Derridian notion of constitutive outside that I want to press into service is useful precisely because it is a nondialectical or postdialectical mediation of difference (distinct from a postmodern notion of difference), which in this case is reflected in the spacing or hybridity that the separation of work and home inscribes within collective identities and social totalities.

CRITIQUE OF THE *CITY TRENCHES* THESIS

The principal weakness of Katznelson's double scheme is that despite the explicit intention to construct explanations that "embrace complexity," and despite considerable success in doing so, the Marxian scaffolding of his urban theory prevents him from fully achieving this goal. Despite the aim of overcoming the "unexamined essentialist assumptions" of working-class historiography by "decongesting" the concept of class, the four-tier class model (unwittingly) presupposes precisely the opposite of what the historical analysis opens up.[31] Thus, the two dimensions that make up the *City Trenches* thesis—the methodological and the substantive—work against each other. This impasse is manifested at several points of the analysis. I will focus on three in particular: the place of state-related variables in the Marxian base/superstructure scheme, the developmental assumptions of the four-tier scheme, and the authorial/textual/discursive privileging of "workers'" identity over against other so-called nonclass groupings and bases of identification.

It is important to recall that Katznelson's response to the difficulties of Marxist theory was to adopt a qualified version of it, which, while retaining the basic model of economic determination of only some "superstructural" features, allowed room for other explanatory variables and approaches. For Katznelson, the justification for retaining Marx's model of the economic mode of production at level one of the model is the decisive importance of capitalist development in the shaping of the modern world: "Both Marx and Weber understood the expansion of market relationships as the central cause of the breakup of precapitalist holistic communities. Weber stressed . . . that the process of *capitalist* development . . . shape[s] the experience of living."[32] Yet faced with the puzzle of the divergent patterns of working-class formation between England and the United States, Katznelson concedes that Marxism has only limited usefulness. The forms of capitalist development and of urban geographies (themselves well explained by forms of capital accumulation and market factors) were largely similar in both the U.S. and English cases, but the outcomes of collective action were different. Marxist theory cannot uniquely explain what we want to know, and as such, cannot furnish the exclusive basis for a critical urban theory. Consequently, Katznelson's historical thesis must treat state-related variables as part of an independent, autonomous dimension of modernity that is as "deserving of comparable theoretical treatment" as the market economy.[33] This is a serious qualification, as Katznelson himself concedes.[34]

Nonetheless, these two moments—economic determinism and a dimension of autonomous state variables—are incompatible. What is required is a way to retain a concept of structure that operates at the same level of abstraction and explanatory force as Marx's mode of production but that can avoid economism by incorporating state-related variables on an equal footing. In the previous chapter, I proposed the Habermasian notion of system as just such a concept. In developing the notion of the first level of class, Katznelson follows Marx in seeing the emergence of an autonomously operating economic subsystem as the basic engine of societal modernization and rationalization. On the other hand, Katznelson does not assimilate the full force of Weber's analysis of the institutions of modernity, for whom capitalism and market exchange formed only one aspect of a larger process of social and systemic rationalization that also included bureaucratic control and power. The Habermasian model provides an alternative theoretical construct that formalizes Katznelson's empirical and historical insight while retaining Marxism's critical edge: modernity possesses not one but two subsystems, the administrative state system and the economic system.[35] The idea of economic exploitation is replaced with the idea of colonization of the lifeworld by processes of bureaucratization (from the state) and commodification (from the market). Katznelson's framework thus lags behind his (more far-reaching) empirical story, relegating power and the state to a superstructural position in the model.

Similar problems appear when we examine the way the four levels of class are related to each other. The purpose of the scheme is to introduce complexity and contingency into the relations among structure, social relations, culture, and agency. To avoid the "reflectionist epistemology" of classical, mechanical Marxism in which social consciousness "reflects" the external reality of social being, and to escape its teleological structure, Katznelson rejects "any notion of degrees of consciousness," so that "the scheme of four levels of class does not imply a series of necessary stages or a natural progression." In fact, he goes further to claim that "no level need be understood or analyzed exclusively in class terms." These and other qualifications prompt an obvious question. If the content of class formation and each level is "left open," by virtue of what criteria can we call the remaining empty scaffolding "class"?[36] The move toward complexity appears to be blocked by an a priori designation of the model in class terms. This results from the lingering residue of precisely those developmental assumptions it sought to avoid. If class and nonclass outcomes are both structural possibilities (although admittedly perhaps not equally likely in any given instance), it seems to be more useful and less constraining to drop the class label and keep the four levels as an important contribution to social-theoretical investigation, leaving the content of each level open to class and nonclass outcomes.

The cost of not doing so is reflected in the asymmetrical treatment given so-called nonclass forms of identity (ethnic, racial, linguistic), as well as in a certain lack of discursive reflexivity about the textual strategies embedded in Marxian discourse. This is most clearly revealed in the way Katznelson's texts, despite the caveats about how class-based outcomes are contingent, privilege a working-class identity *prior* to any given empirical manifestation. Consider the following claims. "There is a range from working classes who see themselves and act wholly on the bases of nonclass understandings to Marx's proletariat." "The working class . . . gave way to a more mixed pattern in which *as workers* they maintained their militant rejectionism but *as citizens* became more incorporated in electoral socialist politics." "Workers appeared in the political arena not as workers but as residents of a specific place or as members of a specific (*nonclass*) group."[37] If the subjects that the text identifies as "workers" can appear or represent themselves in class or nonclass ways, as workers or citizens, in what sense are we justified in calling the entity that does the appearing "workers"? If we say that workers "appeared" as ethnics, as opposed to as workers, does not this imply some judgment as to the more or less "correct" representation? Surely, there is an inconsistency here that goes beyond mere semantics.

Katznelson's response, of course, is that this terminology reflects a basic assumption of the four-tier class scheme. At the levels of class one and class two, "a person's consciousness, culture, and politics do not enter the *definition* of his class position. . . . Not even his behavior is an essential part of it. . . . This level of analysis may tell us how workers exist and live in certain circumstances, but not how they will think or act in those experienced circumstances." Such a distinction is necessary, Katznelson maintains, for any social theory that does not wish to relinquish the project of linking structure and agency in favor of the purely action-oriented perspective common to much discourse and postmodern theory: "Because class . . . lies at the intersection of structure and process, and of being and consciousness, it is impossible to analyze class three, without some objective determination of class two."[38] Katznelson's point here is that the patterning of social relations (at level 2) in "class" ways such as the creation of wage-dependent laborers and the expansion of labor markets is a necessary, but not sufficient, condition for the emergence of "class" types of collective action. In contrast, he correctly points out, a pure action perspective would hold that class-based action, that is, collective action on the basis of the economic category of wage worker, is equally likely or possible under any objective conditions. To say that "there is no objectivity outside discourse" (where discourse means linguistic and symbolic frameworks) is to say that our interpretations (level 3) are arbitrary or unconstrained relative to the "objective" conditions in which we find ourselves, and thus we should not be surprised by any particular outcome. Katznelson's approach parallels in some ways Habermas's, which as we saw in the Introduction, in the discussion of Michael P. Smith's discursive immanentism, holds that the symbolic level of the lifeworld (which is roughly equivalent to Katznelson's level 3) does not exhaust all the mechanisms of societal reproduction. Katznelson is also wary of what he sees to be the implications of a transparent conception of discourse, because he rightly wishes to retain the moment of opacity that clings to experience: We cannot read off the truth of social institutions and history from appeals to intuition and "consciousness," as E. P. Thompson suggests we can. This is an astute critique of those social theoretical approaches that abandon the project of linking structure and agency, and one with which I am sympathetic. Nonetheless, several difficulties remain.

First, it is important to distinguish between the general form of the four-tier scheme and its specific Marxian class content. In my view, the proposal to link the four levels of conceptual framework, social conditions and ways of life, cultural dispositions and values, and organized collective action, is a significant contribution to the agenda of social theory. On the other hand, characterizing the four levels as *class* levels is problematic and is inconsistent with the claims for contingency. If the relationship between levels is fundamentally contingent, nothing substantively is altered in the model if the term "class" is dropped entirely. Either the relationship among structure, disposition, and action is contingent, such that class structures, ways of life, and dispositions may give rise to non-class meanings, collectivities, and organizations—in which case, we cannot speak of "class," necessarily, at different levels; or, in some sense, it is meaningful to talk of class as a unifying theme of all four levels—in which case, the class nature of each level is *necessary*, and we are back to the isomorphism of levels, that is to say, the in-itself/for-itself formulation. To this extent, the four-tier scheme does not depart from the developmental assumptions of classical Marxism or sociological objectivism. To make the passage from in-itself to for-itself more difficult to traverse does not thereby alter either the destination or the idea of a path or a road. If it is a step forward to delineate *four* levels of class, it is still nevertheless four levels of *class*. Every move along or between levels is conceptualized in terms of class structure, class relations, class experience, and class action. The goals of complexity can be more fully achieved if we drop the class labels, retaining, of course, the possibility of class outcomes as one possible set of outcomes.

A second source of the difficulties of the *City Trenches* thesis is that it is unable to break out of the duality of structure and practices, which are then viewed as two independent, exogenous orders. By positing social structures independent of discourse that provide actors with "givens" that are then "mapped," it charts a path between the functionalist reduction of identity to places in the structure and the voluntarist position that cannot distinguish "constraints." Structure and action thus parallel the opposition of being/consciousness. However, by echoing Marx's materialist thesis, this claim embraces the same problematic conclusion: If consciousness is determined by being, then consciousness is not a part of social being. This is precisely the metaphysical presupposition of the model and provides the reason why Katznelson can divorce the "expressions" of subjects (nonclass) from their "being" (class).

To further this critique in a way that will help point us toward an alternative conceptual framework to the Marxian scheme, including a notion of structure that is not seen as wholly external to the realm of agency, consider the implications of extending the notion of contingency from the links between elements (which the *City Trenches* thesis does) to the elements themselves. (Recall that I applied the same analysis to Castells's model of social action above.) Laclau and Mouffe have developed an important critique of approaches such as the *City Trenches* thesis that reject a certain notion of totality by asserting the nonnecessary nature of the links uniting the elements or levels of the totality. These approaches, they observe, raise the question whether the "relations among the internal components of each [level] are essential and necessary." If the answer is "Yes," then we have simply replaced an essentialism of the totality with an essentialism of the elements. This is precisely the transformation characterizing the first and third phases of Castells's work, which ended up in a "theoretically agnostic descriptivism of the 'concrete situations.'" Laclau and Mouffe characterize this move as a "logical pulverization of the social," but one in which the disconnected elements are still conceptually fixed. This captures well the way each level is characterized a priori as class in Katznelson's four-tier scheme. Laclau and Mouffe suggest that the alternative to this logical disaggregation of the totality is "through the critique of every type of fixity, through an affirmation of the incomplete, open, and politically negotiable character of every identity."[39] The reason why even the elements are not fixed is that social identities are characterized by overdetermination, spacing, and hybridity. This is not to say that any outcome is equally likely but rather that we should view the elements of the totality as contingent, just as we view the relations among them.

We can conclude, therefore, that although the thrust of the historical analysis in *City Trenches* is to demonstrate the irreducibility of the distinct basis for identifications and to highlight the "non-class identifications and institutions [that] predominated outside of work" so as to "penetrate beyond such terms as 'working-class community' in order to deal with the content of community culture on its own terms," the four-tier class model undermines the bifurcation thesis of *City Trenches*.[40]

Nonetheless, taken as a whole, Katznelson's work opens the way to new questions and is, in this sense, what Roland Barthes calls a "writerly text."[41] The stress on history, contingency, and heterogeneity is only loosely counteracted by the metanarrative of the transcendental subjectivity of class. By posing the questions of identity, space, and the city in ways that permit an opening, at a certain, if circumscribed, level, for the irreducibility of the moments of work and community, Katznelson moves beyond a closed system of questions and opens out the analysis in terms of the articulation of these two arenas. By insisting on the moment of unification of distinct bases of identity across work and community as problematic and the object and result of struggle, the analysis points toward the overdetermined character of this articulation in spatial terms, as well as toward the hegemonic nature of any given institutionalization of this relationship. Without recourse to the objectivistic and totalizing discourse of the four-tier scheme, the *City Trenches* thesis should be read radically: subjectivity is itself constitutively patterned in a relation of overdetermination and articulation. The radical and far-reaching implications of *City Trenches* lie precisely here: the move toward the historically contingent and constituted basis of subjectivity precludes any recourse to a metanarrative of closure such as is found in the Marxian account of class formation. We are presented, in fact, with the key features of a historical and social-scientific analysis of the radical alterity and heteronomy of identity itself. Yet these insights must be reinscribed outside of the constraints of the four-tier model and draw from the fundamental and often startling implications of the empirical dimension of the *City Trenches* thesis.

Before providing more details of the alternative theoretical framework within which to place these results, in the next section I examine one further weakness of the *City Trenches* thesis, the absence of the role played by gender relations in the constitution of class, space, and the trenches of the city.

ARE THERE ANY WOMEN IN THE TRENCHES?

The central claim of Katznelson's urban theory is that the main explanatory variables accounting for the absence of a holistic working-class identity in the United States (as opposed to the United Kingdom) can be found in the "political context created by state authorities who shaped how the place of residence was understood by the new urban working classes."[42] Elements of the American political regime institutionalized the separate realms of workplace and residential community in ways that divided, rather than permitted, working-class organizations to bridge them.

The *City Trenches* thesis rests on the assumption that the split (in the case of the United States at least) resulted from state-related factors external to the working class, which is seen as defined antecedently and exogenously to the political process. However, if the sorts of vocabularies employed to map the spaces of wage work and community residence are a significant part of the explanation of the "split" in the American understandings of class, this is in part a result of gender assumptions within the broad ranks of organized labor that came to dominate the self-understanding of the labor movement around the beginning of the twentieth century, the same period in which Katznelson sees the crystallization of the "shared rules" of American urban politics. In fact, the institutionalization of the separation between work and community, as with all the spaces of the modern city, was irreducibly gendered and represented a variable internal to the "working class." Incorporating the gender variable transforms the meaning of the story *City Trenches* tells and has implications for the notion of hybrid identity I am proposing.

Despite Katznelson's detailed history of the restructuring of space and settlement patterns, a history that highlights the importance of the relations among workplace, home, and community, and despite his focus on the constitutional basis of the construction of a public sphere in the United States, neither the specific experience of women in the city nor the gender relations within class formation play a part in the story he tells in *City Trenches*. This is important because of the fact that, espe-

cially in the nineteenth century, the workplace as well as the neighborhood associations and institutions on which so much of the case for a
separation between the two rests were predominantly restricted to men.
Thus, the "separation of home and work" overlooks the significance of
nonwaged domestic labor.

Gender relations and their relationship to the languages and images
of working-class identity, however, should be seen as an additional variable, internal to the working class, that reinforced the bifurcation noted
by Katznelson. That is, the manner in which work and community were
institutionalized contained within it assumptions about the meaning and
character of "private" domestic and residential life and its relationship
to the "public" world of wage work.

My aim here is not simply to note the empirical presence or absence
of "women" within the historical narrative. Nor do I wish to claim simply that the activities performed in the household are productive of value
or should also be considered "work." The primary objective is to illustrate the ways in which class as the interpellation of subjects within institutions such as the labor market and labor organizations such as trade
unions can be understood only in a relation of overdetermination and
articulation with the relations of family, gender, and sexuality—sets of
social relations that were spatialized and localized in the residential community, the home, and the workplace. Every attempt to define a class
identity rested on several implicit or explicit assumptions about gender
relations and the relationship between class and gender that paralleled
assumptions about the separation between the workplace and the residential community. I am not contesting the empirical claims of *City
Trenches,* but I am proposing that the story cannot be complete without
considering gender as a variable.[43]

FROM THE STUDY OF WOMEN TO THE ANALYSIS OF GENDER

After at least three decades of historical scholarship writing women
"back into" history, it is no longer very controversial to state that women
have been systematically neglected in most historical writing and that
interpretations of the past have suffered as a result. The critical position
that my analysis has taken vis-à-vis "class," however, is no less applica-
ble to the category "women." Although historical works whose aim is
to render women "visible," to demonstrate that "women were also there"
in strikes and demonstrations, performing productive labor in the home,
creating communities, and so on, is a critically important task, from a

deconstructive perspective, there are also limitations to these approaches. The problem consists of the fact that these accounts aim to (re)insert these subjects into already accepted narratives. Unless we wish to accept gender and sexual identity as biologically given, then we are forced to consider the categories "women" and "men," "masculine" and "feminine," as historically constituted—constituted meanings, moreover, that do not escape the force of the unconscious and fantasy. We must ask what gendered meanings were attached to everyday notions such as class, labor, workplace, and home.

Joan Wallach Scott has gone furthest in introducing these insights for historical analysis, especially in the context of labor history. She calls for a move away from the study of "women" that hitherto has preoccupied feminist social historians and toward the examination of how gendered notions of social being and identity were imbricated in the meanings of everyday life: "The story is no longer about the things that have happened to women and men and how they reacted to them; instead it is about how the subjective and collective meanings of women and men as categories of identity have been constructed."[44] Other historians, such as Sally Alexander, have drawn on Lacanian psychoanalysis as an important tool for the historical study of women and gender, exploring the dimensions opened up by the unconscious and the imaginary. Historians, she writes, "fear that by introducing the unconscious and phantasy into social history is to open a Pandora's box. I only suggest that the persistent problem of femininity . . . indicates that the box is already open."[45]

CITY TRENCHES AND GENDER

The shattering of the unity of everyday life commonly seen as embodied in the artisanal-family household and the medieval city led to the creation of new institutions and forms of association in the residential community spaces that were relatively free from the authority of employers. Katznelson's hypothesis that the opportunities created by these transformations played an instrumental part in the constitution of Western industrial working classes is compelling. At the same time, it is clear that the key institutions of the emerging working-class culture—gangs, firehouses, secret societies, and saloons, to name a few—were restricted to men. The ability to control the institutions of neighborhood life was, according to Katznelson, a defining feature of the development of the new working class; but almost all excluded women from participation, either as a matter of principle or, as in the case of saloons, as a result of social conventions and taboos about "respectable" places for wives, mothers, and daughters to be seen. One historian, for example, has noted that the location of union meetings "over the neighborhood saloon discouraged women from attending."[46]

Katznelson's argument hinges in part on the role that urban political machines played in the political integration of workers and residents. Yet only (white) male workers had the franchise during the formative period of the system of city trenches. Thus, in a nonarbitrary way, women were placed on one side of the system. Similarly, most craft and trade unions were explicitly exclusionary toward women and legitimated themselves in terms of a gendered identity that linked labor with a culture of masculinity, itself represented most immediately in the ideal of the patriarchal family and public power with control over dependents. To claim, therefore, that "workers as citizens did not feel they needed to battle the state, for they were included in its embrace," or that the emerging organizations in the workplace "sought to protect the traditional prerogatives of skilled workers," or to interpret the legislative and moral crusade of the Progressive movement simply in terms of the delivery of services is to underestimate the degree to which these developments not only had differential impacts on male and female members of the working class but also rested on many gendered assumptions.[47] As Carol Pateman, among many others, has demonstrated, the emerging social contract of political citizenship was founded on, and in its formative stages was explicitly modeled on, the patriarchal system of control over (primarily) female dependents. This brought together "men as men," to use Heidi Hartman's expression, men of all classes, since this gender division was an issue that cut across class boundaries.[48] Artisanal households may have been more integrated and cooperative, but they were nevertheless deeply structured upon an asymmetry of power and control invested in the male head of household and legitimated both culturally and legally. Faced with the shattering of *this* particular unity, late-nineteenth-century artisans defended "traditional prerogatives" that were crucially structured by gender identifications: to be an independent artisan was not only to have control over one's means of labor but also to have control as the head of a family; that is to say, control over dependents' labor and autonomy.

Most male workers did not merely confront an objective separation between the identities and institutions that governed community and workplace as an exogenous fact: the very fabric of that objectivity was woven with threads that included self-representations of how a supposed autonomized workplace should relate to the now-separated family household—

representations that an accelerating suburbanization soon would envelop and define as the preserve of a consumptionist femininity. Not only did the system of city trenches limit the content of class for workers, but the limiting of class by workers was also a determinant of that system of trenches. It is not sufficient to observe that trade unions conceived of workers as "labor." We must interrogate how labor itself was conceived. One key aspect of the shared assumptions (liberal or otherwise) was the gendered discourse of the spaces of work and family.

The division between the "private" and the "public" was often reinforced and defended by predominantly male craft and trade unions, in some cases in alliance with the state and employers. Rather than "false consciousness" on the part of working-class men, this reflected an antagonism organized on the basis of gender relations. The salient fact of the continuing bifurcation between work (male, public) and home and community (female, private) then took on an added dimension. This gendered space represented a further division within the working class, which, if we follow the logic of *City Trenches*, would thereby have weakened its capacity as a class and its ability to promote a holistic identity. Katznelson calls for "crisp distinctions among three axes of differentiation of working-class members: (a) workers relatively privileged at work . . . [;] (b) workers with different styles of life in residential communities . . . [;] and (c) workers who provided the political leadership for trade unions, pressure groups, and political parties."[49] However, the relations between men and women—or more accurately, the social relations that organize the gendered nature of subjects—constitute a fourth axis of differentiation.[50]

COUNTERHYPOTHESIS:
GENDER AS A DESTABILIZING VARIABLE

Several historians have convincingly demonstrated the intimate relationship between the emerging housing and labor markets of industrialized urban centers and the gendered framework within which these took place. Jeanne Boydston, for example, has argued that the "pastoralization" of housework in the early republic linked the home and the activities increasingly performed exclusively therein to a sacred ideal of motherhood. She provides extensive historical evidence of the internal and metaphorical nature of the meanings of "home" and "work" in the modern urban period. For example, she claims that "the labor and economic value of housework ceased to exist in the culture of [the] antebellum Northeast.

It became work's opposite." Indeed, the discursive poles of the separation were an object of contestation, as Boydston has pointed out, and thus retained the traces of the other pole: "The language of the ideology of spheres was the language of gender, but its essential dualism was less precisely the opposition of 'female' and 'male' than it was the opposition of 'home' and 'work,' an opposition founded on the gendering of the concept of labor."[51]

The most extensive treatment of the gendered dimensions of the transformations of urban culture has been provided by Elizabeth Blackmar's work on Manhattan in the period between Independence and the Civil War, a period central to Katznelson's historical thesis. She provides detailed evidence to support the argument that what Katznelson interprets as the shared assumptions of urban politics and the patterning of authority and social control in New York and other emerging cities was irreducibly tied to the gendered nature of authority and control:

> The nineteenth-century language of housing came to rest on polarized categories—home and workplace, private and public, respectable and immoral, necessity and luxury—that sought to define and fix the cultural value of one of the city's most unstable and tension-worn social institutions. . . . Yet, precisely because rhetorical oppositions deny qualifications and contradictions, they offer a powerful means of affirming shared cultural values in the face of uncertainties and repeated challenges. . . . By the mid-nineteenth century its vocabulary had become a mainstay of the bourgeois language of both class and gender.[52]

The autonomized private order was seen as the basis of the social order more generally, and the ability to control one's dwelling, a domain now set off from the workplace, "emerged as a new measure of persona, independence and respectability." Parallel to my argument against the conflation of workplace and community in terms of class, she continues, "not the least problem with conventional interpretations of the industrialization of nineteenth-century cities is the tendency to treat housing as a derivative cultural 'sphere' or arena of 'consumption' that merely reflected rather than helped construct the new material social relations of capitalist society. Far from being 'removed' from the marketplace, the home stood at the heart of new property and labor relations."[53] Like Boydston, Blackmar rejects the view that the physical separation of workplaces and residences is merely an objective feature of urbanizing and industrializing societies and argues that this spatial transformation necessarily entails particular interpretations. What is important is the discursive status given to the activities that, as a result of contentions fought on axes of class and gender, as well as race, became institutionalized in the diverse spaces of the capitalist city. It is worth quoting her again at length:

> The cultural construction of housing as a home separated from a workplace did not emerge simply with reference to men's departure to workshops, offices, and stores. Female family members who performed household "duties" were culturally defined against the figures of both "immoral and ungrateful" servants who grudgingly performed "work" and female out-workers who "took away work from men." Although the points of reference were vastly different for propertied and working-class New Yorkers, the language with which they interpreted housing relations was often the same. Unable to eliminate the tensions of waged employment, keeping boarders, or sweated labor within their domestic quarters, New Yorkers insisted on housing's identity as a home, defined family work as a labor of love, and spoke of domestic relations as they "ought" to be.[54]

Integral to this forged consensus, therefore, was the struggle "internal" to the working class over the gendered distribution of tasks and the relationship between the collective identities of class at the workplace and those enmeshed in the home. Blackmar thus concurs with other feminist historians in claiming that, faced with new historical possibilities, "rather than embrace new concepts of domesticity attached to the dwelling, journeymen sought to preserve the values of artisan housekeeping."[55]

In the period between the Civil War and the New Deal, the content of urban working-class identity created by craft and, later, industrial unions continued to embody gender assumptions, and as a consequence, gender relations persisted as a contributing factor to the bifurcation of identity between workplace and community. The terms in which male garment workers in the 1880s in New York responded to the controversy over home-based work versus shop work demonstrate how union understandings of "class" were very much tied up with assumptions about home, community, and family as the other of "work," thus defining work in a particular "gendered" way. The somewhat unique case of a union-sponsored cooperative apartment project in New York City in the 1920s also shows how a progressive, socialist union, even when unconventionally embracing housing as part of its organizational mission, was typical in its treatment of the housing realm, at least when it came to gender issues. If we understand "class" here to refer to both Katznelson's class two and class three, to both the organization of labor markets, embracing nonwaged domestic labor as well as waged factory and shop work, and the self-representation or language of the union, expressing certain "masculinist" assumptions, a brief look at the intersection of class and gender issues in these cases will help illustrate my claim that class is "always already" gendered in ways that fissures or bifurcates the identity of class from the inside.[56]

WORK, SPACE, AND GENDER: A BRIEF LOOK
AT THE NEW YORK GARMENT WORKERS' UNIONS

In the first two decades of the twentieth century, the nature of the garment workforce in New York changed dramatically in its composition, compared with the preceding two decades. Between 1880 and 1900, men replaced many women in the women's and men's garment trades. Immigration also played an important role. Predominantly Jewish workers from Eastern Europe in the 1880s and Italian immigrants a decade later began to replace mostly Irish women needle workers. Whereas Jewish women tended to share with their Irish counterparts the cultural resources to avoid the most rigorous strictures of the cult of domesticity and femininity, Italian women were less prone to work outside the home, thereby reinforcing the physical separation between home and work.

By the last decade of the nineteenth century, large contractors had set up factories for the production of garment goods. However, the nature of the industry and its competitive pressures were such that subcontractors could substantially cut production costs through the use of outside labor, most notably in the tenements of the poorer sections of the city. By 1893, almost 25 percent of men's ready-made clothing was completed in rooms that were both shop and home. The majority of home workers were women, whereas the majority of workers in the shops were men.[57]

These demographic and industry changes also led to changes in the organizations representing workers. The United Garment Workers of America (UGW) had represented garment workers since 1891 but came under increasing criticism from the new immigrant urban labor force that dominated New York by the time of the escalation of labor militancy in the 1909–1914 period, which included the famous shirtwaist-makers' strike. The International Ladies Garment Workers Union (ILGWU) had been founded in 1900, followed by the Women's Trade Union League (WTUL) two years later, in great measure as a response to the aspirations of the new workforce. Whereas the UGW's leadership based in the Midwest was conservative and "nativist," the garment workers of New York were radical and mainly immigrants. The tension between the two constituencies led to a split in the UGW that led to the formation of the Amalgamated Clothing Workers of America (ACW) in 1914, under the leadership of Sidney Hillman.[58] Despite many differences, however, there was a significant continuity between the old and new unionism in the way they articulated class and gender.

UGW TAILORS

The leadership of the UGW represented tailor artisans whose status and security were most threatened by industrialization and mass production. They declared at their founding convention, "[T]he peaceful and independent tailor of history is no more. His former standing in the community like the physician, the pastor or simple artisan is replaced by the factory hand."[59] These tailors focused their insecurities on the increasing tenement-based immigrants from Eastern and Southern Europe,[60] calling for legislation to eliminate sweatshops operated through subcontractors and for the curtailment of immigration. In the preamble to the constitution adopted at the convention, it was announced: "We shall endeavor to abolish the sweating system [and] to supplant tenement house work." The statement of objectives of the UGW included the desire "to discontinue the practice of working in our homes . . . and to elevate the moral, social and intellectual condition of our members."[61]

The UGW drew a telling distinction between "inside" and "outside" shops: the former referred to the relatively autonomous (and recent) work spaces away and distinct from the home, structured formally through the wage contract ("independent"), while the latter was seen as irreducibly imbricated with(in) the space of the family, home, and community. Union rules dictated that eligibility for a union label required all workers in the "inside" shops to be unionized. As a result, there was an effort to recruit women workers into these shops. Men retained leadership positions, and negotiations with employers tended to differentiate by "skill," admitting the tasks associated with men but excluding, for example, the women buttonhole makers, who worked for longer hours and lower wages.[62] Even though women did organize a few women-only locals, the dominant union culture not only prevented the themes of gender from being raised, but were openly against even the inclusion of women in locals.[63]

To enforce the discursive differentiation between work and home, spheres threatened by the potential recognition of the workplace at home, the tailors proposed to issue a union label only to products of "inside" shops that were in "acceptable surroundings." The criteria of what was or was not acceptable principally concerned wages and hourly rates. Nevertheless, we would be mistaken to overlook the role played by the exteriorization of family and sexual relations represented by "the home" for the self-definition of the public, class identity of "workers" and "work." Indeed, throughout this period, the need to differentiate the identity of the workers from any connection with the home was a persistent theme of garment workers' struggles. The striking tailors of 1913, for example, again demanded an end to tenement-house work.[64] Nor were they alone in this demand. One of the central themes of the Progressive reform agenda was the elimination of "work" from the home through legislation banning child labor, home-based work, and so on.[65] Their insistence that labels could go only to "inside" shops implied that there was a clear articulation of place—that is, of what constituted "acceptable surroundings"—with the definition of work, which of course could be raised only in the context of the separation between home and work.

Thus, the nature of "work" as something external to the home and family was integral to the union's self-representation. The division between wage labor and family labor, Christine Stansell writes, limited women's "consciousness of themselves as workers: there was little room in the emerging plebeian women's sphere for women to develop a sense of themselves as individuals through common self-interest in the workplace. [Female] home workers were literally 'outside' the arena of public life where working men were developing the mutual associations which were the basis for a new kind of politicized community in the Victorian city."[66] By making the distinction between "inside" and "outside" shops, the tailors were at the same time forging an identity through representations that embodied gendered and normative assumptions about the forms of articulation between the spaces and structures of labor and sexuality, assumptions regarding the appropriate elements for a "class" or "workplace-based" identity. We cannot fully grasp what tailors (or other artisans more generally) understood by "traditional" status without recognizing the way that this depended on the arrangements by which domestic power was distributed and controlled. This was organized to a significant degree on gender lines, although, as we saw, this could vary by ethnic group. Certainly, as a normative representation of what virtuous work and class identity comprised, all the terms of the discourse related exclusively to the figure of the traditional male artisan.[67]

The "new unionism," embodied most dynamically in the ACW and its founders, envisioned a labor movement combining industrial unionism, class consciousness, and socialist ideology. (Along with the ILGWU and other radical unions, the ACW was an early supporter of the ill-fated Socialist Party in New York.) Fania Cohn offered a stirring paean to the new direction promised by the garment unions: "The Labor Movement stands consciously or unconsciously for the reconstruction of society. It strives towards a new life. It dreams of a world . . . where society will be organized as a Cooperative Commonwealth and where love, friendship, and fellowship will replace selfishness."[68] It was also envisioned by the female rank and file, as well as by the female leadership, which included the WTUL, that the break from craft traditionalism "offered women workers greater opportunities to develop programs suited to their specific needs."[69] The new unionism did indeed break with many of the positions espoused by the "old" unionism dominated by the American Federation of Labor (AFL). But not with all.

Many of the goals that women labor activists and reformers articulated came up against resistance to reconstruction precisely at the portals of the home, where they collided with assumptions about gender relations. Unlike the AFL unions, which tended not to support the entry of women into the labor force, the ACW and ILGWU formally supported women in their ranks.[70] Nonetheless, this was resisted by the locals, and at any rate, the idea that women worked out of necessity and would return home when able was never seriously contested. One of the most exhaustive analyses of the ACW has concluded that "the ACW's inability to answer the 'women's question' within its own ranks was further evidence that social criticism dared not trespass across the borders of the 'holy family.'" Dorothy Jacobs Bellanca, a leading ACW activist, persistently tried to establish a women's bureau within the union, but when a bureau was set up in 1924 with Bellanca as the first director, it soon folded. The leadership did not support what in their view was a potentially divisive new organization. Hillman's own position, for example, was that women were well enough represented.[71] In her study of Bellanca's experience with the ACW, Nina Asher concludes that the union men "generally had no wish to change societal roles; they did not doubt that women ultimately belonged in the home."[72] Similarly, Fraser concludes that the place of the family within the labor movement and "the wider world of social welfare reform" was as "an object of tutelary and defensive protection . . . to save the family from moral and material devastation."[73] If correct, this lends support to the thesis that the trench dug along the axis of gender was as strongly defended and maintained by forces within the Amalgamated Clothing Workers of America as those without.[74]

Women's organizations such as the WTUL accepted the gendered nature of work defended by the labor movement either in principle or by default.[75] They did not challenge the character of the (already constituted) work roles but struggled for the inclusion of women within those roles.[76] As far as the rank-and-file immigrants in the ACW were concerned, they generally shared the same assumptions as the UGW before them: low wages for women were justified by the presumption that women would work only as a temporary measure before marriage and that men would save what they could so as to open up their own "inside" shop—outside the home. Even though the majority of workers in both the men's and ladies' garment trades were women, they had virtually no women representatives. More important, the issues raised by housework and its relation to the labor organization's agenda never succeeded in challenging the consensus of what by the mid-1920s was becoming the basis for the "suburban compromise," thus affirming Nancy Cott's observation that "even in progressive circles, the belief that women could and should combine family life with outside employment was very distinctly a minority viewpoint."[77]

This is reflected in the union-sponsored cooperative apartment projects started in the mid-1920s. Although the ACW espoused some of the broadest and most far-reaching agendas among the labor unions in the decade, the fact that the initiative to construct a housing cooperative would lack any innovative thinking along the dimension of gender is at least suggestive, given several contemporary efforts to introduce gender into the agenda of social reform. Turn-of-the-century New York had seen a series of efforts by socialists, feminists, and others to put housing and urban space forward as a legitimate object of political action and reform—efforts of which activists in the ACW no doubt would have been aware. Indeed, Dolores Hayden has traced throughout this period what she contends amounts to a tradition of "material feminists" whose goal was to carry out a "grand domestic revolution" at the heart of which was a challenge to

> two characteristics of industrial capitalism: the physical separation of household space from public space, and the economic separation of the domestic economy from the political economy. In order to overcome patterns of urban space and domestic space that isolated women and made their domestic work invisible, they developed new forms of neighborhood organization including housewives' co-ops as well as new building types. . . . By redefining housework and the housing needs of women and their families, they pushed architects and urban planners to reconsider the effects of design on family life.[78]

This movement was distinctive in the explicitness with which it confronted and challenged the consequences of the new urban landscape for the sexual division of labor. Ranging from the campaign for paid housework in the late 1860s, to Charlotte Perkins Gilman's ideas for apartment buildings for single, urban women, to the designs inspired by the New York Feminist Alliance in the mid-1910s, to the Settlement House movement,[79] and to designs for kitchenless homes, these groups of men and women differed from the other more dominant forces of the time by rejecting the idea that a woman's emancipation depended solely on her taking a "man's" job in the factory or office. They did not look principally to state legislation as the key to social transformation. A very spatial appreciation of the dangers of isolated home life instead provided a set of ideas and reforms that highlighted the negative aspects of both industrialization and urbanization.

It is safe to assume that the activists in the ACW, with their ties to socialist and other progressive circles, would have had access to the various housing experiments and projects of the time and to the controversies surrounding the direction of progressive social reform, which, it should be recalled, the ACW to a large extent claimed as its own. For example, Max G. Heidelberg, a radical New York architect active on housing issues for the Cooperative League of America (which had collaborated with the ACW since 1919) as well as within socialist and feminist interests, was hired by the Feminist Alliance to design innovative apartments, collective housekeeping facilities, and so forth.[80] Max Eastman, the publisher of *The Masses,* was connected with both feminist and socialist circles, as well as with the ACW.

These parallel developments indicate at the very least that the ideological field of the time was not devoid of these critical ideas. One historian, discussing a similar union-sponsored cooperative project in Philadelphia completed less than a decade after the first Bronx projects, noted that in conversations among the architects, union activists, and officials, "no subject was off limits: socialism, communism, none of the 'isms.'"[81] But "feminism"?

Feminism (a term that initially signified a set of issues broader than the nineteenth-century idea of the improvement of women) was potentially of great importance, and of course a great challenge, to the labor movement, both because of the movement's androcentrism and because of the New Unionism's belief in the utopia of productivity supposed to be brought about by the administrative regimes of Frederick Winslow Taylor and Henry Ford.[82] Mary Jo Buhle has argued that in contrast to the more established women's movements, such as the WTUL, "Feminists chose to wage their battles elsewhere—within the interstices of private life. In redefining the ultimate goal as self-realization rather than advancement, Feminists drastically altered the teleology of woman's mission."[83] By espousing the antirationalist philosophy associated with the French philosopher Henri Bergson, feminists presented perhaps the most radical critique of the most progressive sectors of the labor movement at the time, including the ACW.

The ACW was unable to use its brief encounter with an urban housing project to reveal and challenge the trenches that in the end, to follow Katznelson's interpretation, limited their own mission and identity. The ACW was committed to both the "Age of the Machine" and, by default, what might be called the sexualizing regime of modern urbanism. The problem is that these two impulses converged to such a degree and were espoused with such conviction that the ACW, an important player in the Congress of Industrial Organizations and in the transformation of American unionism before the New Deal, possessed no ideological resources to combat the consolidation of the mechanization and objectification of the house as the container of the equally mechanized and instrumentalized body of the new suburban subject: consumptionist femininity.[84] As Fraser has trenchantly concluded,

> The Amalgamated, and the radical labor movement more generally, were, after all, the apostles of modern times[,] . . . believers in the bourgeois utopia of self-fulfilling productivity, discerning in it the ultimate historical fate of the proletariat. . . . It was as well indifferent to the modernist assault on the bourgeois rationalism, committed instead to progressive efficiency with its penchant for treating the body as a kind of human motor subject to the general laws of thermodynamics. Modernism, whether originating in the diffidence of preindustrial social groups or in the dissociation and nihilism of middle-class intellectuals, was fundamentally antithetical to the objectivism, standardization, and realism of modern times, and to its central institutions—the factory and the bureaucracy. As such it found no expression in the Amalgamated's cultural and educational program. For that matter it left no enduring traces anywhere in the labor movement.[85]

The residential communities that the ACW sponsored in the Bronx did not derive their socialist content from the legacy of Fourier and the utopians, for whom the space of home and work and living relations were central to an emancipatory vision, or from the worker republicanism of the fading craft unions. Rather, they are best understood as part of labor's role in developing a "Fordist" welfare state that would attempt to regulate production and consumption (or reproduction) in a more coherent and extensive way than ever before.[86] The industrial, rather than craft, tradition of the ACW did address a new constituency. But the ACW's move away from a narrow economism was carried out in the terms of a novel and powerful form of corporatism. This "social" union-ism was itself premised on a corporatist closure of identity within a dis-course of productivism and economic growth. The surplus of identities that were excluded, but nonetheless implicitly present, notably gender identities, but in different ways also those of a broader conception of cit-izenship and race, had to struggle in the post–New Deal era for their own political projects, and to do so for the most part outside and against this new social unionism.[87]

Three conclusions follow from the foregoing discussion, in increasing order of generality. First, the way that gender relations within the work-ing class were understood and acted upon comprise an important part of the answer to the question of why American workers before the New Deal did not pose their demands in the workplace and in the commu-nity in the same idiom of class. In addition to the several state-related variables persuasively highlighted by Katznelson, the dominant gender assumptions prevalent in even the most progressive urban unions rein-forced the divided nature of American urban politics. "Class" was restricted to the workplace in part because of how class was understood as the organizational collective identity of a predominantly male domain, the workplace outside the home. That the idea of purely separate spheres for men and women was a myth for many working-class families where women participated in the labor force does not lessen the fact that unions often fought and organized on explicit gender issues, such as the family wage.

Admittedly, the foregoing discussion cannot be taken as a full demon-stration of the role played by the intersection of gender relations and urban space in working-class formation. Determining the precise man-ner in which gender relations contributed to the bifurcated nature of American urban class politics would need to answer questions that I can only raise but not answer here. One question concerns the extent to which the support of women in working-class families helped support and strengthen working-class solidarity, for example, in the case of strikes. Historians have shown instances where ethnic solidarity has helped to promote, rather than to fragment, working-class militancy through communal social networks that provided resources for offset-ting the costs of workplace conflict.[88] Thus, we need to explore under what circumstances gender relations help to promote, rather than detract from, class solidarity. But in exploring this question, it is necessary to keep in mind an important distinction: working-class familial solidarity may promote greater militancy on the part of workplace-based workers, but this is more about the degree of working-class militancy vis-à-vis employers than about the kind of action involved. It is not about bridging or dividing the workplace and the community.

Given Katznelson's comparative analysis of holistic and bifurcated working-class identities in England and the United States, I can imagine two further objections to this initial conclusion. First, if I am right that gender works to pattern class relations across work and home, then why did not apparently similar gender relations in England lead to a similar split there, as in the United States? Second, if the claim about the hybrid nature of urban consciousness is correct, then despite the apparent holism of the English case, was class also bifurcated there? The first question can be answered only through an empirical analysis comparing the role of gender relations in the U.S. and English cases. The answer to the second question must be "Yes and no." Yes, because this holism was bought at the cost of the exclusions of gender, and no, because the patterning of identity is only a structural possibility opened up by the modern city and not a necessary empirical outcome. The way in which this structural possibility was understood and institutionalized was variable. The holism of the English case should thus be viewed as a result of the hegemonizing of community identities by workplace identities and not the true mapping of an essential potential identity without a "constituent outside."

A further set of questions for which understanding the role of gender relations in the transformations of urban space should prove important concerns what Mathew Edel, Elliot Sclar, and Daniel Luria have called the "suburban compromise" between capital and labor. They have claimed that, parallel to the well-known compromise reached on the shop floor in the New Deal, capital and labor struck an earlier and equally significant compromise where they lived. In their view, at the turn of the century, labor agreed to trade workplace militancy in urban areas for greater access to home ownership in burgeoning working-class suburbs, where after World War II the cult of domesticity and consumption gained full expression.[89] Their analysis suggests the following question: To what extent did gender assumptions within organized labor beyond the economic interest in an expanded economy and construction jobs contribute to labor's role as a willing partner in the creation and unfolding of the suburban ideal in the United States, and as a result, to the shape of the postwar suburban transformation of space, itself an important development of postwar class identity?

Beyond the specific historical hypothesis, the second and more general conclusion to be drawn from the case of the garment workers' unions is that the Marxian class concept necessarily embodies an implicit gender dimension. The critique of androcentrism (a term first popularized by Charlotte Perkins Gilman)[90] suggests that "class" is always already structured by gender in the sense that it is an irreducible constitutive limit of the spatial embodiment of class identity, once the separation between work and home has been generalized and institutionalized, although the precise form of this "gendering" is historically variable. A concept of class predicated on the unification of the multiple spaces of identity is therefore both spatialized and gendered.[91] To say simply that trade unions represent class identities needs to be recast so as to raise the question of what exclusions this representation rests upon. This is not in itself a criticism. It is to concede that any given identity, especially if it is institutionalized and organized, necessarily rests on exclusions and the exercise of power. It is not a question of eliminating power from representation, but of assessing which exclusions are preferable or strategically required and the types of institutions that can organize this power.

Finally, and most generally, this result is only one expression of the characteristic of social identities marked by alterity, hybridity, and overdetermination, and whose specific character (be it ethnic, racial, class, territorial, or whatever) does not express an essential identity but is a result of hegemonic articulations. This implies, for example, that "high" classness, in its full Marxian sense as the unification of community and workplace (indeed, of all the relevant spaces of the everyday), should not be viewed in terms of the "true" representation of an extradiscursive reality (class two) but as the hegemonizing of the community residence by workplace identities.

I would push Katznelson's argument even further to suggest that the links between categories of individuals, their identities, and their behavior have become not only contingent, but, in the Derridian sense, undecidable. This makes his cognivitist notion of "mapping" less useful, or at least in need of qualification. The idea of "mapping the city" central to urban theory involves assumptions about both the nature of space (that it is geographical and clear, with clear boundaries demarcating distinct zones of experience and meaning) and the subjects that are to do the mapping (that they are capable of fusing structure and agency into a totality with a fixed meaning). The notion of spacing complicates this sense of mapping. If identities arise in part from a mapping of the spaces of the city, the fluidity and fuzziness of the boundaries of spaces render identities potentially fuzzy and undecidable as well. This does not imply that mapping or identity is impossible, only that the subjects and objects of the mapping of space are best understood along different lines. Mapping is probably better viewed as the "reweaving of webs of belief" about the world and about ourselves, to use Richard Rorty's term, than as the mapping of an external given social reality.[92] The claim in *City Trenches* that "class has been lived and fought as a series of partial relationships" thus needs to be extended.[93] It is not merely class but the city and modernity that have been lived as potentially hybrid and polyvalent, marked by the anxieties produced by the instability of boundaries between spaces of self, other, and strangers.

But such a notion of identity is incompatible with Marxian and other perspectives that either take identities as empirically given or refer back to an antecedently constituted identity. Is it possible to retain the deconstructive insights of the *City Trenches* thesis while dropping the Marxian class scheme? Is there a theoretical model of identity and agency that can replace the Marxian one, that can make sense of the dilemmas of *City Trenches*, allow for a more complex notion of space, and moreover incorporate gender as a constitutive, rather than supplementary, element?

BEYOND ESSENTIALISM IN STRUCTURE, AGENCY, AND IDENTITY

The trouble with the Marxian account of structure and agency is that it narrows the content of these terms to the economic transformations brought on by capitalist development and to the variety of working-class behaviors. I have argued that we should broaden these to incorporate the dual structuring force of the state (bureaucratization) and the economy (commodification). I also proposed that Habermas's theory of systemic rationalization and its separation from the lifeworld provides the best available model that simultaneously retains Marx's critical insight about the overreaching of systemic forces and avoids reducing these to economic forces. At the same time, I suggested that we bypass Habermas's account of the lifeworld based on universal speech pragmatics because (Habermas's own disclaimers notwithstanding) it is too closely tied to foundationalist assumptions of a community of consensus over meaning, goals, values, and so on. Instead, I have found ideas drawn from poststructuralism, deconstruction, and other anti-essentialist perspectives to be more relevant for capturing the hybridity and alterity distinctive of urban cultures. Still, I have found Katznelson's argument for maintaining the agenda of social theory in terms of the linking of distinct levels of analysis (conceptual framework, social conditions, relations and institutions, beliefs and dispositions, and collective action) to be powerful and persuasive. What this implies is that we still need a way to link the forms of structure and agency in a way that is consistent with an anti-essentialist theory of social identities.

LACLAU AND MOUFFE

The work of the political theorists Ernesto Laclau and Chantal Mouffe provides some key elements of the kind of alternative model of structure and agency that urban theory requires. Their approach is attractive because it provides a post-Marxist framework within which to interpret social movements, social conflict, and social change in contemporary societies in terms of the increasing salience and centrality of contingency and alterity.

Laclau's and Mouffe's work has been the subject of much controversy. Some critics have not welcomed their explicit endorsement of a post-Marxist socialist political position based on abandoning a revolutionary strategy both anchored in labor organizations and entailing a qualitative break with liberal democratic institutions. Instead, Laclau and Mouffe favor a political strategy of extending and deepening democratic principles of liberty and equality in more and more areas of social life through the linking of the progressive elements of different social movements. Other critics have dismissed their reliance on unfamiliar philosophical perspectives—Derridian deconstruction, Lacanian psychoanalysis, the Wittgensteinian philosophy of language games—as idealist, obscurantist, and political impotent. While the first objection hardly seems relevant to contemporary political life in most countries, the increasing application of these new theoretical directions in critical cultural studies should make them more familiar. (Their usefulness is another matter altogether.) After all, Hegelian dialectics and Feuerbachian views of human development could hardly be seen as less elaborate than these new perspectives. At any rate, Laclau and Mouffe have drawn imaginatively from a variety of theoretical positions to address many of the problems faced by critical social thought in the contemporary period, problems that are also reflected in Marxian urban theories. Indeed, their approach has informed much, if not all, of the argument here so far.

There are three interrelated elements of Laclau's and Mouffe's anti-essentialist understanding of political identities: identity as "lack," structure as a "failed objectivity," and "dislocation," the "constitutive outside," and "antagonism" as central features of social relations.[94] For Laclau and Mouffe, the key distinction between essentialist and non-essentialist approaches to social agency lies in viewing identities as respectively either expressing an antecedent, fully self-determining self-sufficiency, which they call "positive," or failing to do so, which they call "negative." For Laclau, complete objectivity is defined as a situation in which the permanence or stability of a subject's essential meaning is not threatened by or dependent upon any other force or entity. However, if a subject's identity is somehow prevented from becoming objective by a feature internal to the subject, rather than simply by being limited by an outside force, the subject is best seen as negative, as a failed objectivity. To understand this more clearly, it is necessary to turn briefly to Lacan's theory of the subject, which underlies much of Laclau's approach.

Paralleling the deconstructive critique of "presence" found in the work of Derrida and others, the Lacanian theory of subjectivity or agency is based on the critique of the idea that an individual expresses or represents an essential or "full" identity. Lacan argues that the passage from the period of infancy, in which the child does not distinguish itself from external objects and possesses no distinct sense of self, to the infant's assumption of an "identity" in the social world of other subjects is marked by a paradoxical problematizing of identity itself: the mirror stage. Lacan uses the metaphor of a mirror in which a child sees her presence reflected (or imitated by others) to capture the first moment in which subjectivity is inaugurated. The child comes to recognize herself as a unified being through her identification with an image. In acquiring a sense of self through an imaginary identification with an external representation or image, the subject becomes permanently split. For Lacan, this paradoxical moment is both inevitable and tragic. Although the desire for the fictional unity of self and image continues throughout social life, embodied for instance in utopian impulses and the merging of selves in love, there is in fact no possibility of total self-presence, of a complete coincidence between essence and appearance. Desire is "impossible" since it is directed toward a unity and coherence that is rendered unattainable by the nature of subjectivity as self-difference and lack. To desire one's image is thus at the same time to desire an Other set off by spatial and temporal dislocations.[95] In a parallel argument, Derrida notes that "the speaking subject discovers his irreducible secondarity, his origin that is always already eluded; for the origin is always already eluded on the basis of an organized field of speech in which the speaking subject vainly seeks a place that is always missing."[96] This understanding converges with the account of class and community identities I introduced in Chapter 1 as structured in terms of "constitutive outside" that undermines the self-sufficiency and unity of each identity as self-presence.

Laclau has extended this understanding of identity to reformulate the problem of structure and agency. Laclau's aim is to develop a notion of structure that is consistent with the idea of identity or agency as lack and as overdetermined. He contrasts his approach with conventional treatments that posit the domains of structure and agency as two orders external to each other, such that the structure is "objective" and presses against or limits "subjective" identities from the outside. Because they rest on assumptions about the closed nature of each domain, these approaches result in an oscillation between polarities such as objectivism and subjectivism in sociology, and between viewing historical change as the result of structural contradictions or of class struggles in Marxist thought. This impasse arises principally because, strictly speaking, there is no relation of determination between these two orders, only one of limitation. To overcome this difficulty, Laclau argues that it is necessary to avoid the reintroduction of the totality or structure itself as fixed entity, a new essence, for example, as in structuralism, in which a system of differences is itself fully determining of the definition of each element.

For Laclau, the view of actors as overdetermined, or hybrid, is inconsistent with the notion of structure as a positivity (that is, as fully objective) in which actors are wholly determined by the structure. This arises from the definition of an actor: I possess a freedom to act to the extent that I am not determined by the structure. But, and this is the crucial anti-essentialist step, the reason why I escape determination by the structure is not because I possess an essence or quality independent from the structure, which would be the case if identities were objectively defined, and which is how identity appears in intuitive or existentialist accounts of experience, but because, paradoxically, my identity is constituted through a "radical heteronomy," a patterning or spacing blocking the possibility of an objective identity.[97] If I did achieve such a total objectivity, I would in fact become an internal moment of the structure. I would cease to be an actor in any meaningful sense of the term. Thus, the space of identity is in fact the lack, the missing aspect of the structure that it would need for itself to constitute itself as a coherent whole.

Subjectivity is the locus that escapes determination by the structure. And to the extent that there is a space that does escape determination by the structure, then the structure is also a precarious totality, since it derives its objectivity only from the degree to which it manages to "suture" or fix the differential elements within a fixed system of relations. The structure is a "failed" structure because dislocations resulting from the processes of commodification and bureaucratization of everyday life (the two system imperatives) create antagonistic forces that create multiple power centers that seek to hegemonize and structure their immediate relations. These antagonisms, in turn, provide the spaces within which, through the mechanism of identification, "subject positions" crystallize and upon which the subjects thus constituted may potentially act in response to the dislocations (for example, in trade unions on antagonistic employment relations, or in community organizations on contradictory consumption and spatial relations). The structure as a single determining totality in which the meaning of each individual element is fixed is decentered, not in the sense that there is an absence of structure, as critics often try to claim, but in the sense that there are multiple and undecidable sites of antagonisms, and hence multiple power centers. The space of collective identities, in this view, is a space that attempts, but that always fails, to reach a point beyond antagonism, to transform itself from a negative to a positive value. But since identities are relational in the first place, and derive their character from dislocations in the structure and in relation to other identities, this remains an unachievable goal.[98]

Laclau states that the implications for social analysis of viewing agency and structure in terms of lack, antagonism, and undecidability are as follows: "The field of social identities is not one of full identities, but of their ultimate failure to be constituted. A realistic analysis of sociopolitical processes must therefore abandon the objectivistic prejudice that social forces are something, and start from an examination of what they do not manage to be." The question we need to ask, Laclau suggests, is: "To what extent does a society manage to conceal the system of exclusions on which it is based?"[99]

THE BIFURCATION THESIS RECONSIDERED

If we return to the *City Trenches* thesis in the light of these ideas, we can draw out a rather different and more fruitful dimension from its tensions. Recall its positing of a bifurcation or "radical separation in people's consciousness, speech and activity of the politics of work from the politics of community" and Katznelson's claim that "what is distinctive about the American experience is that the linguistic, cultural, and institutional meaning given to the differentiation of work and community . . . has taken a sharply divided form." This bifurcation can now be understood in a radically different way that does justice to Katznelson's desire to "embrace complexity" and to overcome "developmental assumptions," a way that could not be achieved via the four-tier model.

Drawing on Laclau's political theory, the link between meaning and difference can now be appreciated in a way that problematizes and does not merely depend upon the assumption of a prior collective identity. If we relinquish the conception of an a priori unified identity and instead begin from the position that meaning and subjectivity arise only from the ways in which the multiple elements of social identity are hegemonized and articulated into a provisional totality, the arguments of *City Trenches* can be interpreted as an outline of how this latter conception may look within the social and historical sciences. This approach furnishes us with a more rigorous way of understanding the dilemma of Marxian urban theory in terms of two incompatible conceptions of class agency that we analyzed in Chapter 1. Class is best understood in terms of the hybrid notion of identity and hegemonic concept of agency. In this case, for example, we would say that to assume a subject position (such as "worker") is to *identify* with an imaginary subject that is the addressee of political-organizational discourses—in this case, labor organizations. Similar to many popular commercial discourses, such as is used in advertising, what is addressed in the discourse of the labor movements and trade unions is an imaginary subject ("You" the worker, "You" the consumer) with which a subject must identify.[100] We saw in Chapter 2 how a trade union represents "workers" by naturalizing the concept of worker as if it were a given objective identity without "spacing" or an outside on which its mythical (or "imagined") unity depends. Yet this representation persistently produced a "surplus" identity (women, races, neighborhood or housing interests) excluded from the formal representation and yet from which they nevertheless could not completely disassociate. To secure a class identity paradoxically necessitates the extension of the chain of demands to encompass these surplus identities. The consequence of this chain of articulations is to transform the identities of each element, because no identity exists outside of these articulations.

For example, the identity of the "worker" who defines himself only as a seller of labor power for wages is threatened by several forces outside the workplace. First, the separations of workplace, community, and home inscribe distinct divisions within this individual subject. Second, the dislocations of the capitalist city also threaten the objectivity of the worker: increasing housing costs threaten the identity forged at the workplace, state-sponsored relocation and urban renewal threaten the stability gained from the market exchange relationships between employer and employee, women entering the labor force upset settled background assumptions on which class was defined, and so on. The list could be multiplied, but the point should be clear. There is no objectivity of identity other than in overdetermined relationships with other spaces and other temporalities. To secure the identity "worker" requires the articulation of workplace demands with housing, territorial, urban, and gender demands, among others. Unity is the result of the exercise of power to hegemonize a series of differences, but, because identity is itself a consequence of the dislocations of the system, these differences cannot be permanently closed off and eliminated. I have tried to show that gender is one such set of exclusions upon which the unity of working-class identities is based.

To avoid "incoherence" and relativity, Katznelson is thus not obliged to posit the subject as an a priori unity that identifies as such at the workplace but otherwise elsewhere, which is the strategy of the four-tier model.[101] Agency or the subject is necessarily patterned, and it is the value of *City Trenches* to have demonstrated the social and historical basis of that patterning. Moreover, since the notion of patterning is not restricted to a dichotomous set of identities, the idea of bifurcation should be read as a special case of a more plural character of urban identities.

Indeed, the dilemmas generated by the separation of work and home in all three of our authors can be seen as a motif revealing the complexity and alterity defining the urban experience. The recognition of the bifurcation of work and home identities presses up against this realization, yet is strictly delimited by its Marxian scaffolding. The alternative approach I have outlined should help us remove the Marxian scaffolding without the danger of collapse into an incoherent heap.

In fact, the danger of incoherence rests more directly with Marxian urban theory itself than with alternatives that jettison its certainties and metaphysical presuppositions. Indeed, Katznelson concedes as much in declaring in the first sentence of *Marxism and the City* that "Marxism has broken down as ideology and as a guide to governance." As we have seen, the book ends up with a rather unsatisfactory juxtaposition of

Marxian and non-Marxian elements, with its Marxist elements restricted to the explanation of the economic dimensions of urban development and transformations in the West. But shorn of normative and strategic value, Marxism loses its distinctive claim as a way to change the world. Neither of the assumptions of Marxian urbanism—that core agents of contemporary societies are classes and that the key structural feature of modern societies is primarily the economy—is tenable. Beyond that, the strategic implication of the Marxian model—that progressive strategies to accomplish socialist goals require a simplification of the identity of social groups in two opposing camps—is neither plausible nor desirable anymore. By contrast, radical democratic strategies to deepen democratic reforms imply not the simplification but the proliferation of sites of social antagonism and of the types of social actors. What this implies is an approach to the problems of fragmentation, difference, and pluralism that does not rest on the essentialism of Marxism, with its dichotomy between fragmentation and a total unification. Seen in this light, *City Trenches,* with its dilemmas, is emblematic of one response to the problems of difference in the capitalist city, resting on the dream of identity and agency as transcending plurality. Daniel Bell's comment in "The Failure of American Socialism," written over two decades before *City Trenches,* could be read as a prescient critique of the latter's Marxian presuppositions: "In the here and now, people do not live at the extreme (in the 'entirety' which was Sorel's myth) but they live 'in parts,' parceling out their lives amidst work, home, neighborhood, fraternal club, etc."[102]

Katznelson has helped us see how these trenches were dug and patterned across the modern capitalist city. But the idea of an identity unifying the totality is neither plausible nor desirable.

In his most recent work on liberalism and democratic theory, Katznelson has not only moved farther away from the revolutionary goals of Marxian socialism, he has conceded the primordiality of difference, drawing on John Locke's psychological pluralism to buttress his case for a liberalism that is attentive to difference.[103] At any rate, Katznelson's move away from Marxism proper, following Castells's and Harvey's trajectory, surely marks the exhaustion of the discursive convergence of Marxism and urbanism since the 1960s. What may lay ahead I leave for the next and concluding chapter.

CHAPTER 4

Difference, Democracy, and the City

Ideally, scholarly work can be cast as journey from "explanation" to "response." Whereas explanation tends toward monologue, exposition, and critique, response is an invitation to carry on the conversation with the widest range of interlocutors—in the public sphere, if you will. Radical democratic ideas are clearly inspired by this goal of openness to the voice, dignity, and autonomy of the other, of not decrying the fact that there are more questions than answers. I follow writers such as Marshall Berman, Richard Sennett, Iris M. Young, and others in thinking that the complex modern city is connected in important ways to this ideal, that the city offers perhaps "the only kind of environment in which modern values can be realized."[1]

In what follows, I would like to attempt this move from explanation to response and to ground my ideas in the worlds that I inhabit. To do this, I will outline my views in response to several possible challenges that could be posed. I address them as a means of clarifying ambiguities in my arguments, as well as to point to new directions for research and inquiry. Therefore, after providing a brief summary of the main arguments of the book, the remainder of this conclusion grapples with some continuing questions and dilemmas in thinking about the contribution that urbanism can make to the goals of democracy and justice. While I cannot treat all these problems with the detail they deserve—which would require further theoretical and empirical research—I would like to address them briefly and indicate directions for future work.

THE PROSPECTS FOR URBAN SOCIAL THEORY

A key task of critical urban social theory, and the one this book represents, is to provide an analytical framework for understanding how identities, space, and structure interact to shape the cities in which we live and influence the experience of living in them. (Because it is so hard to generalize about cities, my remarks here will concern, in general, North American cities.) Such a perspective must provide answers to three connected sets of questions: What is the nature of the identities and actors that inhabit the city? What are the types of spaces—of action, of power—that constitute the urban? What are the key structural dimensions that both constrain and form the context of everyday life?

Such a framework must be built upon concepts appropriate for the social, spatial, and political conditions that we face today. First, continued global immigration flows have created a heightened degree of cultural, ethnic, and linguistic pluralism among the identities of the city's inhabitants. In conjunction with vastly expanded communication technologies and media, this has led to intensified exposure to other cultural identities, resulting in conflict, mutual influence and interpenetration, or forms of accommodation. This is not a wholly new phenomenon. It is an acceleration of dynamics that have characterized much of modern history, but we do need new ways of understanding it.

Second, the transformation of urban space (especially in the United States) from the concentric industrial city to a low-density metropolitan network means that the relevant spaces within which individuals create meaning and that structure their world are more numerous, fluid, and overlapping than in the past. As a consequence, "urban" space can no longer be restricted uniquely to the physical place of the immediate residential community. For immigrants, for example, these spaces encompass their ethnic neighborhood enclaves, but also take in the material and cultural connections with faraway places. Global economic elites, on the other hand, occupy the network of flows of capital and commerce, as well as enclosed urban spaces such as gated suburban communities.

Finally, the dilemmas and negative effects of state bureaucratic intervention in many spheres of social life that cannot be reduced to economic processes (lessons learned from the experiences of both the welfare state in the Western nations and the bureaucratic statism in the former communist states) imply that state power and the market economy should be treated as relatively autonomous subsystems, in varying combinations of influence and importance forming the context of social action.

The underlying rationale for undertaking the theoretical exploration found in these pages arose from the fact that Marxian-inspired urban theory, the paradigm that has gone furthest in developing a coherent framework capturing the three dimensions of identity, space, and structure, has reached an impasse. For a period of about two and a half decades, between the late 1960s and the early 1990s, Marxian urban theory was accepted by many to be the key to unlock the puzzles of class, space, and power in capitalist cities. However, today the Marxian political imaginary has lost its grip on the imagination and provides little guidance to problems of governance, and its theoretical framework has lost interpretive power. Through a critique of the work of the three most important theorists of this school of thought, we saw that the answers offered by Marxian urban theory to the questions of identity, space, and structure—economic class actors, a physically bounded notion of urban space, and the economy as the determining feature of the social—were unsatisfactory.

As alternatives, I have proposed three concepts: hybridity, spacing, and the system/lifeworld distinction. First, urban identities should be viewed in terms of hybridity, overdetermination, and undecidability—theoretical terms highlighting the fact that modern urban identities are "mixed up," never reducible to one thing, registering the influence of other identities, and the fact that the boundaries that delimit and shape identities are permeable. Second, I proposed the notion of spacing, which both encompasses the idea of geographical or physical space and is broader than this. It reflects the active, unfinished, and layered quality of the spaces we inhabit (and that inhabit us), the spaces within which we create meaning. Here the notion of the border is important. I have suggested that we view urban space not merely as what is inside borders (of neighborhood, city, or other jurisdictions) but also as the margins or the borderlands, themselves important places of meaning and social life. Third, I have suggested that the structuring dimension of society reflected in Marxian theory's use of the economy is best replaced with the idea of a system consisting of relatively autonomous economic and administrative subsystems that stand in contrast to an analytically distinct sphere, the lifeworld, site of the symbolic reproduction of identities, cultures, and institutions of everyday life.

These three concepts are drawn from different intellectual traditions: poststructuralism, Habermasian systems theory, and comparative and feminist social science and history. Together, they prompt an important question about the feasibility of this kind of eclectic conceptual strategy. It might plausibly be objected that there is a greater degree of incompatibility between them than my approach acknowledges. But this poses less of a problem than may appear at first glance. The notion that there is something deficient about eclecticism has force only in contrast to a totalizing theory or paradigm. I criticized this totalizing stance in Chapter 2 when I showed how Harvey linked epistemological eclecticism to his negative assessment of the diversity of (urbanized) identities, both of which he saw as something to be overcome. Harvey's assessment drew its force from the totalizations of Marxian philosophy and Marxian class theory. However, once we let the latter go and acknowledge that there is no Archimedean point or metatheory from which to distinguish a pure discourse from an eclectic one, all we are left with is to decide between the usefulness and interpretive power of different types of syncretisms. What unifies the present critique is the conjunctural coherence brought about by the problem at hand—interpreting the discourse of critical urbanism.

While I thus do not think that eclecticism necessarily creates fatal methodological problems, I have not been able here to develop more fully the ways in which the different dimensions of my alternative framework articulate with each other. However, I would like to indicate briefly one possible line of argument that does so. Consider two of the key results of the preceding analysis, the concepts of articulation and the distinction between system and lifeworld. These have been seen by many commentators to be incompatible. Social-scientific critics of poststructuralism claim that these two concepts are incompatible because, given that articulation and concepts such as overdetermination were intended to displace the notion of the "expression" of an extradiscursive or essential realm, the nonrepresentational character of these concepts fails to grasp adequately one of the enduring features of modern societies: the power over everyday life of seemingly objective institutions, reflected above all in market and administrative-bureaucratic structures. Placing articulation and the system/lifeworld distinction together in fact accepts these criticisms to the extent of acknowledging that each can grasp what eludes the other. In that sense, however, they are supplementary, not incompatible. There is, however, no simple way to resolve their differences, particularly since writers in neither tradition have considered the others' key claims at an adequate level of detail.

What is clear is that a critical social theory cannot dispense with either an account of agency or an account of structure. This is because it clearly cannot dispense with the need to speak of "commodification" and "bureaucratization" as processes with a history and a force. Habermas is no doubt correct to claim that "it is not a matter of indifference to a society whether and to what extent forms of social integration dependent on consensus are repressed and replaced by anonymous system-integrative sociation."[2] Yet I am not aware of any social-scientific deployment of poststructuralism or deconstruction that offers a theoretical elaboration of these structural dimensions. It is true that these processes of differentiation, which are removed from direct control of communities, can no longer be read as pure expressions of fetishized objectivity for all the reasons discussed in Chapter 2. So, while positions influenced by deconstruction, such as in the work of Laclau, would eschew any notion of objectivity in terms of social phenomena outside discourse—a position I endorse—they typically are less successful in accounting for the seemingly intractable quality of precisely these features of modernity.[3] This I consider to be a significant drawback, which I suspect cannot be accommodated within the terms of discourse theory as it is presently cast. So the problem becomes how to develop an account of the "objectivity" of social systems while at the same time to avoid theorizing this objectivity as a dimension external to discourse.

A solution might be found if we make a distinction between processes that are discursively constituted and those that are discursively regulated. While all social phenomena are constituted discursively, not all are regulated in this way. The market, for example, is discursively constituted—it is a socially constructed institution—but it is regulated through money, whose key characteristic is precisely that it is not discursive. That is because money, in Habermas's terms, is a "medium" that abstracts from the directly redeemable validity claims that constitute the basis of everyday speech and communication and thus appears to work behind the back of participants' lifeworlds. (This is the insight captured in the phrase the "invisible hand" of the market.) Of course, media themselves are discursively constituted,[4] but their operations now structure quasi-autonomous domains of social life. This is incidentally one explanation for the possibility of and (partial) effectiveness of instrumental policy interventions. Looked at in this way, the concepts of articulation and overdetermination derived from poststructuralist theory and insights of Habermasian systems theory can be made compatible with each other.[5]

OBJECTIONS

Several possible objections exist to the alternative framework introduced in the preceding chapters and summarized above. These can be gathered together into two broad claims: first, that I underestimate the influence of economic class forces on urban space, and, second, that I overestimate the relevance of hybridity and complexity for understanding urban experience. As we will see, the latter is a more complex matter, covering several different kinds of problems. In addressing these concerns I will make two principal counterclaims: first, that rejecting economism does not, and should not, discount the market economy as a crucial shaper of urban space and of urban life, and, second, that hybridity and spacing have important implications for everyday life, for city planning practice, and for the design of local political institutions.

UNDERESTIMATING THE INFLUENCE OF ECONOMIC FORCES

The first objection might be articulated, I imagine, by policy makers, city planners, and activist citizens frustrated by the "privileged role of businesses" in societies like that of the United States. It argues that the theoretical critique of Marxian urban theory underestimates the empirical, practical dominance of economic forces in shaping urban space as well as in limiting the possibilities for a just and liberatory urbanism. The former point is clearly seen in the following plaint of a U.S. urban planner: "My city is driven by the private sector. We can help the private sector get things done, but the private sector is really making decisions that affect form, function, physical character, and life within the city. With very few exceptions, the private sector is calling the tune within American cities."[6] Further support for this position could point to the increasing presence of fortified enclaves and gated communities that exclude on the basis of wealth and income—one of the most worrying developments in urbanism today, which can be seen in cities from São Paulo to Los Angeles. Should this not be interpreted as a class structuring of urban space? Is this not an example of an explicit mapping of urban space in class terms and thus of the bolstering of class-based identities and agents?

Without doubt, it is crucial for a normative critical urban theory not to lose sight of the destructiveness of the market; but as Young and others have argued, economic exploitation cannot be the only basis of a theory of justice. Therefore, given that I have no objection to these empirical claims, the central question is whether recognition of these trends provides support for an interpretation of urban development and the patterning of collective identities on the basis of specifically *Marxian* class categories.

The answer, I think, is "No." While it is correct to interpret socioeconomic spatial segregation in class terms, it is not useful to see these in Marxian class terms. Indeed, a rigorous Marxian class theory instructs us not to confuse relations of production with mere market categories of stratification such as income, occupation, or education.[7] The difficulty for proponents of Marxian class analysis has been to connect their categories with the more obvious everyday dimensions of stratification. Socioeconomic stratification, along with the dimensions of race, ethnicity, or gender, is one of the defining markers of spatial segregation and one of the fault lines of local political discourse. Of course, this "hermeneutic" approach should not blind analysis to ideological and systemic distortions of societal mechanisms that are not immediately available to actors' consciousnesses, but at a practical analytical and political level, the geography of capitalist modernity is hard to read through Marxian class categories.

Consequently, while it is correct to argue that there are class mappings of space, these classes are more Weberian than Marxian ones. After all, economic groupings of people having organized to further their interests or defend themselves from oppression go back at least to Spartacus. There is nothing new about that. However, for Marx, classes were more than that: they carried the weight of a world-historical project. But I do not see the advantage of attributing to these groups a significance deeper than selfishness, bigotry, shortsightedness, helplessness in the face of a lack of political options, or an adolescent desire for an environment purified of the unexpected.

Acknowledging that spatial class segregation is a type of (exclusionary) difference points to another type of problem, however: the moral ambiguities in the concept of difference employed positively by many variants of postmodern theory and cultural studies. For example, urban theorists such as Michael Dear, Edward Soja, Michael P. Smith, and others, have advocated postmodernism as the most appropriate perspective for analyzing the new forms of urbanism because it values difference along a range of different characteristics, such as culture, ethnicity, or territory. Such a perspective is necessitated, according to Allen J. Scott and Soja, by the new urban landscape in the United States since the 1970s, which has been constituted by a "a very different urbanization process, much less susceptible to traditional forms of analysis."[8] A central task of postmodern urban theory thus is the illumination of "heterotopias," "absolutely Other and differentiated social spaces," as positive features of urban life.[9] Understanding these new spatial realities is necessary if we are to forge a new type of politics, which Soja describes as "a new politics of location and a radical spatial subjectivity and praxis that is postmodern from the start."[10] Similarly, Dear argues that by putting difference and representation to the fore of analysis, postmodern approaches are better equipped to read the contemporary American city, in which the legibility of space is more complicated and hierarchies are more despatialized than in the classic modern city mapped by the Chicago School.[11]

However, it is unclear what purchase the focus on urban difference has for analyzing the increasing socioeconomic segregation of space, the creation of fortress cities, gated communities, walled enclaves, or "privatopias." The objection could be raised that segregated ghettos and even old essentialist economic class inequality could be equally understood as forms of difference. A weakness of postmodern urban theory's stress on difference lies here, in its inability to differentiate analytically between different types of difference, between types of difference that we should advocate for and those that we should try to dismantle or weaken.

On the other hand, this charge cannot be leveled at the notion of hybridity, which I distinguish from the more typical use made of the concept of difference within postmodern urban theory. In the Introduction, I took pains to distinguish my own position from what usually is associated with the postmodern celebration of *absolute* difference. This latter kind of pluralism, one of a piece with identity politics, is what I called an "essentialism of the elements" in the last phase of Castells's work. It was precisely this perspective I also found problematic in the work of Michael P. Smith, as well as in Soja's "heterotopic" critical geography. By contrast, poststructuralist thought, to which I am more indebted, complicates our understanding of identity politics by suggesting that politics should not be about establishing and affirming identities but about destabilizing them. It is a politics, in the apt formulation of Eli Zaretsky, "that aims to subvert or decenter, rather than to conquer or assert."[12]

The notion of spacing I have proposed implies that all forms of social identity should be seen as necessarily overdetermined. From this point of view, spatial segregation and economic stratification should be seen as attempts to shut out the contingency of identity. Although creating borders may create difference, at the limit, it denies hybridity. Laclau has put it this way: "The ideological would not consist of the misrecognition of a positive essence, but exactly the opposite: it would consist of the non-recognition of the precarious character of any positivity, of the impossibility of any ultimate suture."[13]

For urbanists, this denial of hybridity rounds out Sennett's idea of a purified community, free from the unexpected and serendipitous, and free from experiences that can be emotionally threatening, dislocating, and painful. For example, in *The Uses of Disorder,* Sennett discusses several communities whose residents had in general very little to do with each other. Yet he shows that as soon as a black family moved in, or an outside researcher challenged their degree of cohesion, they closed ranks around a mythical sense of solidarity, claiming a unity that was "willed" but not "experienced." In interpreting the phenomenon of "false gemeinschaft," Sennett does not define positively what an urban enclave is, for to do so would be to miss the key point: this false community was defined by what it failed to be, in terms of an outside force that, paradoxically, disturbed something that did not exist in the first place. These fantasies of community are reactions to a fundamentally complicated world and seek to stabilize and retain the idea of a subject "without pain or paradox," to live a pastoral version of modernity hiding from the fact that "to be modern is to live a life of paradox and contradiction."[14]

Against this impulse, it should be the task of critical urban praxis to emphasize the fact that the complexity of the city provides the concrete opportunities for citizens to mature into what Berman and Rorty have called "ironists"—those who have developed a sense of the contingency of their own identities and have learned to grow out of what Habermas refers to as "willed immaturity." Thus, any attempt at complete (imagined and mythical) closure around an ethnic, economic, racial, or territorial group is an attempt to deny the relational and hybrid basis of all identities.

This does not mean that groups cannot try to exclude and indeed succeed in excluding. The history of suburbanization in America is in large part the story of transforming public into private space. Gated communities are only the logical culmination of this trend. Below I will discuss how this antiurban and ultimately antidemocratic impulse in the United States has been institutionalized through legislative and juridical support for the strengthening of jurisdictional borders around municipalities. This institutionalization of the imagined local community has contributed to the inability of social-policy reform and progressive urban planning to advance an alternative radical democratic conception of community in terms of spacing, hybridity, and reciprocity.

OVERESTIMATING THE RELEVANCE OF COMPLEXITY AND A NEW THEORY OF SELF FOR AN EFFECTIVE URBANISM

Several further challenges would suggest that the framework I have proposed overestimates the value of the notions of hybridity and spacing.

This objection applies to three issues in particular: the value of the experience of hybridity and spacing for the everyday city life of individuals and groups, their value as concepts to guide public discourse and city planning options, and, more generally, their value for public policy and the design of local political institutions. I will address these briefly in turn.

The urban theory I have proposed in the preceding pages builds upon the idea that the promise of the city for the everyday life of individuals and groups lies in its complexity and fluidity, that is, in the way in which it offers the self a terrain of identifications and possibilities that are flexible, hybrid, and undecidable. The theory echoes Berman's claim that only this kind of urban environment can lead to the "modernization of the soul," which, ironically, he tells us, is the ability to make oneself at home, if only provisionally, in the midst of contradiction and paradox. We see this notion articulated clearly in Sennett's early work, as well as in Jane Jacobs's call for mixed-use urban spaces. There are virtues to the disorder and chaos of the city.

Despite its appeal, this proposal must address several plausible challenges. I will address two in particular, the first voiced (I imagine) by a "realist" everyman, the second from a more philosophical position. The first argues that the complexity of the city overestimates the average person's tolerance for complexity, confusion, and ambiguity, for the perpetual renegotiation of identity, for the testing of who we are. For most people, this critic would claim, there has to be a balance between adventure and certainty. There has to be a balance between a space where we feel safe enough to take stock of the world around us and come to some settled, if provisional, interpretations of who we are and a space where, armed with these ideas, we embrace the stranger, the unknown, the challenging. Park's famous metaphor of the city as a "mosaic of little worlds" offers precisely this solution. From this point of view, then, what I have dubbed the promise of the city is not very palatable to most people. Indeed, support for this "realistic" position is not hard to come by: surveys have consistently demonstrated people's desire to reside in smaller, quieter, and less demanding environments. Big cities in the United States have lost population continuously throughout this century as households searched for less dense and less challenging environments. Walter Lippmann's comment on Governor Al Smith of New York's failed bid for the presidency in 1928 is telling: "Quite apart from the objection to Tammany, the sectional objection to New York, there is an opposition to Smith which is authentic. . . . It is inspired by the feeling that the clamorous life of the city should not be acknowledged as an American ideal."[15] One could conclude from this line of reasoning that modern urban forms, with their mosaic of relatively homogeneous neighborhoods and plurality of homogeneous suburbs, are a reflection of this general disposition toward the need for a haven amid the chaos of the city, and as such are necessary ingredients of modern urbanism.

The second objection I find equally challenging. I imagine this objection being voiced by a so-called liberal ironist, a proponent of American neopragmatist philosophy. Her argument might go as follows: "I have no real disagreements with your critique of Marxian urban theory, or with your use of deconstruction or systems theory. My difficulty is that you share with Laclau, Derrida, Sennett, and Michael Sandel the mistaken idea that only by understanding the 'deep' nature of the self can we forge a progressive politics that can create the good city. Although I agree with you that possessing a sense of irony and contingency about one's final vocabulary—about what gives meaning to one's life—is admirable, I tend to the opinion that Robert Park's model of the city as little 'island' communities is perhaps all we should hope for in a complex and diverse world. As Rorty has pictured it, we should 'urge the construction of a world order whose model is a bazaar surrounded by lots and lots of exclusive clubs.'[16] Even Will Kymlicka, who knows a lot about the real-life problems of institutionalizing multiculturalism in Canada, apparently holds this view.[17] The priority of democracy (that is, of liberty and equality) over philosophy (that is, over one's ultimate beliefs and values) is characteristic of modern liberal democracies and suggests that we should dissociate liberty and equality from thick notions of fraternity, from beliefs about the 'good' community. The good city is not one that can be built on a given idea of self (or what you call 'identities'), even hybrid ones, but one that ties together ethnocentric communities into an overlapping consensus to respect each others' private turf.[18] It is not only that this is the only way to ensure social peace, but once we abandon the Enlightenment notion of a universal community, there is nothing left but relativist, contingent worldviews and the necessity for solidarity, as opposed to the revelation, or even forging, of a common essence. In fact, there is something odd about your use of poststructuralism as a critique of totalizing ideas of community. As I see it, a city à la deconstruction would be no longer be 'lumpy,' with spaces of different truths and worldviews. It would become 'flat,' with everyone equally hybrid, equally other to each other's other. When I think of African Americans and Jews living side by side in Crown Heights in New

York, Muslims and Hindus in Bombay, or the Balkan republics, after all the violence and hostility of the riots and wars there, the 'little islands' model is a lot more realistic than the psychologically challenging one you, the early Sennett, or Julia Kristeva have in mind."

"The contingency or hybridity of identity you speak of," she might continue, "is an admirable goal for the private pursuit of autonomy, to become what Harold Bloom calls a strong poet, a rewriter of the narrative of one's own life. But for public purposes of solidarity with those who suffer economically, socially, and personally, all we need are better public policies and to persuade more people to support the goals of equality and liberty and dignity for all. Of course, I agree with you that this will never amount to a class movement in the Marxian sense, but the post-Marxism you espouse is too abstract and theoretical for the kinds of issues a progressive social agenda should be constructing. It tends to fall into the cultural politics of Left academia in the United States, which in general have been marching on their academic departments while the Right has been marching on the government. At worst, poststructuralism (or postmodernism) makes a theoretical virtue out of the cultural symptoms of capitalist restructuring. By suggesting as you do that today there is no clear urban space to map and no subject to map it, since both space(s) and identity(ies) are fuzzy, overdetermined, and multiple, you rob us of the critical power to grasp a sense of urban reality that is necessary for social mobilization. Rather than provide us the tools to map a new social space, in the way Harvey and Fredric Jameson have tried to do, you have submitted to the 'impulse to make ephemerality, fragmentation, and plasticity internal to social theory' and to the temptation 'to mimic the bewilderment of the situation on the ground.'"[19]

These are salient points. There is indeed a need for balance, and this requires a degree of homogeneity and spaces for it, or at the very least requires stability and predictability. However, this should not lead us to accept as an ideal the description of the city as a "mosaic of little worlds that touch but do not interpenetrate." It may be composed of little worlds, perhaps, but surely they interpenetrate, and at least overlap, as well as touch. Exploring and illuminating the ways in which boundaries or borders are both productive and subversive of identity, rather than simply lines of demarcation between mutually exclusive groups or communities, brings to light the promise of the city in what Iris Marion Young has called "social differentiation without exclusion." She sees city neighborhoods as an ideal of multiple, fuzzy spaces: everyone seems to know that there is a neighborhood, but no one really knows where the borders are. Moreover, although there may be a predominant ethnic or class profile to its residents, members of other groups also live there. We do share the streets, the airwaves, the parks, as well as the "imagined" space of a national or even international community. At these levels, our boundaries begin to blur. We should acknowledge and value this blurring, rather than hide from it. In so doing, we acknowledge the constructed and contingent nature of individual or group identities and rely less on appeals to defend our borders or to exclude. As citizens, our particularities make sense only in the context of a broader community in which we are responsible to others.

One of the contributions of poststructuralism is to offer ways of responding to this challenge of borders in urban life other than that which we find in the work of urban sociologists such as Lyn Lofland or Claude S. Fischer, philosophical liberals such as Richard Rorty, or pluralists such as Robert Dahl. Fischer's otherwise compelling subcultural theory of urbanism adopts Lofland's notion of the city as composed of an integrated and functional private realm juxtaposed with a world of strangers who are unfamiliar and dissimilar, a world that we can know only categorically (via "stereotypes") and that creates anxiety and fear.[20] However, another way of looking at this problem (and I have drawn on Derridian and Lacanian theory to do so) is to say that the city is a place where individuals integrate the multiple dimensions of their subjectivity by integrating the different worlds of the city—the place where everyone can say, with the fourteenth-century Persian poet Hafiz of Shiraz whose verse forms this book's epigraph, "through life's disheveled strands was my meaning found." In Jonathan Raban's evocative formulation, this is the "soft city" that awaits an imprint of identity.[21]

Gogol's writing on nineteenth-century St. Petersburg captures this process poignantly: the tensions between the different spaces of the city are reflected in two narrative styles, one surrealistic, the other realistic. For Marshall Berman, this tension reflects "two spatially contiguous but spiritually disparate aspects of modern city life. On the side streets, where Petersburgers live their everyday lives, normal rules of structure and coherence, of space and time, of comedy and tragedy apply. On the Nevsky [the main public space] however, these rules are suspended, the planes of normal vision and the boundaries of normal experience are shattered, people step into a new frame of space and time and possibility." But for Berman, these passages also warn of the danger of the city and the necessity of some form of personal integration: "The Nevsky can enrich Petersburgers' lives spectacularly, so long as they know how to take the trips it offers them and then come back. But those who cannot integrate the city's two worlds are likely to lose their hold on both, and hence on life itself."[22] To make the most out this urban journey, therefore, one needs to step into the maelstrom of public space and life with what Dostoyevsky called "minimal egoism" so as to be able to transform the reality of not being a unified subject from the pain and suffering of dissociation into a form of confident play. A hybrid individuality thus needs a sense of self or integration, but it would not be the subjectivity associated with an individual or group space autonomous from the context surrounding it, or with a transcendence of these conditions to a universal community. Instead, it would acknowledge that forms of identity are contingent and historical. It would also recognize that while identities are constructed, like the whole symbolic order of the lifeworld, they cannot be fully reduced to the conscious intentionality of subjects. Like the many streets and byways that we know to exist in our cities and through which we might one day pass, yet cannot map totally in our consciousness, the selves we are always becoming are a mixture of what structures us now and the possibilities and paths that await us.[23]

There is indeed something inevitable about the "lumpiness" of groups, communities, and spaces, especially in complex, multicultural societies. Network analysis and the so-called subcultural theory of urbanism have provided one powerful explanation of why this is so. At the same time, there are several difficulties with the idea of seeing cultures, groups, or different spaces as separate islands.[24] First, as Park himself noted in 1937, "the great world—intertribal, interracial, international—[has] brought about everywhere an interpenetration of peoples and a fusion of cultures."[25] Affirming this insight, Katznelson has observed that the idea of little worlds that do not penetrate underestimates the "mutual constitution of cultural contact and the tendency for all cultures to change and develop in interaction with others."[26] Second, it overestimates the internal homogeneity of cultures, neighborhoods, indeed, of any social grouping. Third, it lends itself too readily to the legitimation of oppressive practices and discrimination within any group. These considerations add up to the conclusion that hybridity, in the structuring context of a market/state system, is at the core of what I call the urban experience.[27]

Despite the obvious exclusions, our worlds do interpenetrate—rich and poor neighborhoods, cities, and suburbs, different countries and cultures. Of course, it is important that cities be safe, clean, and attractive so as to break the link in the popular imagination, so marked in the United States, between difference and danger. It should be the goal of urbanists to explore how these boundaries structure thought, action, and policy, as well as to show how they reinforce privilege, inequality, and power. Balancing the tension between similarity and difference, while perhaps obvious to say, has seemed hard to achieve institutionally. Attention should be focused on how to design cities—physically and institutionally—that can take advantage of this tension, in addition to ensuring economic and bureaucratic efficiency and accountability.

HYBRID IDENTITIES AND PUBLIC POLICY

The theoretical framework outlined here has several implications for how we think about ways to deepen the democratic aspects of urban political institutions. Contrary to the critique of hybridity as irrelevant for public purposes, a sense of one's identity as contingent and hybrid—as urban, in my usage—can play a crucial role in forging more effective public outcomes.

The hybridity of identities can further radical democratic public policies because the complex differentiations characteristic of the city and the multiple groups and identities that it concentrates provide the setting for a social learning process that creates citizens who possess a reflective, mature, and contingent sense of self, tolerant of a high degree of ambiguity and difference. This hybrid sense of self is capable of envisioning, formulating, and supporting more enlightened and more rational preferences and collective decisions regarding a range of pressing social problems, which will lead to a more effective and socially just set of public policy outcomes.

The importance of linking hybrid identities, institutions, and public policy is motivated by the acknowledgment that the current set of institutional mechanisms—above all, fragmented local government and the juridically protected mobility of capital—is inadequately fulfilling the key tasks of democratic institutions, which are to generate collective decisions that are rational and reasonable for the common good and that can lead to solutions to persistent social and urban problems.[28] Despite the assumption of democratic theory that political participation will lead to an enlightened citizenry, the alienation of the electorate from increasingly corrupt and distant politicians, especially at the local level, the distrust of state authority (especially police authority in poor and minority urban areas), and the use of welfare bureaucracies to "regulate the poor" and induce dependence and compliance with a low-wage labor market—

all these have not led to more effective urban public policy preferences or policies. Indeed, few urban policy initiatives have managed to challenge the "voices of decline" in relation to the problems of American cities.[29]

In general, the response by progressives to the reality of poor government decision making has been to advocate the extension of the principle of democratic participation to be more inclusive either of persons (women, blacks, gays, and so on) or institutions (cities, community groups, community districts, schools, hospitals, and so on), or both. However, this quantitative extension of democracy may no longer be effective as a means of achieving more rational outcomes.[30] First, it is no longer clear who the relevant populations with the right to participate in any given instance should be. Consider the example of the siting of a hazardous waste facility in the South Bronx of New York City: should participation in decision making be restricted to those directly (chemically) affected, to the local community district, the borough, or the city of New York as a whole? Or even should it include the poor black community in Virginia that will be the ultimate recipient of the waste? Second, in cases where the issue is the protection of minority rights (such as the siting of a homeless shelter or a home for the mentally ill), having "all" participate could be counterproductive, given the possibility of a NIMBY (Not In My Backyard) reaction. This is a relevant consideration for recent proposals for the creation of metropolitan government or regional legislatures in the United States. Simply enlarging the unit of governance to include more of the affluent and the poor will not guarantee greater predispositions toward redistributive and rational policies. Finally, it is by no means clear that simply greater participation at the local level will lead to more enlightened outcomes. Motives for participation can include short-term gain, rather than well-considered judgments about what is best for all. Nor should we expect "community"-based mobilizations to be necessarily egalitarian and inclusive. They can be reactionary, parochial, and exclusionary.

Claus Offe and Ulrich Preuss have examined this impasse and have concluded that solutions cannot be limited to the quantitative extension of the egalitarian principle to more and more categories of the population or to more and more institutional sectors of society. What is required instead is the improvement of the quality of citizens' individual and group decision making and preferences, not with respect to any substantive content, but relative to three criteria of political rationality: decisions and citizen's attitudes should be fact-regarding, future-regarding, and other-regarding, in contrast to being ignorant, myopic, and selfish.[31] They characterize this alternative as the radicalization of the principle of democratic participation, a "third wave" of democratization,

> enfranchising, as it were, the various preferences that exist within the individual citizens/voters so as to organize an orderly social conflict not just between majorities and minorities (or for that matter, between workers and managers in the case of "economic democracy") but, in addition, an inner conflict between what the individuals themselves experience as their more desirable and less desirable desires. Such a radicalization of the democratic principle would aim at stimulating deliberation not just between agents, but within subjects themselves.

Institutional arrangements thus should be evaluated against their capacity to "encourage reflexive and deliberative modes of preference learning and preference revision." By reflective preferences, they mean "preferences that are the outcome of a conscious confrontation of one's own point of view with an opposing point of view, or of the multiplicity of viewpoints that the citizen, upon reflection, is likely to discover within his or her own self." In place of the liberal-individualist or communitarian definitions of solidarity, Offe and Preuss propose that the principle of reciprocity is most consistent with the goal of creating a "multi-perspectival mode of forming, defending, and thereby refining our preferences."[32]

Two examples demonstrate the relevance of these reflections for urban policy in the United States. Consider, first, the policy issues raised by the problems of political fragmentation and local governance in the United States. Anthony Downs has shown how the dominant pattern of metropolitan growth there—unlimited, low-density sprawl—is so riddled with internal contradictions that it creates problems that undermine the initial goals of the vision (the so-called American Dream) and "threaten the long-term viability of American society." This model, which Downs concedes is premised upon an unconstrained individualism, has five key components: single-family home ownership on spacious lots; individual automobile ownership with empty freeways; low-rise workplaces in bucolic settings, each with its own parking lot; small residential communities with their own local governments; and an environment free from the signs of poverty. But the attempt to achieve these goals has led directly to a set of familiar, interrelated urban ills that are inconsistent with the ambitious goals the dominant vision promises: lack of affordable housing, excessive traffic and congested highways, too much absorption of open space, no clear mechanisms to resolve the problems of locally undesirable land uses (LULUs), no way to compel people to pay the costs generated by their behavior (for example, the cost of lowering the supply of affordable housing as a result of exclusionary large lot zoning, or of pollution due to long auto trips), and so on. Downs's conclusion is pointed: "Most Americans do not realize that success in attaining these goals is responsible for other results they abhor."[33]

Thus, it is not simply a question of the redistribution of the costs of urban development or of compromising with other interests that is at stake in the project of democratizing the city. If Downs is right, the only logical conclusion that can be drawn is that "enlightened" preferences alone can resolve these dilemmas, preferences resulting from actors facing the contradictions of their own choices and actions. An acknowledgment and awareness of the spatial manifestations of these contradictions in the context of egalitarian values is what would constitute a critical spatial praxis.

Yet the institutional framework within which most American's spatial preferences are formed and articulated does not encourage hybrid, complex perspectives. Quite the contrary, the well-known ability of groups to incorporate their own cities and surround themselves with walls, preventing their taxes from being redistributed to poorer sections of the metropolitan area, creates a form of identity or agency that is monological, instrumental, and atomistic, rather than dialogical or hybrid. The ability to throw up borders around municipalities does not reflect a natural ecological order—they are anchored in everyday life through juridical and legislative authority, motivated and reinforced through unequally distributed economic resources.[34] Political institutions such as juridical boundaries institutionalize a given sense of self or identity.[35] To draw on a well-known formulation, they organize some identities in, and some out.[36] This should not be mistaken for a criticism of spatial patterns of social differentiation in which individuals or groups congregate together. Urban theory has shown that such lumpiness, when it involves ethnic or other voluntary characteristics, is integral to city life. It is when social differentiation is associated with exclusion of others from political, economic, and social resources that the criterion of hybridity is violated. This is because the homogeneity of spaces, the creation of borders, reinforces an instrumental, atomistic, and monological sense of self, one that is not obligated to others in a *public* sense, a sense of sharing the processes of preference and identity formation. The "possessive individual" possesses both a private sense of self and a face presented to the society at large. It is both private and public, and it is hard to imagine that transforming the public self would not require some kind of change in the private.[37]

Seen in this light, the focus of critical urban praxis should be on the design and implementation of institutions that can foster this sense of inner deliberation. Cities offer important lessons in this venture: their dilemmas—posed by markets, politics, bureaucracies, and the diverse needs of communities—have provided many experiments and have much to teach us about what to avoid and what to emulate in this project.[38]

The second example of contemporary relevance that illustrates the link between public policy and a complex sense of identity and public space concerns the "new urbanism" movement in urban planning and urban design in the United States and its conception of the role and meaning of "community" in contemporary urban planning and architectural practice. The movement's key objective is the promotion of a more organic sense of community through better physical design and land use. Many of these principles have been developed in reaction to the dominant form of urbanism discussed above. For example, in place of low-density and highly segregated residential and work spaces linked by long, expensive highways, the new urbanism seeks compact development containing a greater mix of functions and income groups, making the use of public transportation and walking feasible. The underlying premise of the new urbanism is that unchecked urban development has contributed to the erosion of community in the United States. Conversely, by providing people with a sense of locale and place, social capital or civic capacity can be increased and strengthened.

But consider some of the dilemmas of "community." I have argued that two key factors are important to preserve and promote in cities for influencing and shaping the economic and political institutions that mediate between lifeworld and system: an open sense of identities and spaces to resist the forces of homogeneity and segregation and a civil society or lifeworld robust enough to defend itself against encroachments such as gentrification and real estate speculation by the market and imposed solutions such as urban renewal and authoritarian city planning by state bureaucracies.[39] But are these two objectives always compatible? For Richard Sennett, the popular approach of decentralizing land-use planning decisions, devolving them on smaller local communities and giving them formal, autonomous power, carries with it several dangers that are best avoided. Emphasizing smaller units of governance in the name of "community" control, according to Sennett, has the paradoxical effect of weakening the sense of public space and public life that is necessary for a radical democracy because it reinforces the (false) notion that identities are more authentic if they are face-to-face and parochial. This idea is built on the essentialist idea that the best basis of community is similarity.[40] The false sense of power and identity (in the singular) over larger societal forces adopted by these groups leads to resentment and divides the city, instead of creating a public sphere capable of multiperspectival preferences. Promoting the idea that authentic community and identity can be derived only from intimacy (both physical and emotional) can only backfire; civil, urbane sociability can occur only if people have some barriers between each other. This is a corollary of overdetermination: if hybridity means that my identity as totally separate from others is impossible because it depends in part on what falls outside its boundaries, it also implies that total identification is also impossible. Ignoring this can lead to "uncivilized" destructiveness, fantasies of a purified community, and the inability to listen to outside voices. The "open town" of Celebration, Florida (built by the Disney Corporation), and myriad gated communities are good examples of what to avoid. Mixed-income housing and neighborhoods are better than ones homogenized by class.[41]

A contrasting position has been developed by Richard Dagger, for whom the problem in American cities is not enough civic community and ethical citizenship. Several factors in addition to the urban political economy account for this, including the large size of metropolises, fragmented political authorities, and high mobility rates leading to a loss of local connection and "civic memory." He points to at least four types of measures that could be adopted to address these problems. First, he suggests that experiments with city size can be undertaken, with government policy promoting medium-sized cities with populations from 20,000 to 200,000 that are small enough to be "mapped" by an individual but large enough to allow diversity. Although people cannot be coerced into moving anywhere they don't want to go, government can eliminate housing and highway subsidies that promote suburban sprawl and high mobility, substituting other subsidies such as those for high-speed rail links that allow access but prevent sprawl. Second, civic participation can be encouraged through the support and involvement of decentralized, community-based organizations, the redesign of local governance structures so as to involve many more people in elected offices, and the creation of metropolitan governments to overcome fragmented authority and reduce confusion in the minds of residents who want to be more involved. Third, civic design such as that associated with the new urbanism can promote a greater sense of belonging by designing better public spaces—parks, community centers, recreational facilities, schools, and playgrounds in each neighborhood—where people would feel safe to gather, socialize, and build social networks.

The precise mix, tensions, and shortcomings of these two different approaches cannot be prescribed. They have to be tried, and then assessed pragmatically. Indeed, these ideas may not have immediate practical significance, but by describing the dilemmas and parameters facing urbanists, the considerations they bring to the fore can clarify the terms within which synthetic solutions can be assessed and interpreted. In sum, these two examples help to demonstrate, albeit schematically, the way new ideas of urbanism can be informed by the theoretical perspectives I have offered in this book.

Linking a complex, urban image of the self with the public goal of progressive social policy suggests the limitations of recent attacks on poststructuralist thought for a radical democratic agenda. For these critics, the emphasis on the hybridity, incompletion, or complexity of identities promotes only hopelessness and is useless for the purpose of relieving suffering through public policy.[42] On the contrary, the enclave consciousness of suburbs, gated communities, or racist neighborhoods that either ignore or fear their fellow citizens living outside their borders suggests the importance of stressing the ambiguity and porousness of all boundaries, around either territorial communities or individual selves. Boundaries cannot be eliminated, of course, but we need to transform them from being brittle and defensive, as they increasingly are, to being supple and productive. The idea of hybridity can be a normative guide to how we might go about reforming institutions that shape urban identities and to the kinds of goals we might aim for in doing so. The defense of fragmented local government in the United States as the preferred arena of public choice is problematic precisely here because it eliminates the idea of a public sphere composed of multiple publics that nonetheless share a common fate.[43] Even efficient fiscal arrangements for economic redistribution based on autonomous political-territorial units cannot substitute for deliberation on the fate of our poor cities and neighborhoods. By contrast, the ideas I have highlighted here—the benefits of an urban hybrid sensibility, a focus on the virtues and dangers of markets and bureaucracies, and the vastly more fluid, complex spaces, global, regional, local, that we are creating and that define us in turn—I hope might contribute to a spatially attuned radical democratic agenda.[44]

The city, as I have treated it here, is not so much a territory or a place as it is a promise, a potential, built on an ethics of respect for the hybrid spaces of identities. If city air can still make us free, this is no longer the liberation of a previously concealed individuality, but, paradoxically, it is the freedom to glimpse our own hybridity, our own contingency.

Notes

PREFACE

1. Ira Katznelson, *City Trenches: Urban Politics and the Patterning of Class in the United States* (Chicago: University of Chicago Press, 1982).

2. Ernesto Laclau and Chantal Mouffe, *Hegemony and Socialist Strategy: Towards a Radical Democratic Politics* (London: Verso, 1985).

3. Jürgen Habermas, *The Theory of Communicative Action,* vol. 1, *Reason and the Rationalization of Society,* trans. Thomas McCarthy (Boston: Beacon Press, 1984), and *The Theory of Communicative Action,* vol. 2, *Lifeworld and System: A Critique of Functionalist Reason,* trans. Thomas McCarthy (Boston: Beacon Press, 1987).

4. Robert E. Park, "The City: Suggestions for the Investigation of Human Behavior in the Urban Environment," in Robert E. Park and Ernest W. Burgess, *The City: Suggestions for the Investigation of Human Behavior in the Urban Environment* (1925; Chicago: University of Chicago Press, 1967), 40. See Richard Sennett's discussion of Rousseau's critique of city life in *The Fall of Public Man: On the Social Psychology of Capitalism* (New York: Vintage, 1976), 115–22.

5. Julia Kristeva, *Strangers to Ourselves,* trans. Leon S. Roudiez (New York: Columbia University Press, 1991), 13.

6. Richard Sennett, *The Uses of Disorder: Personal Identity and City Life* (New York: Norton, 1970), 108, 82, 132. Although it was published in 1970, in many ways Sennett's book prefigured the postmodern turn in the study of the city with an incisiveness and relevance not matched by many current discussions.

INTRODUCTION

1. On the racialized dimension of class identity, see David Roediger, *Wages of Whiteness* (New York: Verso, 1991).

2. Stanley Aronowitz, *The Politics of Identity* (New York: Routledge, 1992), 32. Emphasis in the original. My position converges in many (but not all) respects with Edward W. Soja's eloquent arguments for replacing radical political economy with a postmodern cultural politics as the basis of critical urban theory. See "Margin/Alia: Social Justice and the New Cultural Politics," in *The Urbanization of Injustice,* ed. Andy Merrifield and Erik Swyngedouw (New York: New York University Press, 1997).

3. My aim here, it should be emphasized, is not to show, yet again, the inadequacy of class reductionism. More than enough has been written about this issue, although I will discuss it at several points throughout what follows, where doing so appears necessary to the larger argument.

4. "Men make their own history, but they do not make it just as they please; they do not make it under circumstances chosen by themselves, but under circumstances directly encountered, given and transmitted from the past." Karl Marx, *The Eighteenth Brumaire of Louis Bonaparte,* in Karl Marx and Friedrich Engels, *Selected Works in One Volume* (London: Lawrence & Wishart, 1968), 96.

5. See, for example, Manuel Castells, *The Power of Identity* (Malden, Mass.: Blackwell, 1997).

6. See Aristide Zolberg and Long Litt Woon, "Why Islam Is Like Spanish: Cultural Incorporation in Europe and the United States," Negotiating Difference Series, ICMEC Working Papers, International Center for Migration, Ethnicity, and Citizenship at the New School for Social Research, June 1997.

7. These trends are not so new. As early as 1937, Robert Park spoke about hybridity, migration, and the interpenetration of cultures. *Race and Culture* (Glencoe, Ill.: Free Press, 1950), 373.

8. See Anthony Giddens, *Modernity and Self-Identity* (Stanford, Calif.: Stanford University Press, 1991).

9. Craig Calhoun, "Social Theory and the Politics of Identity," in *Social Theory and the Politics of Identity,* ed. Craig Calhoun (Oxford: Blackwell, 1994), 23.

10. Individualism can be seen as an extreme variant of the politics of difference (atomism), but it is also an example of a universalism in which everyone is reduced to an identical basis. On the convergence of individualism and communitarianism, see Iris Marion Young, *Justice and the Politics of Difference* (Princeton, N.J.: Princeton University Press, 1990), chapter 8.

11. As Craig Calhoun has put it, these perspectives reflect the reduction (particularly in the West) of the high levels of "systematicity of identity schemes" characterizing earlier, more communitarian social formations. *Social Theory,* 11.

12. See Madan Sarup, *Identity, Culture, and the Postmodern World* (Athens: University of Georgia Press, 1996).

13. Ivan Illich, *H₂O and the Waters of Forgetfulness: On the Historicity of Stuff* (Dallas: Dallas Institute of Humanities and Culture, 1985), 8.

14. See Mathew Edel, Elliot Sclar, and Daniel Luria, *Shaky Palaces: Homeownership and Social Mobility in Boston's Suburbanization* (New York: Columbia University Press, 1984), chapters 9–11.

15. Castells's recent formulation of the Network Society remains trapped within a physicalist conception of space. In his view, the central conflict in the

network society is between the "space of flows" and the "place of being" or meaning, or as he puts it, between "the Net" (of cybernetic self-regulating systems) and "the Self" (of experience and meaning). Castells defines "flows" as the "purposeful, repetitive, programmable sequences of exchange and interaction between physically disjointed positions held by social actors in the economic, political, and symbolic structures of society." This abstract logic of flows and the Net is counterposed to the "place of meaning," which is defined as "a locale whose form, function, and meaning are self-contained within the boundaries of physical contiguity." *The Rise of the Network Society* (Cambridge, Mass.: Blackwell, 1996), 412, 423. What this fails to capture is the manner in which the spaces of resistance and meaning today, for example, in diasporic communities, span many spaces that are not contiguous. Castells discusses the Parisian neighborhood of Belleville as a bounded space of meaning. But many analysts have shown the manner in which North African Muslim migrant workers give meaning to their "locale" through complex layers of association with local institutions and networks, as well as through continuing ties to their countries of origins. See the essays in Barbara Metcalf, ed., *Making Muslim Space in Europe and North America* (Berkeley: University of California Press, 1996).

16. Michael Kearney, "The Effects of Transnational Culture, Economy, and Migration on Mixtec Identity in Oaxacalifornia," in Michael Peter Smith, *The Bubbling Cauldron: Race, Ethnicity, and the Urban Crisis,* ed. Michael P. Smith and Joe R. Feagin (Minneapolis: University of Minnesota Press, 1995), 229.

17. Elijah Anderson, *Streetwise* (Chicago: University of Chicago Press, 1990), for example, chapter 6.

18. Claude S. Fischer, *To Dwell among Friends: Personal Networks in Town and City* (Chicago: University of Chicago Press, 1982); Barry Wellman, "The Community Question," *American Journal of Sociology* 84 (March 1979).

19. Jacques Derrida, *Positions,* trans. Alan Bass (Chicago: University of Chicago Press, 1981), 81.

20. Charles Tilly, *Big Structures, Large Processes, Huge Comparisons* (New York: The Russell Sage Foundation, 1984), and *The Contentious French* (Cambridge, Mass.: Belknap Press, 1986), 272.

21. See Edward W. Soja, "Los Angeles, 1965–1992," in Allen J. Scott and Edward W. Soja, *The City: Los Angeles and Urban Theory at the End of the Twentieth Century* (Berkeley: University of California Press, 1996); and Manuel Castells, *The Informational City* (New York: Blackwell, 1989).

22. Sharon Zukin, *The Culture of Cities* (Cambridge, Mass.: Blackwell, 1995), chapter 1.

23. Saskia Sassen, *The Global City* (Princeton, N.J.: Princeton University Press, 1991); Susan Fainstein, *The City Builders* (Cambridge, Mass.: Blackwell, 1995).

24. John R. Logan and Harvey Molotch, *Urban Fortunes: The Political Economy of Place* (Berkeley: University of California Press, 1987).

25. Castells, *The Network Society,* 467.

26. See Charles Tilly, *Coercion, Capital, and European States, A.D. 990–1990* (Cambridge, Mass.: Blackwell, 1990); and Ira Katznelson, *Marxism and the City* (Oxford: Clarendon Press, Oxford University Press, 1992), especially chapter 5.

27. The project is "critical" in the sense that it is sensitive to the forces block-ing greater democratic transformations, "urban" because of the centrality of spa-tiality to its analysis of social forms (not merely because it takes its object as the "city"), and "theory" in that it retains the (modernist?) hope of synthetic, pos-itive knowledge. Although recent developments in philosophy and social theory have posed serious challenges to the program of theoretical narratives, there are still important grounds for maintaining such a research program, particularly if it can integrate within it the postmodern suspicion of the real and a nonreduc-tive approach to representation.

28. Mike Savage and Allen Warde, *Urban Sociology, Capitalism, and Moder-nity* (New York: Continuum, 1993), 31.

29. See Susan Fainstein and Clifford Hirst, "Urban Social Movements," in *Theories of Urban Politics,* ed. David Judge, Gerry Stoker, and Harold Wollman (London: Sage, 1995).

30. Claus Offe, "New Social Movements: Expanding the Boundaries of Insti-tutional Politics," *Social Research* 52, no. 4 (winter 1985).

31. Manuel Castells has described these tensions in *The City and the Grass-roots* (Berkeley: University of California Press, 1983), part 2.

32. Alain Touraine, *The May Movement, Revolt and Reform: May 1968—The Student Rebellion and Workers' Strikes—The Birth of a Social Movement,* trans. Leonard F. X. Mayhew (New York: Random House, 1971), 23 ; Daniel Singer, *Prelude to Revolution: France in May 1968* (New York: Hill and Wang, 1970), x.

33. See Guy Debord, *The Society of the Spectacle* (New York: Zone Books, 1994), and Henri Lefebvre, *Le Droit a la ville* (Paris: Anthropos, 1968).

34. Manuel Castells, *The Urban Question: A Marxist Approach* (Cambridge, Mass.: MIT Press, 1977), 1–2, viii.

35. It is obvious that a formulation such as the separation between work-places and community residential spaces harbors implicit gender assumptions, such that "work" occurs only outside the home. I use the formulation not because I neglect this gender dimension of space and class but because it is the point of departure for my critique of the androcentric assumptions of Marxian urbanism in Chapter 3.

36. Erik Olin Wright et al., *The Debate on Classes* (New York: Verso, 1989), 207.

37. David Harvey, *Consciousness and the Urban Experience: Studies in the History and Theory of Capitalist Urbanization* (Baltimore: Johns Hopkins Uni-versity Press, 1985), 37; Ira Katznelson, *City Trenches: Urban Politics and the Patterning of Class in the United States* (Chicago: University of Chicago Press, 1982), 6, 9; Castells, *The City and the Grassroots,* 68–69.

38. I do not provide more than a schematic overview here. For more com-prehensive assessments related to the many subareas, such as economic geogra-phy, urban culture, and urban politics, see variously, Katznelson, *Marxism and the City,* which remains the most extensive and positive evaluation; Savage and Warde, *Urban Sociology;* Peter Saunders, *Social Theory and the Urban Ques-tion,* 2d ed. (New York: Holmes & Meier, 1986); Chris G. Pickvance, "Marxist Theories of Urban Politics," in *Theories of Urban Politics,* ed. David Judge, Gerry

Stoker, and Harold Wollman (London: Sage, 1995); and Mark Gottdiener, *The Social Production of Urban Space* (Austin: University of Texas Press, 1985).

39. Neil Smith, *The New Urban Frontier: Gentrification and the Revanchist City* (London: Routledge, 1996).

40. See Merrifield and Swyngedouw, eds., *The Urbanization of Injustice.*

41. Mike Savage, Review of *Marxism and The City,* by Ira Katznelson, *International Journal of Urban and Regional Research* 17, no. 1 (1993): 139.

42. Nigel Thrift, "An Urban Impasse?" *Theory, Culture, and Society* 10 (1993): 229–38. This review essay itself harbors some curious ambiguities. While taking Zukin and others to task for remaining too faithful to the framework of political economy, he seems to imply that the "impasse" refers not to these approaches but to the new work that is seeking to break away from it. He then ends up confusingly suggesting that it is the work of these very political economists (Sassen, Zukin) that can help us out of the impasse!

43. Although see the debate within economic geography in Richard Walker, "Regulation and Flexible Specialization as Theories of Capitalist Development: Challenges to Marx and Schumpeter?" in *Spatial Practices,* ed. Helen Ligget and David Perry (Thousand Oaks, Calif.: Sage, 1995).

44. Katznelson, *Marxism and the City,* chapter 4.

45. Anthony D. King, for example, argues for this emphasis on culture as representing a paradigm shift from the political economy orientation of the earlier period. "Introduction: Cities, Texts, and Paradigms," in *Re-Presenting the City: Ethnicity, Capital and Culture in the Twenty-first-Century Metropolis,* ed. Anthony D. King (New York: New York University Press, 1996), 2. See also the essays in this collection, which are presented as examples of this new paradigm.

46. See Helen Liggett, "City Sights/Sites of Memories and Dreams," in *Spatial Practices,* an intriguing attempt to bring Barthes and Lefebvre together for urban analysis.

47. For example, Dennis Cosgrove and Mona Domosh, "Author and Authority: Writing the New Cultural Geography," in *Place/Culture/Representation,* ed. James Duncan and David Ley (London: Routledge, 1993). Many of the other papers in this collection of the new cultural geography, especially the essays by Derek Gregory and John Agnew, deal with related themes.

48. Edward W. Soja, *Thirdspace: Journeys to Los Angeles and Other Real and Imagined Places* (Cambridge, Mass.: Blackwell, 1996).

49. Christine Boyer, *Dreaming the Rational City: The Myth of American City Planning* (Cambridge, Mass.: MIT Press, 1983), for example, xi.

50. Zukin, *The Culture of Cities,* 1–15.

51. Manuel Castells, *The End of the Millennium* (Malden, Mass.: Blackwell, 1998), 168.

52. David Harvey, *Justice, Nature, and the Geography of Difference* (Cambridge, Mass.: Blackwell, 1996); Fredric Jameson, "The Cultural Logic of Late Capitalism," in *Postmodernism, or The Cultural Logic of Late Capitalism* (Durham, N.C.: Duke University Press, 1991).

53. Mike Davis, *City of Quartz: Excavating the Future in Los Angeles* (New York: Vintage, 1992).

54. Stephen Elkin, *City and Regime in the American Republic* (Chicago: University of Chicago Press, 1987); Ira Katznelson, "Social Justice, Liberalism, and the City," in *The Urbanization of Injustice,* ed. Andy Merrifield and Erik Swyngedouw (New York: New York University Press), 1997.

55. Derek Gregory, "Interventions in the Historical Geography of Modernity: Social Theory, Spatiality, and the Politics of Representation," in *Place/Culture/Representation,* ed. James Duncan and David Ley (London: Routledge, 1992).

56. Nancy Duncan, ed., *BodySpace: Destabilizing Geographies of Gender and Sexuality* (London: Routledge, 1996); Doreen Massey, *Space, Place, and Gender* (Minneapolis: University of Minnesota Press, 1994).

57. This problematic of the postmodern fascination with surfaces is a theme found throughout Slavoj Žižek's writings. For a clear early discussion, see Žižek's "Beyond Discourse Analysis," in Ernesto Laclau, *New Reflections on the Revolution of Our Time,* trans. Jon Barnes (London: Verso, 1990).

58. Jacques Derrida, *Writing and Difference,* trans. Alan Bass (Chicago: University of Chicago Press, 1978), 237.

59. Savage and Warde, *Urban Sociology,* 133.

60. Kaja Silverman, *Threshold of the Visible World* (New York: Routledge, 1996), 1–2.

61. Michael Peter Smith, "Postmodernism, Urban Ethnography, and the New Social Space of Ethnic Identity," *Theory and Society* 21 (1992): 493–531.

62. See Judith Butler's interesting analysis of the "production of the visible" in the Rodney King affair, "Endangered/Endangering: Schematic Racism and White Paranoia," in *Reading Rodney King, Reading Urban Uprising,* ed. Robert Gooding-Williams (New York: Routledge, 1993).

63. Michael Peter Smith, "Postmodernism," 509.

64. Lawrence Grossberg has made the most explicit argument against perspectives that seek to deconstruct binary oppositions, for they remain trapped, he claims, within the modernist framework that from the beginning constituted itself in terms of its difference with its other, namely, tradition and the ancients. "Identity and Cultural Studies—Is That All There Is?" in *Questions of Cultural Identity,* ed. Stuart Hall and Paul du Gay (London: Sage, 1996).

65. See, for example, Gayatri C. Spivak, *The Post-Colonial City: Interviews, Strategies, Dialogues,* ed. Sarah Harasym (New York: Routledge, 1990), 51.

66. Jacques Derrida, "Différance," in *Margins of Philosophy,* trans. Alan Bass (Chicago: University of Chicago Press, 1982).

67. Patricia Clough, "Poststructuralism and Postmodernism: The Desire for Criticism," *Theory and Society* 21 (1992): 543–52.

68. See Renato Rosaldo's analysis of "borderland" individuals, communities, and institutions, in chapter 9 of *Culture and Truth,* 2d ed. (Boston: Beacon Press, 1993).

69. Smith appears to conflate concepts such as "global," "macro," "structure," and so on, with each other. See Janet Wolff, "The Real City, the Discursive City, the Disappearing City: Postmodernism and Urban Sociology," *Theory and Society* 21 (1992): 553–60.

70. Louis Althusser, *Reading Capital,* trans. Ben Brewster (New York: Verso, 1979), 188.

71. Lest the mention of Althusser in a not wholly unsympathetic tone set off alarm bells in some readers, it should be emphasized that in my view, the theoretical contribution of the notion of "contradiction and overdetermination" can be, and should be, separated from the political positions he embraced, as well as the "philosophy" of Marxism as the science of science that he used to rationalize these positions.

72. Michael Peter Smith, "Postmodernism," 504.

73. Jürgen Habermas, *The Theory of Communicative Action,* vol. 2, trans. Thomas McCarthy (Boston: Beacon Press, 1987), 149.

74. See Michael Peter Smith and Joe R. Feagin's introduction to *The Bubbling Cauldron,* 5.

75. I have taken the concept of the "imaginal" geography from the much-neglected work of Henri Corbin, *Spiritual Body and Celestial Earth: From Mazdean Iran to Shi'ite Iran,* 2d ed., trans. Nancy Pearson (Princeton, N.J.: Princeton University Press, 1977), and the notion of "stuff" from Ivan Illich's discussion of Bachelard's *The Poetics of Space* in his poetic *H_2O and the Waters of Forgetfulness.*

76. Striking in this regard is Castells's intellectual trajectory. Having "abandoned" Marxism in *City and the Grassroots,* his subsequent work comes close to embracing a technological determinism straight out of volume 3 of *Capital.* More on this in the next chapter.

77. For one exception (although only partly influenced by poststructuralist ideas), see Michael Piore, *Beyond Individualism* (Cambridge, Mass.: Harvard University Press, 1995).

78. For example, Uwe Becker argues that Laclau's and Mouffe's reformulation replaces essentialism with subjectivism: "Class Theory: Still the Axis of Critical Social Scientific Analysis?" in Erik Olin Wright et al., *The Debate on Classes,* 134. And see Katznelson, *Marxism and the City,* 89, where he claims that they reject structure in favor of agency. As will become clear, I do not think these criticisms are valid, even though Laclau's and Mouffe's presentation can lend itself to misinterpretation.

79. Dominick LaCapra, *Rethinking Intellectual History: Texts, Contexts, Language* (Ithaca, N.Y.: Cornell University Press, 1983), 20–21.

80. I have adopted this approach as a structural device to avoid repetition as much as possible. This is not to suggest, for example, that only Castells's work can be charged with essentialism or Harvey's with functionalism. Indeed, the work of each also can be interpreted in terms of the critiques of the others.

81. This procedure is coincident with what in Althusserian terms would be the "production of the concept" of Marxian urbanism. It is consistent, as I understand it, with Savage and Warde's plea for analytical approaches that break with narrativization.

82. The chapters do not claim to be a comprehensive analysis of each author's writings. Their work is treated only in reference to the specific problem at hand.

CHAPTER 1

1. It goes without saying that the city encompasses within it much more than a certain type of identity relation. What I am saying is that what is specifically urban about the city is the possibility of the space of hybridity. I suggest we resist

categorizing this as a *cultural* definition of cities or urbanity. The space of hybridity is something that is instead constitutive of the economic, political, and cultural realms. The precise forms of these effects have yet to be explored, something I touch on briefly in the final chapter.

2. As I noted above, I distinguish this view from the now popular idea that subjects merely possess multiple roles or identities. The criterion for this approach being the "best" is not derived from a metaphysical claim as to the "true" nature of the person, which would contradict the critique of essentialism I undertake in the chapter. Rather, it comes from the idea that the concept of hybridity is best suited to capture the democratic possibilities of our rapidly changing cities.

3. Metaphysical individualism holds, first, that individual agents are the primary components of social life and that their agency cannot be attributed to supra-individual entities or forces such as social structures or historical tendencies. Sociological holism, by contrast, holds that individuals derive their identities and motives for action from being normatively integrated into the social structure of which they are a part. On these doctrines, see Chandran Kakuthas and Philip Petit, *Rawls: A Theory of Justice and Its Critics* (Stanford, Calif.: Stanford University Press, 1990); Andrew Levine, Elliott Sober, and Erik Olin Wright, "Marxism and Methodological Individualism," *New Left Review* 162 (1987).

4. See Teresa de Laurentis, "Upping the Anti in Feminist Theory," in *Cultural Studies Reader,* ed. Simon During (London: Routledge, 1993), 75. See Diana Fuss, *Essentially Speaking: Feminism, Nature, and Difference* (New York: Routledge, 1989), and Terry Eagleton, *The Illusions of Postmodernism* (Oxford: Blackwell, 1996), 97.

5. Manuel Castells, *The Rise of the Network Society* (Cambridge, Mass.: Blackwell, 1996), and *The Power of Identity* (Oxford: Blackwell, 1997), 64.

6. Castells, *Power of Identity,* 1–4.

7. Manuel Castells, *The Urban Question: A Marxist Approach* (Cambridge, Mass.: MIT Press, 1977).

8. See, for example, Ira Katznelson, *Marxism and the City* (Oxford: Clarendon Press; Oxford University Press, 1992), and Peter Saunders, *Social Theory and the Urban Question,* 2d ed. (New York: Holmes & Meier, 1986).

9. Louis Althusser, "Contradiction and Overdetermination," in *For Marx* (London: New Left Books, 1977), 113.

10. For the most extensive review and discussion of the literature, see *Marxism and the City*, chapters 4 and 5; and Leo Schnore, "The City as a Social Organism," *Urban Affairs Quarterly* 1 (1966). It is possible that new informational technologies will blur the boundaries of work and home in significant ways in the future.

11. Erik Olin Wright, "Exploitation, Identity, and Class Structure," in *The Debate on Classes,* ed. Erik Olin Wright et al. (New York: Verso, 1989), 207.

12. "When it came to the quality of everyday experience . . . the most important single change in French life over four centuries was probably the proletarianization of work—the declining control of households over their own means of production and the increasing dependence of those households on the sale of their labor power. Proletarianization was part and parcel of the development of

capitalism." Charles Tilly, The *Contentious French* (Cambridge, Mass.: Belknap Press, 1986), 5.

13. Castells, *The Urban Question*, 2. This difficulty would hold equally for any of the so-called new social movements.

14. Ibid., 445.

15. Manuel Castells, "Theoretical Propositions for the Experimental Study of Urban Social Movements," in *Urban Sociology: Critical Essays*, ed. Chris G. Pickvance (New York: St. Martin's, 1976), 148, emphasis in the original.

16. Castells, *The Urban Question*, 445.

17. Ibid., 129.

18. Ibid., 130.

19. Ibid., 243, 95; Castells, "Theoretical Propositions," 163.

20. Castells, *The Urban Question*, 92, 93.

21. Manuel Castells, "Is There an Urban Sociology?" in *Urban Sociology: Critical Essays*, ed. Chris G. Pickvance (New York: St. Martin's, 1976), 42.

22. The necessity of breaking with experience to produce "knowledge" is the subject of the remarkable chapter "Marxism Is Not a Historicism" in Louis Althusser, *Reading Capital*, trans. Ben Brewster (New York: Verso, 1979).

23. Castells, *The Urban Question*, 220.

24. Ibid., 110, 111.

25. Ibid., 180–81.

26. See Ernesto Laclau and Chantal Mouffe, *Hegemony and Socialist Strategy: Towards a Radical Democratic Politics* (London: Verso, 1985), 104. "Suture" is the Lacanian concept for the relationship between a subject and its identification with a lack in the structure, although here it is employed to describe the moment of closure, as in "stitched up good and proper." I take this up further in Chapter 3. See Kaja Silverman, *The Subject of Semiotics* (New York: Oxford University Press, 1983).

27. Castells, *The Urban Question*, 268. "Meaning must await being said or written in order to inhabit itself, and in order to become, by differing from itself, what it is: meaning." Jacques Derrida, *Writing and Difference*, trans. Alan Bass (Chicago: University of Chicago Press, 1978), 11.

28. Of course, there are many other dimensions and purposes of Castells's work than that examined here. For example, they develop a fruitful political sociology of consumption and state provision that opened the way for many concrete research programs.

29. Manuel Castells, *City, Class, and Power*, trans. supervised by Elizabeth Lebas (New York: St. Martin's, 1978), 16.

30. For a now-classic statement of the bureaucratic inequalities in urban housing provision, see Ivan Szelenyi, *Urban Inequalities under Socialism* (New York: Oxford University Press, 1983).

31. Castells, *City, Class, and Power*, 23, 19. Castells confusingly lumps under the "political" both the public sphere of moral discourse, e.g., institutionalized in parliaments, associations, etc., and the administrative system.

32. Ibid., 34–35, 36.

33. Ibid., 41, 35.

34. It may not even have been true at that time, although space prohibits a full exposition of the reasons why.

35. Castells, *The Urban Question*, 2.

36. Recall, by way of contrast, the position of *The Urban Question*: "Constructing new social relations [can be achieved only] through the revolutionary . . . class struggle . . . and . . . the dictatorship of the proletariat." Further examples: A theory of urban social movements "requires a point of departure bound up with the working-class movement and its practice." Urban issues, which are "secondary structural issues . . . not directly challenging the production methods of a society . . . become social movements insofar as they become one component of . . . the workers' movement [and linking] with political conflicts still dominated essentially by the current forms of the capital-labor confrontation." Ibid., 89, 6, 376–77.

37. Castells, *City, Class, and Power*, 36, 61, 144.

38. A possible objection should be addressed at this point: that what was being criticized was not the concept of relative autonomy but its incompatibility with the concept of an ultimate determination by the economy. Without such an essentialist assumption of a center in a structured totality, a relationship between two elements that cannot be subsumed within a higher unity, as in the Hegelian notion of the dialectic, requires a new, nondialectical concept of relation. This concept is the constitutive outside, derived from Derrida's and Laclau's work.

39. Castells, *City, Class, and Power*, 147–48.

40. Ibid.

41. Castells's work up till 1983 can indeed be considered a unity, rounding out his preoccupation with developing a theory of urban social movements and its relationship to urban political economy and Marxian theory. Castells, personal communication. Nonetheless, the similarities between the analyses of social movements in *The City and the Grassroots* of 1983 and *The Power of Identity*, published in 1997, suggest that it would not be inappropriate to view these two works as constituting the third phase of his work on social movements. See *The Power of Identity*, 60–64.

42. For these criticisms, see Savage and Warde, *Urban Sociology*, 156–58.

43. "If there is an underlying theme . . . of this book, it is precisely our conviction that class analysis is an insufficient approach to the understanding of urban change throughout history." And: "Class relationships and class struggle . . . are not by any means the only primary source of urban social change. The autonomous role of the state, the gender relationships, the ethnic and national movements, and movements that define themselves as citizen, are among the alternative sources of urban change." *The City and the Grassroots*, 4, 291.

44. Castells, *The City and the Grassroots*, 68.

45. It is important to note that the issue of the relation between class dimensions and urban dimensions is only one aspect of the larger question of the relationality of all identities within the urban field, be they class, territorial, ethnic, religious, or political. This larger question is the unresolved focus of *The Urban Question* and *City, Class, and Power*, namely, the problem of how to conceptualize the overdetermination of identities.

46. Castells, *The City and the Grassroots*, 111.

47. Ibid., 116.

48. Although interesting and provocative, the full details and ramifications of the model are not relevant to my argument. However, I will return to the theoretical assumptions underlying this model to help pursue our analysis of the problems of essentialism below.

49. It is worth noting that Castells's explanation should be understood in the context of several other notable attempts to account for the limited nature of U.S. urban politics. In addition to Katznelson's *City Trenches: Urban Politics and the Patterning of Class in the United States* (Chicago: University of Chicago Press, 1982), which I discuss in detail in Chapter 3, see, for example, Paul Peterson, *City Limits* (Chicago: University of Chicago Press, 1981), and Roger Friedland, Frances Fox Piven, and Robert R. Alford, "Political Conflict, Urban Structure, and the Fiscal Crisis," in *Marxism and the Metropolis: New Perspectives in Urban Political Economy,* 2d ed., ed. William K. Tabb and Larry Sawers (New York: Oxford University Press, 1984).

50. Also see in this regard Sallie Marston and George Towers, "Private Spaces and the Politics of Places: Spatioeconomic Restructuring and Community Organizing in Tucson and El Paso," in *Mobilizing the Community: Local Politics in the Era of the Global City,* ed. Robert Fisher and Joseph Kling (Newbury Park, Calif.: Sage, 1993).

51. Castells, *The City and the Grassroots,* 171.

52. Katznelson, *Marxism and the City,* 134–39.

53. It should be pointed out that I am not here concerned with criticizing Castells's interpretation of the failure of the Mission Coalition Organization to transform the disparate elements into a new "totality" (granting for the moment that was their intention), although there are several other equally if not more compelling accounts of the limits or trenches of U.S. cities. I am concerned with analyzing the underlying assumptions concerning the logic of the articulation of distinct identities that is revealed by this case and with what it can teach us about how to think about a nonessentialist form of identity.

54. See Chapter 2 for more about this in terms of the distinction between system and lifeworld. The figure is taken from Castells, *The City and the Grassroots,* 125.

55. Ibid., 349.

56. Recall the phrase in *The Urban Question:* "meaning has meaning only outside of itself," 286.

57. "If any one of the dimensions expands separately [there results] a social movement that integrates in its basic definition the other dimensions under a subordinate form: an urban social movement (based upon CY), or a class struggle (based on CL), or an ethnic social movement (based on R)." Castells, *The City and the Grassroots,* 349. In the absence of any additional hypotheses or assumptions securing the necessity of the "expansion" of any one dimension over the others, the model represents a clear move away from a monistic, teleological structure.

58. Ibid.

59. "Urban struggles [involve] issues *over and above* those of production process." Castells, *The City and the Grassroots,* 68. Moreover, by separating the urban (i.e., consumption) from class in this way, and projecting this understanding back into history, Castells loses sensitivity to how before (or during)

the separation the defense of one's home and community *was* the defense of economic interests. Before housing and land were reduced to consumption items,
there was an amalgamation between the two, and artisans defended the one to
defend the other. See Eli Zaretsky, *Capitalism, the Family, and Personal Life*
(New York: Harper & Row, 1973).

60. Castells, *The City and the Grassroots*, 68–69.

61. We can observe this logic operating in the analysis. For example, the reasons why the community organizers "were unable to raise the level of self-definition
and organization to a point that would have created *unity*" concerned the obstacles
"against raising the practice of an urban movement above [each] one of [its] dimensions," namely, of neighborhood, poverty, culture. Castells, *The City and the Grassroots*, 129. Each factor was intimately connected with elements and factors that
went beyond the bounds of the local Mission case. Despite being "present," they
were not "fully present," since part of what went into defining their characteristics
exceeded any conceivable unity that may have been achieved locally.

62. This phrase is taken from Laclau and Mouffe, *Hegemony*, 120.

63. Serge Moscovici and Willem Doise, *Conflict and Consensus: A General
Theory of Collective Decisions*, trans. W. D. Halls (London: Sage, 1994), 8.

64. Laclau and Mouffe, *Hegemony*, 104.

CHAPTER 2

1. See David Harvey, *The Urban Experience* (Baltimore: Johns Hopkins University Press, 1989), xii.

2. Manuel Castells, *The Urban Question: A Marxist Approach* (Cambridge,
Mass.: MIT Press, 1977). The afterward to the 1975 English edition, however,
does attempt to justify the emphasis on collective consumption by way of Marx's
writings, particularly in the *Grundrisse*.

3. David Harvey, *Consciousness and the Urban Experience: Studies in the
History and Theory of Capitalist Urbanization* (Baltimore: Johns Hopkins University Press, 1985), 37.

4. See Doreen Massey, "Flexible Sexism," and Rosalyn Deutsche, "Boy's
Town," both in *Environment and Planning: D, Society and Space* 9 (1991):
31–57 and 5–30, respectively.

5. See "Paris, 1850–1870," in *Consciousness and the Urban Experience*. The
following section is drawn from Ira Katznelson's lucid discussion of Harvey in
Marxism and the City (Oxford: Clarendon Press; Oxford University Press,
1991),119–34.

6. Charles Tilly, *Coercion, Capital, and European States*, A.D. 990–1990
(Cambridge, Mass.: Blackwell, 1990), 30; Theda Skocpol, *States and Serial Rev-
olutions* (Cambridge: Cambridge University Press, 1979), 24–25; Katznelson,
Marxism and the City, 119–34.

7. See Ira Katznelson, "Social Justice, Liberalism, and the City: Considerations on David Harvey, John Rawls, and Karl Polanyi," in *The Urbanization of
Justice*, ed. Andy Merrifield and Erik Swyngedouw (New York: New York Uni-

versity Press, 1997), and Richard Dagger, *Civic Virtues: Rights, Citizenship, and Republican Liberalism* (New York: Oxford University Press, 1997), chapter 10.

8. Roger V. Gould, *Insurgent Identities* (Chicago: University of Chicago Press, 1995), 4. Although Gould's methodology and conclusion are not fully convincing, they raise several unresolved questions. For example, he uses marriage records to show that the degree of interclass social contact was still substantial just before the commune uprising and that workers "were not sealing themselves off from the bourgeoisie" (86). Gould thus rejects Harvey's argument that new (working-)class-homogeneous communities had emerged after the urban reforms and that they formed the significant core of the commune. To the extent that new neighborhood enclaves did emerge, they were defined more by a sense of place and neighborhood than by occupation. In another instance, Gould points to the differences between the clienteles of wine shops and nightclubs in the center of the city and in the outskirts. Whereas the former, often located in craft-specific districts, drew occupation-specific crowds, the neighborhood bars drew from all local residents, suggesting that the former should be viewed as class institutions, whereas the latter cannot. Although there is not space for a full assessment of Gould's work, we might ask why the presence of middle-class witnesses to marriages between working-class couples is an adequate indicator of the increased class homogeneity of the new neighborhoods. For example, is it reasonable to assume that cross-class friendships would have disappeared within one or two decades (by 1869, the date of Gould's marriage data), even if individuals were forced to move due to Haussmann's reforms? Furthermore, Gould's interpretation rests on the contrast between the class nature of the 1848 uprising and the urban character of the 1871 event. But this is potentially misleading, since it appears to underestimate the extent to which working-class collective action was a growing feature of the French urban scene throughout the latter part of the nineteenth century and well into the twentieth. See, for example, Charles Tilly, *The Contentious French* (Cambridge, Mass.: Belknap Press, 1986).

9. See the discussion of these writers and a discussion of the literature on European state building in relation to capitalism and a defense of the Marxian position in Alex Callinicos, *Making History: Agency, Structure, and Change in Social Theory* (Ithaca, N.Y.: Cornell University Press, 1988). See also Maurice Godelier, *The Mental and the Material,* trans. Martin Thom (London: Verso, 1985).

10. All pages cited refer to the reprinted versions in David Harvey, *The Urbanization of Capital* (Baltimore: Johns Hopkins University Press, 1985) and *Consciousness and the Urban Experience.*

11. "The question I began with over a decade ago now, was roughly this: can we *derive* a theoretical and historical understanding of the urban process under capitalism *out of a study of the supposed laws of motion* of a capitalist mode of production? I quickly became convinced that the answer was yes." Harvey, *The Urbanization of Capital,* 185.

12. Ibid., 2.

13. Ibid., 1–2.

14. Harvey, *Consciousness and the Urban Experience,* 37, 50; *The Urbanization of Capital,* 15.

15. Harvey, *Consciousness and the Urban Experience,* 37, 48–49, emphasis in the original; *The Urbanization of Capital,* 30.

16. Harvey, *Consciousness and the Urban Experience,* 57, 48, and especially *The Condition of Postmodernity: An Enquiry into the Origins of Cultural Change* (Oxford: Blackwell, 1989), 108; *The Urbanization of Capital,* 27, 156.

17. Raymond Williams, *The Year 2000* (New York: Pantheon, 1983), 132–33, quoted in Sydney Plotkin, "Enclave Consciousness and Neighborhood Activism," in *Dilemmas of Activism: Class, Community, and the Politics of Local Mobilization,* ed. Joseph M. Kling and Prudence S. Posner (Philadelphia: Temple University Press, 1990), 236.

18. See Max Weber, "Basic Sociological Terms," in *Understanding and Social Inquiry,* ed. Fred Dallmayr and Thomas McCarthy (Notre Dame, Ind.: University of Notre Dame Press, 1977).

19. Harvey writes, "The problems of proportionality involved in the aggregative production of means of production and means of consumption are examined. . . . The objective here is to show the potential for crises of disproportionality within the production process." *The Urbanization of Capital,* 4.

20. Jürgen Habermas, *The Theory of Communicative Action,* vol. 2, *Lifeworld and System: A Critique of Functionalist Reason,* trans. Thomas McCarthy (Boston: Beacon Press, 1987), 117.

21. The most detailed analysis of Marx's own work from this perspective is Jean Cohen, *Class and Civil Society: The Limits of Marxian Critical Theory* (Amherst: University of Massachusetts Press, 1982). See also Jürgen Habermas, *Legitimation Crisis,* trans. Thomas McCarthy (Boston: Beacon Press, 1976).

22. "In the middle of the nineteenth century the theoretical connotation of the concept of proletariat, defined in terms of separation of means of production, corresponded closely to the intuitive concept of proletariat conceived in terms of manual, principally industrial laborers. . . . One simply knew who were the proletarians." Adam Przeworski, *Capitalism and Social Democracy* (Cambridge: Cambridge University Press, 1985), 57, 56.

23. Harvey, *Consciousness and the Urban Experience,* 38.

24. For an answer via the critique of essentialism carried out in language philosophy, see Jacques Derrida, "Ltd Inc abc . . . ," in *Limited Inc.,* ed. Gerald Graff, trans. Samuel Weber and Jeffrey Mehlman (Evanston, Ill.: Northwestern University Press, 1988), 93.

25. The consistency with which Harvey uses labor and capital as actors that make decisions, experience violence, organize collectively, and so on, recalls Marx's own critique of the use of hypostatized economic categories in "an enchanted, perverted, topsy-turvy world in which Monsieur Le Capital and Madame La Terre, who are social characters as well as mere things, do their danse macabre." *Capital,* vol. 3 (London: International, 1974), 108.

26. Harvey, *Consciousness and the Urban Experience,* 62.

27. Ira Katznelson, *City Trenches: Urban Politics and the Patterning of Class in the United States* (Chicago: University of Chicago Press, 1982), 19.

28. On the former, see Jürgen Habermas, *On the Logic of the Social Sciences,* trans. Shierry W. Nicholsen and Jerry A. Stark (Cambridge, Mass.: MIT Press, 1988), and Karl-Otto Apel, *Understanding and Explanation* (Cambridge, Mass.:

MIT Press, 1984), 71–76. On the latter, see Jean Baudrillard, *The Mirror of Production* (St. Louis: Telos Press, 1975); Cohen, *Class and Civil Society,* chapter 6; and Habermas, *The Theory of Communicative Action,* vol. 2, 334–43.

29. See Chris G. Pickvance, "The Structuralist Critique in Urban Studies," in *Cities in Transformation,* ed. Michael Peter Smith (Beverly Hills, Calif.: Sage, 1984).

30. Harvey, *Consciousness and the Urban Experience,* 263.

31. Ibid.

32. Ibid., 263–64.

33. Ibid.

34. Harvey, *The Urbanization of Capital,* 185, x.

35. Ibid., xi.

36. Ibid., 1.

37. Ibid., 262.

38. Of course, property speculators use real estate for its market value, but "this is a very different use from that described under 'use-value' and it implies that money is to be made through market operations with respect to housing." David Harvey, "The Nature of Housing," in *The Manipulated City,* ed. Stephen Gale and Eric Meure (Chicago: Maaroufa Press, 1975), 133. Is not this categorization of what really is and is not use value arbitrary, determined more by a kind of moral purity reserved for processes not tainted by the market and the stamp of money? In my view, there is just such a moral condemnation of money throughout Harvey's writings—although never quite as explicitly or as colorfully as can be found in the writings of Marx himself: "Money is the *pimp* between need and object, between life and man's means of life. . . . It is the universal whore, the universal pimp of men and peoples." "Economic and Philosophical Manuscripts," in *Early Writings,* trans. Rodney Livingstone and Gregor Benton (London: Penguin Books, in association with *New Left Review;* first Vintage Books edition, 1975), 375, 377, emphasis in the original.

39. Harvey, "The Nature of Housing," 133.

40. See Karl Polanyi, Conrad Arensberg, and Harry Pearson, eds., *Trade and Market in the Early Empires* (Glencoe, Ill.: Free Press, 1957), 250–56. As in the case of Marx, I am not concerned with the accuracy of Harvey's appropriation of Polanyi. Suffice it to say there are several grounds for criticism on this score. Polanyi's discussion of the three modes of integration—for better or worse—is restricted to the economy in the first place. Thus, he does not use the expression "mode of economic integration" at all, using only "forms of integration" of the economy, whereas Harvey applies the three modes to society in general, not just the economy. As we will see, this is not a trivial distinction.

41. Morton Fried, *The Evolution of Political Society* (New York: Random House, 1967).

42. David Harvey, *Social Justice and the City* (Baltimore: Johns Hopkins University Press, 1973), 209.

43. Polanyi writes that "reciprocity assumes for a background symmetrically arranged groupings." See "The Economy as an Instituted Process," in *Trade and Market in the Early Empires.* It is true that the model of a capitalist market of free individuals also could be conceived under the concept of "symmetrically arranged

groupings" and that this can be one institutionalized context for the economic exchange of goods. But this would be to miss the point, not least if we wish to follow Harvey's critique and not simply confirm the capitalist fetish of commodities.

44. Jürgen Habermas, *The Theory of Communicative Action,* vol. 1, *Reason and the Rationalization of Society,* trans. Thomas McCarthy (Boston: Beacon Press, 1984), 390.

45. Ibid., 392.

46. Jacques Derrida, "Remarks on Deconstruction and Pragmatism," in *Deconstruction and Pragmatism,* ed. Chantal Mouffe (London: Routledge, 1996), 83.

47. David Harvey, *Justice, Nature, and the Geography of Difference* (Cambridge, Mass.: Blackwell, 1996).

48. Harvey, *Social Justice,* 209, 281.

49. Karl Marx, *Grundrisse,* trans. Martin Nicolaus (London: Penguin Books, in association with *New Left Review,* 1973), 164; Harvey, *Consciousness and the Urban Experience,* 3.

50. "The inhabitants of a modern metropolis are independent in the positive sense of the word . . . even though . . . their relationship [to each other] is completely objective and is only embodied in money." Georg Simmel, *The Philosophy of Money,* trans. Tom Bottomore and David Frisby (London: Routledge & Kegan Paul, 1978), 300.

51. Ruth Laub Coser, "The Complexity of Roles as a Seedbed of Individual Autonomy," in *The Idea of Social Structure: Papers in Honor of Robert K. Merton,* ed. Lewis A. Coser (New York: Harcourt Brace Jovanovich, 1975).

52. "In that the purely money relationship ties the individual very closely to the group as an abstract whole and in that this is because money . . . is the representative of abstract group forces, the relationship of individual persons to others simply duplicates the relationship that they have to objects as a result of money." Simmel, *The Philosophy of Money,* 301, 303.

53. Harvey, *Consciousness and the Urban Experience,* 4.

54. Harvey, *The Urbanization of Capital,* x.

55. Harvey, *Consciousness and the Urban Experience,* 31–61, 18.

56. Ibid., 53.

57. See Harvey, *Social Justice,* 93.

58. Ibid., 93–94.

59. Jürgen Habermas, *Autonomy and Solidarity: Interviews,* ed. Peter Dews (London: Verso, 1986), 46.

60. "Price-fixing markets require participants who are antagonistic to each other and who operate in the medium of exchange value." Harvey, *Social Justice,* 241.

61. "Reciprocity comes closest to performing its traditional function in the neighborhood and in the local community. . . . [W]orking-class communities typically evolved a neighborly warm-hearted reciprocity that did much to assuage the worst ravages of an insensate wage system. In the early stages of the industrial urbanization reciprocity was typically based on extended kinship relations, ethnic or religious identifications." Ibid., 281.

62. "The criteria of moral worth inherent in the older rank [and egalitarian] societies provide an apparent relief to counter the impersonal and dehumanizing criteria of the market place." Ibid., 279.

63. Claus Offe, "Two Logics of Collective Action," in *Disorganized Capitalism: Contemporary Transformations of Work and Politics* (Cambridge, Mass.: MIT Press, 1985).

64. Strategic action is defined as entailing "at least two goal-directed acting subjects who achieve their ends by way of an orientation to, and influence on, the decision of other actors. Success in action is also dependent upon other actors, each of whom is oriented to his own success and behaves cooperatively only to the degree that this fits with his egocentric calculus of utility. . . . This model is often interpreted in utilitarian terms; the actor is supposed to choose and calculate means and ends from the standpoint of maximizing utility. It is this model of action that lies behind decision-theoretic and game-theoretic approaches in economics, sociology, and social psychology." On the other hand, the concept of normatively regulated action or reciprocity as it is used by Harvey "does not refer to the behavior of basically solitary actors who come upon other actors in their environment, but to members of a social group who orient their action to common values. . . . The concept of *communicative action* refers to the interaction of at least two subjects capable of speech and action who establish interpersonal relations. . . . The actors seek to reach an understanding about the action situation and their plans of action in order to coordinate their actions by way of agreement. The central concept of *interpretation* refers in the first instance to negotiating definitions of the situation which admit of consensus. . . . Language is given a prominent place in this model." Habermas, *Communicative Action* 1, *Reason,* 87–88, 85, 86. For a discussion of the problem of dualism in Habermas's version of the theory of action, see Richard Munch, *Theory of Action: Towards a Synthesis Going Beyond Parsons* (London: Routledge & Kegan Paul, 1987). See also Jürgen Habermas, *The Philosophical Discourse of Modernity: Twelve Lectures,* trans. Frederick Lawrence (Cambridge, Mass.: MIT Press, 1987), 63.

65. Cohen has characterized self-regulation as the idea that "the capitalist mode of production reproduces itself, its social actors, and their necessary motivations out of its own economic logic." *Class and Civil Society,* 192.

66. Harvey, *Social Justice,* 212, emphasis in the original.

67. Ibid., 282.

68. Ibid. In the context of the history of "flesh-and-blood" working-class movements, the suggestion that labor movements do not take on "mixed political coloration" and never respond in policies or programs to changing circumstances surely can find no empirical support.

69. Harvey, *The Urbanization of Capital,* 225; *Consciousness and the Urban Experience,* 2.

70. Harvey, *Social Justice,* 200; Jacques Derrida, *Writing and Difference,* trans. Alan Bass (Chicago: University of Chicago Press, 1978), 162.

71. Habermas, *The Philosophical Discourse of Modernity,* 339, emphasis in the original.

72. Harvey, *The Urbanization of Capital,* 225.

73. Claus Offe, "New Social Movements: Challenging the Boundaries of Institutional Politics," *Social Research* 52, no. 4 (winter 1985): 845–46.

74. See Marshall Berman, *All That Is Solid Melts into Air* (New York: Penguin, 1988), 9–12. There is an ongoing debate over where and how to draw the

line between modernism and postmodernism. Writers such as Walter Benjamin and Marshall Berman have interpreted modernism in art, literature, architecture, and urbanism that stress the fragment and perspectivalism. Fredric Jameson, however, has offered an influential argument as to what sets off these earlier attempts to represent difference from contemporary "postmodern" projects. See Berman, *All That Is Solid*, and, for example, Walter Benjamin, "Notes on Paris," in *Reflections*, ed. Peter Demetz, trans. Edmund Jephcott (New York: Schocken, 1978), and Fredric Jameson, "The Cultural Logic of Late Capitalism," in *Postmodernism, or The Cultural Logic of Late Capitalism* (Durham, N.C.: Duke University Press, 1991).

75. Harvey, *Justice, Nature, and the Geography of Difference*, 311, 322.

76. See Kian Tajbakhsh, "Postmodernism, Postmarxism, and the Question of Class," *Social Scientist* 19, nos. 3–4 (March–April 1991).

77. See Andrew Levine, Elliott Sober, and Erik Olin Wright, "Marxism and Methodological Individualism," *New Left Review* 162 (March–April 1987).

78. Offe gives the following examples: "voluntary membership, a more or less bureaucratic structure of decision making, dependence upon material and motivational resources, efforts to change the respective environments into more favorable ones, and so forth." Claus Offe, *Disorganized Capitalism*, 175.

79. Ibid., 183, 184.

80. Ibid., 204.

81. It depends on a recognition of common interests only in part, however, since we cannot assume that the bonds of solidarity can be traced back to a common reason for joining a group. Many people may join the same collectivity for different reasons.

82. "The problem here is that once the *recognition of common interests on the part of individuals* is thought to play a decisive role in class action then, as Weber correctly maintains, there is no reason why other 'common interests,' nationality, religious belief, 'race,' etc., should not play an equally decisive role in non-class forms of collective action. To conceive of class as a form of communal action, therefore, is to conceive it as one among many of the possible forms of communal action. Class action cannot then be accounted for by reference to class interests since some further explanation is required of why those interests and not others provide the basis for communal action." Anthony Cutler et al., *Marx's Capital and Capitalism Today* (London: Routledge & Kegan Paul, 1977), 188, emphasis in the original.

83. Przeworski, *Capitalism and Social Democracy*, 70, 67.

84. Offe, *Disorganized Capitalism*, 151–52, emphasis in the original.

85. Ibid. It is of course an open question whether all other bases of organization exhibit such a characteristic and whether trade unions will always do so. However, if unions ceased to act on this assumption entirely, we would be faced with a significant transformation of the political nature of industrial society.

86. Ibid., 152, emphasis in the original.

CHAPTER 3

1. E. P. Thompson, *The Making of the English Working Class* (Harmondsworth: Penguin, 1968).

2. Michael Kazin, "Daniel Bell and the Agony and Romance of the American Left," introduction to Daniel Bell, *Marxian Socialism in the United States* (Ithaca, N.Y.: Cornell University Press, 1996), 24.

3. Lawrence Goodwyn, *The Populist Moment* (Oxford: Oxford University Press, 1978); Thomas Bender, *Community and Social Change in America* (Baltimore: Johns Hopkins University Press, 1982); Harry Boyte, *Backyard Revolution* (Philadelphia: Temple University Press, 1980).

4. Robert Dahl, *Who Governs?* (New Haven: Yale University Press, 1961).

5. See John R. Logan and Harvey L. Molotch, *Urban Fortunes: The Political Economy of Place* (Berkeley: University of California Press, 1987); Clarence Stone, "The Study of Politics in Urban Development," in *The Politics of Urban Development,* ed. Clarence Stone and Heywood Sanders (Lawrence: University of Kansas Press, 1987).

6. See Paul Peterson, *City Limits* (Chicago: University of Chicago Press, 1981).

7. David Robertson and Dennis Judd, *The Development of American Public Policy: The Structure of Policy Restraint* (Glenview, Ill.: Scott, Foresman, 1989), 9–14.

8. Roger Friedland, Frances Fox Piven, and Robert R. Alford, "Political Conflict, Urban Structure, and the Fiscal Crisis," in *Marxism and the Metropolis: New Perspectives in Urban Political Economy,* 2d ed., ed. William K. Tabb and Larry Sawers (New York: Oxford University Press, 1984).

9. This is reflected in Hobsbawm's assertion that "we know of societies which have the same material base but widely varying ways of structuring their social relations, ideology, and other superstructural features." Eric. R. Hobsbawm, "Marx and History," *New Left Review* 143 (January–February 1984): 44, cited in Ira Katznelson, *Marxism and the City* (Oxford: Clarendon Press; Oxford University Press, 1992), 83.

10. Katznelson, *Marxism and the City,* 208.

11. Ira Katznelson, "Working-Class Formation: Constructing Cases and Comparisons," in *Working-Class Formation: Nineteenth-Century Patterns in Western Europe and the United States,* ed. Ira Katznelson and Aristide Zolberg (Princeton, N.J.: Princeton University Press, 1986), 21.

12. See the excellent review article by Aristide Zolberg, "How Many Exceptionalisms?" in *Working-Class Formation: Nineteenth-Century Patterns in Western Europe and the United States,* ed. Ira Katznelson and Aristide Zolberg (Princeton, N.J.: Princeton University Press, 1986).

13. Katznelson, "Working-Class Formation: Constructing Cases," 21.

14. Katznelson, *Marxism and the City,* 210.

15. James Vance, "Housing the Worker: The Employment Linkage in Urban Structure," *Economic Geography* 42 (October 1966).

16. This refers to the Marxian class concept. The neighborhoods were class-homogeneous in Weberian class terms. See Katznelson, *Marxism and the City,* chapter 6, and *City Trenches: Urban Politics and the Patterning of Class in the United States* (Chicago: University of Chicago Press, 1982).

17. See Katznelson's discussion of studies of late-nineteenth-century and early-twentieth-century Detroit, *Marxism and the City,* 273–74.

18. Katznelson, *City Trenches,* 19.

19. Ibid., 16.

20. Ibid., 42, 44.

21. Ira Katznelson, "Working-Class Formation and the State: Nineteenth-Century England in American Perspective," in *Bringing the State Back In,* ed. by Peter B. Evans, Dietrich Rueschemeyer, and Theda Skocpol (Cambridge: Cambridge University Press, 1985). See also Stephen Skowronek, *Building a New American State: The Expansion of National Administrative Capacities, 1877–1920* (Cambridge: Cambridge University Press, 1982).

22. Katznelson, *City Trenches,* 58–67; Skowronek, *Building a New American State,* 272–73.

23. Katznelson, *City Trenches,* 51–52, 53.

24. Ibid., 63–64, 67.

25. Ibid., 6, 19.

26. David Harvey, *Consciousness and the Urban Experience: Studies in the History and Theory of Capitalist Urbanization* (Baltimore: Johns Hopkins University Press, 1985), 37.

27. See Katznelson, *City Trenches,* 20.

28. Katznelson, *Marxism and the City,* 213.

29. Charles Stephenson and Robert Asher, "Dimensions of American Working-Class History," in *Life and Labor: Dimensions of American Working-Class History,* ed. Charles Stephenson and Robert Asher (Albany: State University of New York Press, 1986), 3.

30. Katznelson, *City Trenches,* 19.

31. Ira Katznelson and Aristide Zolberg, "Working-Class Formation: Constructing Cases," 13.

32. Katznelson, *City Trenches,* 196, 195.

33. Katznelson recommends that we "explore whether side by side with capitalism we may discover other large-scale social processes that have likewise had a fundamental impact in shaping the modern world. The main candidates for such a parallel status, deserving comparable theoretical treatment, are the development of coherent national states and the emergence of networks of relationships in civil society with a high degree of autonomy from both the economy and the state in the West since the sixteenth century." *Marxism and the City,* 85.

34. This also represents a gradual move away from a unique reliance on Marxism. Earlier in *City Trenches,* Katznelson claimed that "the Weberian failure to treat the relationship of work and community is inherent in the limitations of the social theory, but . . . the Marxist shortcomings are not." *City Trenches,* 200–201.

35. Jürgen Habermas, *The Theory of Communicative Action,* vol. 2, *Lifeworld and System: A Critique of Functionalist Reason,* trans. Thomas McCarthy (Boston: Beacon Press, 1987), 153–98.

36. Katznelson, "Working-Class Formation: Constructing Cases," 17, 22, 21.

37. Katznelson, *City Trenches,* 209; Katznelson, "Working-Class Formation: Constructing Cases," 29; Katznelson, "Social Justice, Liberalism, and the City," 274.

38. Katznelson, *City Trenches,* 205.

39. Ernesto Laclau and Chantal Mouffe, *Hegemony and Social Strategy: Towards a Radical Democratic Politics* (London: Verso, 1985), 103–4.

40. Katznelson, *City Trenches,* 18, 199.

41. Roland Barthes, *The Pleasure of the Text,* trans. Richard Miller (New York: Noonday Press, 1989).

42. Katznelson, *Marxism and the City,* 212.

43. Two points should be kept in mind here. Because I wish to problematize the apparent essential identity of workers, the term "worker" should be read within scare quotes, although I dispense with this convention for sake of convenience. Second, obviously I can do no more in the following discussion than to suggest a series of hypotheses and directions for further historical analysis, rather than a fully completed analysis.

44. Joan Wallach Scott, *Gender and the Politics of History* (New York: Columbia University Press, 1988), 6.

45. Sally Alexander, "Women, Class, and Sexual Difference," *History Workshop* 17 (1984): 125–35.

46. Carolyn Daniel McCreesh, *Women in the Campaign to Organize Garment Workers, 1880–1917* (New York: Garland, 1985), 66.

47. Katznelson, *City Trenches,* 63–64.

48. Carol Pateman, *The Sexual Contract* (Stanford, Calif.: Stanford University Press, 1988); Heidi Hartmann, "Capitalism, Patriarchy, and Job Segregation by Sex," *Signs* 1 (1976): 168.

49. Katznelson, "Working-Class Formation and the State," 264.

50. Katznelson has conceded the absence of gender relations in his and related work. But he argues (justifiably in my view) that to speak of the separation of work and home does not necessarily imply that domestic labor was either nonexistent or historically insignificant. The domestic sphere was both an integral part of the economic structure of capitalist cities and a realm set off from the newly emerging factories and autonomous workplaces. Yet the fact that many labor unions restricted women from their ranks and often fought for economic justice on the basis of a "family wage" is enough to demonstrate the salience of gender and the separation of workplace and home for workers themselves.

51. Jeanne Boydston, *Home and Work: Housework, Wages, and the Ideology of Labor in the Early Republic* (New York: Oxford University Press, 1990), 146, 159.

52. Elizabeth Blackmar, *Manhattan for Rent, 1785–1850* (Ithaca, N.Y.: Cornell University Press, 1989), 113.

53. Ibid., 51–52, 109, 112.

54. Ibid., 126.

55. Ibid., 124.

56. The advantage of drawing upon a psychoanalytical model of identity is that the gendered dimension of the subject is integral to it.

57. McCreesh, *Women in the Campaign,* 12–13. See also Susan Glenn, *Daughters of the Shtetl: Life and Labor in the Immigrant Generation* (Ithaca, N.Y.: Cornell University Press, 1990).

58. Eli Zaretsky, *Capitalism, the Family, and Personal Life* (New York: Harper & Row), 1973.

59. United Garment Workers, *Proceedings of the Founding Convention* (New York, 1891), 1; Jesse Pope, *The Clothing Industry in New York* (1905; New York: B. Franklin, 1970), 223–30; McCreesh, *Women in the Campaign*, 46.

60. See John Bodnar, *The Transplanted: A History of Immigrants in Urban America* (Bloomington: Indiana University Press, 1985), especially chapter 2.

61. United Garment Workers, *Proceedings of the Founding Convention*, 4–6.

62. McCreesh, *Women in the Campaign*, 48; Nancy Cott, *The Grounding of Modern Feminism* (New Haven, Conn.: Yale University Press, 1987), 236.

63. See, for example, McCreesh, *Women in the Campaign*, 117–20, and Roger Waldinger, "Another Look at the International Ladies' Garment Workers' Union: Women, Industry Structure, and Collective Action," in *Women, Work, and Protest: A Century of U.S. Women's Labor History*, ed. Ruth Milkman (Boston: Routledge & Kegan Paul, 1985).

64. Harry Best, *The Men's Garment Industry of New York and the Strike of 1913* (New York: University Settlement Society Press, 1913), 9; Melvyn Dubofsky, *When Workers Strike: New York City in the Progressive Era, 1910–1918* (New York: Quadrangle Press, 1968).

65. Roy Lubove, *The Progressive and the Slums: Tenement House Reform in New York City, 1890–1917* (Pittsburgh: University of Pittsburgh Press, 1962). "Like so many of her Progressive contemporaries, Robins could not conceive of personal fulfillment or self-realization except in terms of social efficacy and civic responsibility. . . . Protective legislation was to safeguard the role for women as mothers, for motherhood guaranteed social bonds and human connections." Elizabeth Anne Payne, *Reform, Labor, and Feminism: Margaret Drier Robins and the Women's Trade Union League* (Urbana: University of Illinois Press, 1988), 145; Stanley J. Lemons, *The Woman Citizen: Social Feminism in the 1920's* (Urbana: University of Illinois Press, 1973), 145–47.

66. Christine Stansell, "The Origins of the Sweatshop: Women and Early Industrialization in New York City," in *Working Class America*, ed. Michael Frisch and Daniel Walkowitz (Urbana: University of Illinois Press, 1983), 97. Yet in her analysis, Stansell oddly attributes no role to working-class men in keeping women "in the home." If she had, she would have been forced also to reconceive class formation in a more fundamental and rigorous way. For she does not interrogate the identity "woman" that plays the central part in her story: it is assumed as a given.

67. Blackmar, *Manhattan for Rent*, 51; Boydston, *Home and Work*, chapter 7.

68. Fania Cohn, *Our Educational Work—A Survey*, quoted in McCreesh, *Women in the Campaign*, 228.

69. Ibid., McCreesh, *Women in the Campaign*, 197, 217.

70. See Alice Kessler-Harris, *Out to Work: A History of Wage-Earning Women in the United States* (Oxford: Oxford University Press, 1982), 153.

71. Steven Fraser, *Labor Will Rule: Sidney Hillman and the Rise of American Labor* (New York: Free Press, 1991), 224.

72. Nina Asher, "Dorothy Jacobs Bellanca: Women Clothing Workers and the Runaway Shops," in *A Needle, A Bobbin, A Strike: Women Needle Work-*

ers in America, ed. Joan Jensen and Sue Davidson (Philadelphia: Temple University Press, 1984), 219.

73. Fraser, *Labor Will Rule,* 224.

74. The Amalgamated Clothing Workers did propose government-funded child care and antidiscrimination legislation against women at the workplace, notably during the "People's Platform" of 1944. See Fraser, *Labor Will Rule,* 509–10. But I am suggesting that these measures are not inconsistent with the defense of the gendered patterning of home/work, public/private.

75. As the founder and president of the WTUL remarked of Hillman, "We saw things alike especially in regard to the Labor Movement." Payne, *Reform, Labor, and Feminism,* 193. See also May Wood Simons, "Cooperation and Housewives," *The Masses: Women's Issue,* no. 1 (December 1911): "The larger part of the agitation, even in the socialist movement, among women have been directed at whom? Why, the girls in industry. Not the housekeepers."

76. There is no judgment implied in this assessment as to the relative importance of these strategies, and it is not meant to suggest that this achievement was not an important accomplishment in itself.

77. See Mathew Edel, Elliot Sclar, and Daniel Luria, *Shaky Palaces: Home-ownership and Social Mobility in Boston's Suburbanization* (New York: Columbia University Press, 1984), especially chapter 9. Cott, *The Grounding of Modern Feminism,* 191. It is perhaps of interest for the argument here to quote William Green, president of the AFL, justifying the labor movement's orientation toward the household economy. "In former days, when each family unit was practically self-sufficient economically, the wife made as objective a contribution to the home as the husband. As changes have come in our social and industrial organization there have come protests against this division of responsibility that it narrowed women's sphere to the home and excluded her from work. . . . As a fundamental principle American labor feels it is far wiser and of greater permanent value to strive to keep the wages of the head of the family adequate to maintain standards of living for the family than to sanction the practice of outside employment for the mother." William Green, "The Husband's Wage," *The Survey,* February 15, 1927, 280; also, Martha May, "Bread before Roses: American Workingmen, Labor Unions and the Family," in Milkman, ed., *Women, Work, and Protest.*

78. Dolores Hayden, *The Grand Domestic Revolution: A History of Feminist Designs for American Homes, Neighborhoods, and Cities* (Cambridge, Mass.: MIT Press, 1981), 1.

79. See Jane Addams, "The Settlement as a Factor in the Labor Movement," in *Hull-House Maps and Papers* (Boston: Thomas Crowell & Co., 1895).

80. See "Feminists Design a New Type Home," *New York Times,* April 5, 1914; "Feminists Debate Plans for a House," *New York Times,* April 22, 1914, 12. See also May Walden Kerr, *Socialism and the Home* (Chicago: Charles H. Kerr & Co., 1901).

81. Cited in Gail Eileen Radford, "Modern Community Housing: New Responses to the Shelter Problem in the 1920s and 1930s" (Ph.D. diss., Columbia University, 1989), 118. The quotation is from William James, a contemporary of the Philadelphia Co-ops. The architect of the Carl Mackley Houses, Oscar Stonorov, a socialist from Vienna, drew on the municipal experiments of that

city as a model for the Hosiery Workers Co-op project. On Vienna, see Peter Marcuse, "A Useful Installment of Socialist Work: Housing in Red Vienna in the 1920's," in *Critical Perspectives on Housing,* ed. Rachel Bratt, Chester Hartman, and Anne Meyerson (Philadelphia: Temple University Press, 1986).

82. Cott, *The Grounding of Modern Feminism,* 3.

83. Mary Jo Buhle, *Women and American Socialism: 1870–1920* (Urbana: University of Illinois Press, 1981), 292.

84. "Consumptionism . . . is the greatest idea that America has given to the world: the idea that workmen and the masses be looked upon not simply as workers or producers, but as *consumers.*" Christine Frederick, *Selling Mrs. Consumer* (New York: The Business Bourse, 1929), 4–5. Frederick and Lillian Gilbreth were perhaps the key ideologues of the antifeminist, proconsumer suburban home movement. See, for example, Lillian Gilbreth, *Management in the Home* (New York: Dodd, Mead, 1959).

85. Fraser, *Labor Will Rule,* 223.

86. Michel Aglietta, *A Theory of Capitalist Regulation: The U.S. Experience,* trans. David Fernbach (London: New Left Books, 1979), 155–69. See also essays in Mickey Lauria, ed., *Reconstructing Urban Regime Theory: Regulating Politics in a Global Economy* (Thousand Oaks, Calif.: Sage, 1996).

87. It is symptomatic of the continuing marginalization of gender, race, or other bases of social identity by the labor movement that one of the most critical treatments of postwar unionism relegates the question of "other" identities into chapters entitled "Other Social Movements in the U.S. Working Class" and "Other Voices." See Kim Moody, *An Injury to All: The Decline of American Unionism* (New York: Verso, 1988). What this overlooks is precisely the way in which these other identities are constitutive of the identity "working class." An important development has been the rise of public-sector unions since the 1970s that have tried to fuse the feminist, civil rights, minority rights, and labor movements. See Deborah E. Bell, "Unionized Women in State and Local Government," in Milkman, ed., *Women, Work, and Protest.*

88. See Katznelson's discussion of Gutman and Greenstone in *City Trenches,* 11.

89. Edel, Sclar, and Luria, *Shaky Palaces,* chapter 9.

90. Charlotte Perkins Gilman, *The Man-Made World, or Our Androcentric Culture* (New York: Charlton, 1911), apparently derives the term "androcentric" from Lester F. Ward's *Pure Sociology* (New York: Macmillan, 1903), which contrasts it with "Gynaecocentric Theory." The *Oxford English Dictionary,* 2d ed. (1989), also cites Ward's as the first usage.

91. On the late-nineteenth-century European linkage of femininity, city spaces, and consumption, see Gillian Swanson, "Drunk with the Glitter: Consuming Spaces and Sexual Geographies," in *Postmodern Cities and Spaces,* ed. Sophie Watson and Katherine Gibson (Cambridge, Mass.: Blackwell, 1995).

92. Richard Rorty, *Objectivity, Relativism, Truth,* Philosophical Papers, vol. 1 (Cambridge: Cambridge University Press, 1991), 120.

93. Katznelson, *City Trenches,* 19.

94. The term "Other" in Lacan's work, in distinction from the common term "other," refers to the symbolic order of language—or more broadly, of culture—within which individuals come to acquire an identity. The symbolic order is con-

stituted linguistically, each term deriving its meaning only in relation to other terms in the signifying chains of language, and thus the subject is constituted in its relation to the Other, and its desire is the desire of the Other.

95. See Laclau and Mouffe, *Hegemony,* chapter 3; Ernesto Laclau, *New Reflections on the Revolution of Our Time* (London: Verso, 1990), chapter 1; Chantal Mouffe, *The Return of the Political* (London, Verso, 1993), chapter 6; Ernesto Laclau, *Emancipations* (London: Verso, 1996), 56–60.

96. Jacques Derrida, *Writing and Difference,* trans. Alan Bass (Chicago: University of Chicago Press, 1978), 178.

97. Jacques Lacan, *Ecrits: A Selection,* trans. Alan Sheridan (New York: Norton, 1977), 172: "The radical heteronomy that Freud's discovery shows gaping within man can never again be covered over."

98. Laclau, *New Reflections,* 61–67.

99. Ibid., 38, 36.

100. See Judith Williamson, *Decoding Advertisements: Ideology and Meaning in Advertising* (London: Marion Boyers, 1978).

101. Katznelson's charge in *Marxism and the City* (303) that Laclau and Mouffe have dissolved the tension between structure and agency is half right. I agree that the latter have not developed an adequate explanation of the large-scale processes that they acknowledge as the source of dislocations of the modern period (that is, commodification and bureaucratization; see, for example, Laclau, *New Reflections,* 51, 53). Because of this, I have sought to supplement their work with systems theory. But, *pace* Katznelson, their inadequacy in this area is not because they dissolve the tension between structure and agency into discourse theory. On the contrary, I hope I succeeded in showing why Laclau's approach is helpful in grasping the tensions between structure and agency as internal to the failed objectivity of each, rather than as two independent orders ranged against each other.

102. Daniel Bell, *The End of Ideology* (New York: Collier, 1961), 298.

103. I leave to another occasion the question of how compatible this approach is with my use of deconstruction and Lacanian notions of alterity and overdetermination.

CHAPTER 4

1. Marshall Berman, *All That Is Solid Melts into Air: The Experience of Modernity* (New York: Penguin, 1988), 318.

2. Jürgen Habermas, *The Theory of Communicative Action,* vol. 2, *Life-world and System: A Critique of Functionalist Reason,* trans. Thomas McCarthy (Boston: Beacon Press, 1987), 186.

3. Laclau, for example, provides no theoretical account of commodification and bureaucratization, although for him they are the central causes of the "dislocations of the social." See *New Reflections on the Revolution of Our Time,* trans. Jon Barnes (London: Verso, 1990), especially 51–54.

4. See Emile Durkheim's comments on the contract, which appears not to be subject to contract. *Division of Labor,* trans. George Simpson (New York: Free Press, 1933), 381–82.

5. I should mention that I omit reference here to the sophisticated "functional structuralism" of Niklas Luhmann. My assertion that Harvey's functionalism neglects the hermeneutic dimension of meaning might be obviated by Luhmann's solution. Luhmann accepts the problem of "meaning" for the social sciences, but "in such a way that it is set within, rather than setting a limit upon, the system-theoretic perspective." Thomas A. McCarthy, *The Critical Theory of Jürgen Habermas* (Cambridge: Polity, 1984), 226. Thus, meaning itself becomes a functionally necessary component of social systems that must deal with overcomplexity. However, to take up this reply would be both forced and too generous to Harvey, who does not deal with this matter at all.

6. From Joseph E. Vitt, Jr., "Kansas City: Problems and Successes of Downtown Development," in *Personality, Politics and Planning: How City Planners Work,* ed. Anthony Catenese and W. Paul Farmer (Beverly Hills, Calif.: Sage, 1978), 109, quoted in Richard Dagger, *Civic Virtues: Rights, Citizenship, and Republican Liberalism* (New York: Oxford University Press, 1997), 171.

7. Alex Callinicos and Chris Harman, *The Changing Working Class* (London: Bookmarks, 1987), 2–5.

8. Edward W. Soja and Allen J. Scott, "Introduction to Los Angeles: City and Region," in *The City: Los Angeles and Urban Theory at the End of the Twentieth Century,* ed. Allen J. Scott and Edward W. Soja (Berkeley: University of California Press, 1996), 16.

9. Edward W. Soja, *Postmodern Geographies: The Reassertion of Space in Critical Social Theory* (London: Verso, 1988), 16–17.

10. Edward W. Soja, *Thirdspace: Journeys to Los Angeles and Other Real and Imagined Places* (Cambridge, Mass.: Blackwell, 1996), 84.

11. Michael Dear, "Intentionality and Urbanism in L.A., 1781–1991," in *The City: Los Angeles and Urban Theory at the End of the Twentieth Century,* ed. Allen J. Scott and Edward W. Soja (Berkeley: University of California Press, 1996). For support of this thesis of a fundamental break in dominant Western patterns of urbanism, see, for example, Mark Gottdiener, *The Social Production of Urban Space* (Austin: University of Texas Press, 1985), and Anthony Downs, *New Visions for Metropolitan America* (Washington, D.C.: Brookings Institution, Lincoln Institute of Land Policy, 1994). For critiques of the thesis, see Robert Beauregard and Anne Haila, "The Unavoidable Incompleteness of the City," *American Behavioral Scientist* 41, no. 3 (November–December 1997): 327–41, and Ira Katznelson, *Marxism and the City* (Oxford: Clarendon Press; Oxford University Press, 1992), chapter 7.

12. Eli Zaretsky, "Identity Theory, Identity Politics: Psychoanalysis, Marxism, Post-structuralism," in *Social Theory and the Politics of Identity,* ed. Craig Calhoun (Oxford: Blackwell, 1994), 200.

13. Laclau, *New Reflections,* 92.

14. Jacques Derrida, "Let Us Not Forget—Psychoanalysis," *Oxford Literary Review* 12, nos. 1–2 (1990): 4. Berman, *All That Is Solid,* 13.

15. Cited by Prof. Michael Ebner, letter, *New York Times,* March 16, 1998, from William Leuchtenburg, *The Perils of Prosperity, 1914–32* (Chicago: University of Chicago Press, 1958), 239–40.

16. Richard Rorty, "On Ethnocentrism: A Reply to Clifford Geertz," in *Objectivity, Relativism, Truth* (Cambridge: Cambridge University Press, 1991), 209.

17. See Will Kymlicka, "Liberal Individualism and Liberal Neutrality," in *Communitarianism and Individualism,* ed. Shlomo Avineri and Avner de-Shalit (Oxford: Oxford University Press, 1992).

18. John Rawls develops the idea of an "overlapping consensus" in *Political Liberalism* (New York: Columbia University Press, 1993).

19. Katznelson, *Marxism and the City,* 303. I discuss the orthodox Marxian interpretation of our "postmodern" culture as merely symptomatic of a fundamentally unchanged structural reality, developed by writers such as Alex Callinicos, Terry Eagleton, Fredric Jameson, and David Harvey in "Postmodernism, Postmarxism, and the Question of Class," *Social Scientist* 19, nos. 3–4, (March–April 1991).

20. Lyn H. Lofland, *A World of Strangers: Order and Action in Urban Public Space* (New York: BasicBooks, 1973) and *The Public Realm: Exploring the City's Quintessential Public Territory* (Hawthorne, N.Y.: Aldine de Gruyter, 1990); Claude S. Fischer, *To Dwell among Friends: Personal Networks in Town and City* (Chicago: University of Chicago Press, 1982), 247–49.

21. Jonathan Raban, *Soft City* (London: Harvill Press, 1998), 3.

22. Berman, *All That Is Solid,* 203.

23. This of course raises the question that in the case of a split or divided self, who then is doing the integrating, who is standing in the spaces? On this conundrum, see Margo Rivera, "Linking the Psychological and the Social: Feminism, Poststructuralism, and Multiple Personality," *Dissociations* 2, no. 1 (March 1989). I would like to thank Dr. Muriel Dimen for bringing this essay to my attention.

24. "Sub-cultural theory holds that urbanism produces Park's 'mosaic of little worlds which touch but do not interpenetrate.'" Claude S. Fischer, *The Urban Experience,* 2d ed. (San Diego: Harcourt Brace Jovanovich, 1984), 37.

25. Robert Park, "Cultural Conflict and the Marginal Man," in *Race and Culture* (Glencoe, Ill.: Free Press, 1950), 373.

26. Ira Katznelson, *Liberalism's Crooked Circle: Letters to Adam Michnik* (Princeton, N.J.: Princeton University Press, 1996), 157.

27. The intellectual history of the concept of "marginality" is an important dimension in the history of sociological thought that deserves greater analysis than I can offer here. In the work of Park, marginality and hybridity meant something closer to what I mean by an interstitial space of becoming: for Park, this borderland was productive and interesting for individuals and for society. After the 1960s, this meaning appears to have been displaced in favor of the idea of marginality as socioeconomic exclusion or cultural outcasts. On the early work, see essays in Park, *Race and Culture,* and for an overview, see H. F. Dickie-Clark, *The Marginal Situation* (London: Routledge & Kegan Paul, 1966), especially chapters 1 and 2.

28. In other words, the deepening of democratic institutions can provide alternatives to the status quo described by Glazer: "The present mood of the United States does not favor a fully developed national system of social policy. It reflects the considered judgment by many Americans that despite the cost in

social disorder that prevails in their society [and cities], they prefer it that way."
See Nathan Glazer, *The Limits of Social Policy* (Cambridge, Mass.: Harvard University Press, 1988), 192. My point here is how to make these mechanisms work better, not that they should be eliminated.

29. Robert Beauregard, *Voices of Decline: The Post-War Fate of U.S. Cities* (Oxford: Blackwell, 1993).

30. For example, Iris Marion Young implies such a quantitative extension: "Empowerment [of localities] means . . . expanding the range of decisions that are made through the democratic process." *Justice and the Politics of Difference* (Princeton, N.J.: Princeton University Press, 1990), 251.

31. Claus Offe and Ulrich Preuss, "Democratic Institutions and Moral Resources," in *Political Theory Today,* ed. David Held (Stanford, Calif.: Stanford University Press, 1991), 156.

32. Ibid., 170.

33. The weakness of Downs's otherwise important work is that while he admits that self-interested individualism is an important cause of the problems he identifies, he explicitly rejects any alternative political or economic model that is not premised upon individual or household self-interest. *New Visions,* 6, 124. Indeed, he appears unaware of this contradiction.

34. For important discussions, see Gregory Weiher, *The Fractured Metropolis: Political Fragmentation and Metropolitan Segregation* (Albany: State University of New York Press, 1991); Jerry Frug, "Decentering Decentralization," *University of Chicago Law Review* 60, no. 2 (spring 1993), and "The Geography of Community," *Stanford Law Review* 48, no. 5 (May 1996); Downs, *New Visions,* chapter 9; Young, *Justice,* chapter 8.

35. It is important to realize that this analysis is thoroughly anti-essentialist, nominalist, and pragmatist as it relates to identity. I am not suggesting that we reform institutions (e.g., toward metropolitan governments) so as to conform better to the true identity of citizens. Rather, the justification for reforms should rest upon the three criteria of political rationality introduced above, because they might help in overcoming the impasses of urban America.

36. Since E. E. Schattscheider's *The Semi-Sovereign People: A Realist's View of Democracy in America* (New York: Holt, Rinehart & Winston, 1960), it has been customary to refer to the "mobilization of bias" thesis that political institutions organize some interests "in" and some "out."

37. This conclusion of the importance of hybridity for a public sense of solidarity converges with Michael Walzer's claim that divided selves and complex democracies presuppose each other. *Thick and Thin: Moral Argument at Home and Abroad* (Notre Dame, Ind.: University of Notre Dame Press, 1994), especially chapter 5, and Frug's critique of local government law in "Decentering Decentralization," *University of Chicago Law Review* 60, no. 2 (spring 1994), and "The Geography of Community."

38. Katznelson's argument that we should not overlook the fact that the development of the modern city (in the West) and modern liberalism's quest for ways to organize difference and tolerance have been mutually constitutive is relevant here. "Social Justice, Liberalism, and the City: Considerations on David Harvey, John Rawls, and Karl Polanyi," in *The Urbanization of Injustice,* ed.

Andy Merrifield and Erik Swyngedouw (New York: New York University Press, 1997).

39. Jean Cohen and Andrew Arato develop a lifeworld/system model to include the institutional dimensions of economic and political societies that mediate between the two dimensions, something missing in Habermas's account. *Civil Society and Political Theory* (Cambridge, Mass.: MIT Press, 1992), chapter 8.

40. Richard Sennett, *The Fall of Public Man* (New York: Norton, 1976). See also Young, *Justice.*

41. On gated communities, see Edward James Blakely, *Fortress America: Gated Communities in the United States* (Washington, D.C.: Brookings Institution Press, 1997), and Gerald E. Frug, *City Making: Building Communities without Building Walls* (Princeton, N.J.: Princeton University Press, 1999). On mixed-income housing, see Alex Schwartz and Kian Tajbakhsh, "The Feasibility of Mixed-Income Housing," *Cityscape: A Journal of Policy Development and Research* 3, no. 2 (1997).

42. Richard Rorty, *Achieving Our Country: Leftist Thought in Twentieth-Century America* (Cambridge, Mass.: Harvard University Press, 1998).

43. See, for example, Elinor Ostrom, "The Social Stratification–Government Inequality Thesis Explored," *Urban Affairs Review* 19, no. 1 (1983): 91–112. The importance of hybridity for a radical democratic agenda also leads me to take issue with Susan Fainstein's recent argument that equality, diversity, and democracy are mutually exclusive values promoted by different perspectives within current urban theory. See "Justice, Politics, and the Creation of Urban Space," in *Urbanization of Injustice,* ed. Andy Merrifield and Erik Swyngedouw (New York: New York University Press, 1997).

44. That is how to create and strengthen "institutions which can gradually reduce the subordination of production to profit, do away with poverty, diminish inequality, remove social barriers to educational opportunities, and minimize the threat to democratic liberties from state bureaucracies." This is Lezek Kolokowski's description of some of the key aims of a democratic socialist project, quoted in Richard Rorty, "A Spectre Haunting the Intellectuals," review of *Spectres of Marx,* by Jacques Derrida, *European Journal of Philosophy* 3, no. 3 (December 1995): 292.

Selected Bibliography

Addams, Jane. "The Settlement as a Factor in the Labor Movement." In *Hull-House Maps and Papers*. Boston: Thomas Crowell & Co., 1895.

Aglietta, Michel. *A Theory of Capitalist Regulation: The U.S. Experience*. Translated by David Fernbach. London: New Left Books, 1979.

Alexander, Sally. "Women, Class, and Sexual Difference." *History Workshop* 17 (1984).

Althusser, Louis. "Contradiction and Overdetermination." In *For Marx*. London: New Left Books, 1977.

———. *Reading Capital*. Translated by Ben Brewster. New York: Verso, 1979.

Anderson, Elijah. *Streetwise*. Chicago: University of Chicago Press, 1990.

Apel, Karl Otto. *Understanding and Explanation*. Cambridge, Mass.: MIT Press, 1984.

Aronowitz, Stanley. *The Politics of Identity*. New York: Routledge, 1992.

Asher, Nina. "Dorothy Jacobs Bellanca: Women Clothing Workers and the Runaway Shops." In *A Needle, A Bobbin, A Strike: Women Needle Workers in America*, edited by Joan Jensen and Sue Davidson. Philadelphia: Temple University Press, 1984.

Barthes, Roland. *The Pleasure of the Text*. Translated by Richard Miller. New York: Noonday Press, 1989.

Baudrillard, Jean. *The Mirror of Production*. Translated and with an introduction by Mark Poster. St. Louis, Mo.: Telos Press, 1975.

Beauregard, Robert. *Voices of Decline: The Post-War Fate of U.S. Cities*. Oxford: Blackwell, 1993.

Beauregard, Robert, and Anne Haila. "The Unavoidable Incompleteness of the City." *American Behavioral Scientist* 41 (1997).

Becker, Uwe. "Class Theory: Still the Axis of Critical Social Scientific Analysis?" In *The Debate on Classes*, edited by Erik Olin Wright. New York: Verso, 1989.

Bell, Daniel. *The End of Ideology*. New York: Collier, 1961.

Bell, Deborah E. "Unionized Women in State and Local Government." In *Women, Work, and Protest: A Century of U.S. Women's Labor History,* edited by Ruth Milkman. Boston: Routledge & Kegan Paul, 1985.

Bender, Thomas. *Community and Social Change in America.* Baltimore: Johns Hopkins University Press, 1982.

Berman, Marshall. *All That Is Solid Melts into Air: The Experience of Modernity.* New York: Penguin, 1988.

Best, Harry. *The Men's Garment Industry of New York and the Strike of 1913.* New York: University Settlement Society Press, 1913.

Blackmar, Elizabeth. *Manhattan for Rent, 1785–1850.* Ithaca, N.Y.: Cornell University Press, 1989.

Blakely, Edward James. *Fortress America: Gated Communities in the United States.* Washington, D.C.: Brookings Institution Press, 1997.

Bodnar, John. *The Transplanted: A History of Immigrants in Urban America.* Bloomington: Indiana University Press, 1985.

Boydston, Jeanne. *Home and Work: Housework, Wages, and the Ideology of Labor in the Early Republic.* Oxford: Oxford University Press, 1990.

Boyer, Christine. *Dreaming the Rational City: The Myth of American City Planning.* Cambridge, Mass.: MIT Press, 1983.

Boyte, Harry. *Backyard Revolution.* Philadelphia: Temple University Press, 1980.

Buhle, Mary Jo. *Women and American Socialism: 1870–1920.* Urbana: University of Illinois Press, 1981.

Butler, Judith. "Endangered/Endangering: Schematic Racism and White Paranoia." In *Reading Rodney King, Reading Urban Uprising,* edited by R. Gooding-Williams. New York: Routledge, 1993.

Calhoun, Craig. "Social Theory and the Politics of Identity." In *Social Theory and the Politics of Identity,* edited by Craig Calhoun. Oxford: Blackwell, 1994.

Callinicos, Alex. *Making History: Agency, Structure, and Change in Social Theory.* Ithaca, N.Y.: Cornell University Press, 1988.

Callinicos, Alex, and Chris Harman. *The Changing Working Class.* London: Bookmarks, 1987.

Castells, Manuel. "Is There an Urban Sociology?" In *Urban Sociology: Critical Essays,* edited by Chris G. Pickvance. New York: St. Martin's, 1976.

———. "Theoretical Propositions for the Experimental Study of Urban Social Movements." In *Urban Sociology: Critical Essays,* edited by Chris G. Pickrance. New York: St. Martin's, 1976.

———. *The Urban Question: A Marxist Approach.* Cambridge, Mass.: MIT Press, 1977.

———. *City, Class, and Power.* Translation supervised by Elizabeth Lebas. New York: St. Martin's, 1978.

———. *The City and the Grassroots.* Berkeley: University of California Press, 1983.

———. *The Informational City.* New York: Blackwell, 1989.

———. *The Rise of the Network Society.* Cambridge, Mass.: Blackwell, 1996.

———. *The Power of Identity.* Malden, Mass.: Blackwell, 1997.

———. *The End of the Millennium.* Malden, Mass.: Blackwell, 1998.

Clough, Patricia. "Poststructuralism and Postmodernism: The Desire for Criticism." *Theory and Society* 21 (1992).

Cohen, Jean. *Class and Civil Society: The Limits of Marxian Critical Theory.* Amherst: University of Massachusetts Press, 1982.

Cohen, Jean, and Andrew Arato. *Civil Society and Political Theory.* Cambridge, Mass.: MIT Press, 1992.

Corbin, Henri. *Spiritual Body and Celestial Earth: From Mazdean Iran to Shi'ite Iran.* 2d ed. Translated by Nancy Pearson. Princeton, N.J.: Princeton University Press, 1977.

Coser, Ruth Laub. "The Complexity of Roles as a Seedbed of Individual Autonomy." In *The Idea of Social Structure: Papers in Honor of Robert K. Merton,* edited by Lewis A. Coser. New York: Harcourt Brace Jovanovich, 1975.

Cosgrove, Dennis, and Mona Domosh. "Author and Authority: Writing the New Cultural Geography." In *Place/Culture/Representation,* edited by James Duncan and David Ley. London: Routledge, 1993.

Cott, Nancy. *The Grounding of Modern Feminism.* New Haven, Conn.: Yale University Press, 1987.

Cutler, Anthony, et al. *Marx's* Capital *and Capitalism Today.* London: Routledge & Kegan Paul, 1976.

Dagger, Richard. *Civic Virtues: Rights, Citizenship, and Republican Liberalism.* New York: Oxford University Press, 1997.

Dahl, Robert. *Who Governs?* New Haven, Conn.: Yale University Press, 1961.

Davis, Mike. *City of Quartz: Excavating the Future in Los Angeles.* New York: Vintage, 1992.

Dear, Michael. "Intentionality and Urbanism in L.A., 1781–1991." In *The City: Los Angeles and Urban Theory at the End of the Twentieth Century,* edited by Allen J. Scott and Edward W. Soja. Berkeley: University of California Press, 1996.

Debord, Guy. *The Society of the Spectacle.* New York: Zone Books, 1994.

de Laurentis, Teresa. "Upping the Anti in Feminist Theory." In *Cultural Studies Reader,* edited by Simon During. London: Routledge, 1993.

Derrida, Jacques. *Writing and Difference.* Translated by Alan Bass. Chicago: University of Chicago Press, 1978.

———. *Positions.* Translated and annotated by Alan Bass. Chicago: University of Chicago Press, 1981.

———. "Différance." In *Margins of Philosophy.* Translated by Alan Bass. Chicago: University of Chicago Press, 1982.

———. "Ltd Inc abc. . . . " In *Limited Inc.* Edited by Gerald Graff. Translated by Samuel Weber and Jeffrey Mehlman. Evanston, Ill.: Northwestern University Press, 1988.

———. "Let Us Not Forget—Psychoanalysis." *Oxford Literary Review* 12, nos. 1–2 (1990).

———. "Remarks on Deconstruction and Pragmatism." In *Deconstruction and Pragmatism,* edited by Chantal Mouffe. London: Routledge, 1996.

Deutsche, Rosalyn. "Boy's Town." *Environment and Planning: D, Society and Space* 9 (1991).

Dickie-Clark, H. F. *The Marginal Situation.* London: Routledge & Kegan Paul, 1966.

Downs, Anthony. *New Visions for Metropolitan America.* Washington, D.C.: Brookings Institution, Lincoln Institute of Land Policy, 1994.

Dubofsky, Melvyn. *When Workers Strike: New York City in the Progressive Era, 1910–1918.* New York: Quadrangle Press, 1968.

Duncan, Nancy, ed. *BodySpace: Destabilizing Geographies of Gender and Sexuality.* London: Routledge, 1996.

Durkheim, Emile. *Division of Labor.* Translated by George Simpson. New York: Free Press, 1933.

Eagleton, Terry. *The Illusions of Postmodernism.* Oxford: Blackwell, 1996.

Ebner, Michael. Letter, *New York Times,* March 16, 1998.

Edel, Mathew, Elliot Sclar, and Daniel Luria. *Shaky Palaces: Homeownership and Social Mobility in Boston's Suburbanization.* New York: Columbia University Press, 1984.

Elkin, Stephen. *City and Regime in the American Republic.* Chicago: University of Chicago Press, 1987.

Fainstein, Susan. *The City Builders.* Cambridge, Mass.: Blackwell, 1995.

———. "Justice, Politics, and the Creation of Urban Space." In *The Urbanization of Injustice,* edited by Andy Merrifield and Erik Swyngedouw. New York: New York University Press, 1997.

Fainstein, Susan, and Clifford Hirst. "Urban Social Movements." In *Theories of Urban Politics,* edited by David Judge, Gerry Stoker, and Harold Wollman. London: Sage, 1995.

Fischer, Claude S. *To Dwell among Friends: Personal Networks in Town and City.* Chicago: University of Chicago Press, 1982.

———. *The Urban Experience.* 2d ed. San Diego: Harcourt Brace Jovanovich, 1984.

Fraser, Steven. *Labor Will Rule: Sidney Hillman and the Rise of American Labor.* New York: Free Press, 1991.

Frederick, Christine. *Selling Mrs. Consumer.* New York: The Business Bourse, 1929.

Fried, Morton. *The Evolution of Political Society.* New York: Random House, 1967.

Friedland, Roger, Frances Fox Piven, and Robert R. Alford. "Political Conflict, Urban Structure, and the Fiscal Crisis." In *Marxism and the Metropolis: New Perspectives in Urban Political Economy,* 2d ed., edited by William K. Tabb and Larry Sawers. New York: Oxford University Press, 1984.

Frug, Jerry. "Decentering Decentralization." *University of Chicago Law Review* 60, no. 2 (spring 1994).

———. "The Geography of Community." *Stanford Law Review* 48, no. 5 (May 1996).

Frug, Gerald E. *City Making: Building Communities without Building Walls.* Princeton, N.J.: Princeton University Press, 1999.

Fuss, Diana. *Essentially Speaking: Feminism, Nature, and Difference.* New York: Routledge, 1989.

Giddens, Anthony. *Modernity and Self-Identity.* Stanford, Calif.: Stanford University Press, 1991.

Gilbreth, Lillian. *Management in the Home.* New York: Dodd, Mead, 1959.

Gilman, Charlotte Perkins. *The Man-Made World, or Our Androcentric Culture*. New York: Charlton, 1911.

Glazer, Nathan. *The Limits of Social Policy*. Cambridge, Mass.: Harvard University Press, 1988.

Glenn, Susan. *Daughters of the Shtetl: Life and Labor in the Immigrant Generation*. Ithaca, N.Y.: Cornell University Press, 1990.

Godelier, Maurice. *The Mental and the Material*. Translated by Martin Thom. London: Verso, 1986.

Goodwyn, Lawrence. *The Populist Moment*. Oxford: Oxford University Press, 1978.

Gottdienier, Mark. *The Social Production of Urban Space*. Austin: University of Texas Press, 1985.

Gould, Roger V. *Insurgent Identities*. Chicago: University of Chicago Press, 1995.

Green, William. "The Husband's Wage." *The Survey*, February 15, 1927.

Gregory, Derek. "Interventions in the Historical Geography of Modernity: Social Theory, Spatiality, and the Politics of Representation." In *Place/Culture/Representation*, edited by James Duncan and David Ley. London: Routledge, 1992.

Grossberg, Lawrence. "Identity and Cultural Studies—Is That All There Is?" In *Questions of Cultural Identity*, edited by Stuart Hall and Paul du Gay. London: Sage, 1996.

Habermas, Jürgen. *Legitimation Crisis*. Translated by Thomas McCarthy. Boston: Beacon Press, 1976.

———. *The Theory of Communicative Action*. Vol. 1, *Reason and the Rationalization of Society*. Translated by Thomas McCarthy. Boston: Beacon Press, 1984.

———. *Autonomy and Solidarity: Interviews*. Edited by Peter Dews. London: Verso, 1986.

———. *The Philosophical Discourse of Modernity: Twelve Lectures*. Translated by Frederick Lawrence. Cambridge, Mass.: MIT Press, 1987.

———. *The Theory of Communicative Action*. Vol. 2, *Lifeworld and System: A Critique of Functionalist Reason*. Translated by Thomas McCarthy. Boston: Beacon Press, 1987.

———. *On the Logic of the Social Sciences*. Translated by Shierry W. Nicholsen and Jerry A. Stark. Cambridge, Mass.: MIT Press, 1988.

Hartmann, Heidi. "Capitalism, Patriarchy, and Job Segregation by Sex." *Signs* 1 (1976).

Harvey, David. *Social Justice and the City*. Baltimore: Johns Hopkins University Press, 1973.

———. "The Nature of Housing." In *The Manipulated City*, edited by Stephen Gale and Eric Meure. Chicago: Maaroufa Press, 1975.

———. *Consciousness and the Urban Experience*. Baltimore: Johns Hopkins University Press, 1985.

———. *The Urbanization of Capital*. Baltimore: Johns Hopkins University Press, 1985.

———. *The Condition of Postmodernity: An Enquiry into the Origins of Cultural Change*. Oxford: Blackwell, 1989.

——. *The Urban Experience*. Baltimore: Johns Hopkins University Press, 1989.

——. *Justice, Nature, and the Geography of Difference*. Cambridge, Mass.: Blackwell, 1996.

Hayden, Dolores. *The Grand Domestic Revolution: A History of Feminist Designs for American Homes, Neighborhoods, and Cities*. Cambridge, Mass.: MIT Press, 1981.

Hobsbawm, Eric R. "Marx and History." *New Left Review* 143 (January–February 1984).

Illich, Ivan. *H₂O and the Waters of Forgetfulness: Reflections on the Historicity of Stuff*. Dallas: Dallas Institute of Humanities and Culture, 1985.

Jameson, Fredric. *Postmodernism, or The Cultural Logic of Late Capitalism*. Durham, N.C.: Duke University Press, 1991.

Kakuthas, Chandran, and Philip Petit. *Rawls: A Theory of Justice and Its Critics*. Stanford, Calif.: Stanford University Press, 1990.

Katznelson, Ira. *City Trenches: Urban Politics and the Patterning of Class in the United States*. Chicago: University of Chicago Press, 1982.

——. "Working-Class Formation and the State: Nineteenth-Century England in American Perspective." In *Bringing the State Back In*, edited by Peter B. Evans, Dietrich Rueschemeyer, and Theda Skocpol. Cambridge: Cambridge University Press, 1985.

——. "Working-Class Formation: Constructing Cases and Comparisons." In *Working-Class Formation: Nineteenth-Century Patterns in Western Europe and the United States*, edited by Ira Katznelson and Aristide Zolberg. Princeton, N.J.: Princeton University Press, 1986.

——. *Marxism and the City*. Oxford: Clarendon Press; Oxford University Press, 1992.

——. *Liberalism's Crooked Circle: Letters to Adam Michnik*. Princeton, N.J.: Princeton University Press, 1996.

——. "Social Justice, Liberalism, and the City: Considerations on David Harvey, John Rawls, and Karl Polanyi." In *The Urbanization of Injustice*, edited by Andy Merrifield and Erik Swyngedouw. New York: New York University Press, 1997.

Kazin, Michael. "Daniel Bell and the Agony and Romance of the American Left." Introduction to Daniel Bell, *Marxian Socialism in the United States*. Ithaca, N.Y.: Cornell University Press, 1996.

Kearney, Michael. "The Effects of Transnational Culture, Economy, and Migration on Mixtec Identity in Oaxacalifornia." In *The Bubbling Cauldron: Race, Ethnicity, and the Urban Crisis*, edited by Michael Peter Smith and Joe R. Feagin. Minneapolis: University of Minnesota Press, 1995.

Kerr, May Walden. *Socialism and the Home*. Chicago: Charles H. Kerr & Co., 1901.

Kessler-Harris, Alice. *Out to Work: A History of Wage-Earning Women in the United States*. Oxford: Oxford University Press, 1982.

King, Anthony D. "Introduction: Cities, Texts and Paradigms." In *Re-Presenting the City: Ethnicity, Capital, and Culture in the Twenty-first-Century Metropolis*, edited by Anthony D. King. New York: New York University Press, 1996.

Kristeva, Julia. *Strangers to Ourselves.* Translated by Leon S. Roudiez. New York: Columbia University Press, 1991.

Kymlicka, Will. "Liberal Individualism and Liberal Neutrality." In *Communitarianism and Individualism,* edited by Shlomo Avineri and Avner de-Shalit. Oxford: Oxford University Press, 1992.

LaCapra, Dominick. *Rethinking Intellectual History: Texts, Contexts, Language.* Ithaca, N.Y.: Cornell University Press, 1983.

Lacan, Jacques. *Ecrits: A Selection.* Translated by Alan Sheridan. New York: Norton, 1977.

Laclau, Ernesto. *New Reflections on the Revolution of Our Time.* Translated by Jon Barnes. London: Verso, 1990.

———. *Emancipations.* London: Verso, 1996.

Laclau, Ernesto, and Chantal Mouffe. *Hegemony and Socialist Strategy: Towards a Radical Democratic Politics.* London: Verso, 1985.

Lauria, Mickey, ed. *Reconstructing Urban Regime Theory: Regulating Politics in a Global Economy.* Thousand Oaks, Calif.: Sage, 1996.

Lefebvre, Henri. *Le Droit à la ville.* Paris: Anthropos, 1968.

Lemons, Stanley J. *The Woman Citizen: Social Feminism in the 1920's.* Urbana: University of Illinois Press, 1973.

Levine, Andrew, Elliott Sober, and Erik Olin Wright. "Marxism and Methodological Individualism." *New Left Review* 162 (1987).

Liggett, Helen. "City Sights/Sites of Memories and Dreams." In *Spatial Practices,* edited by Helen Ligget and David Perry. Thousand Oaks, Calif.: Sage, 1995.

Lofland, Lyn H. *A World of Strangers: Order and Action in Urban Public Space.* New York: BasicBooks, 1973.

———. *The Public Realm: Exploring The City's Quintessential Public Territory.* Hawthorne, N.Y.: Aldine de Gruyter, 1990.

Logan, John R., and Harvey Molotch. *Urban Fortunes: The Political Economy of Place.* Berkeley: University of California Press, 1987.

Lubove, Roy. *The Progressive and the Slums: Tenement House Reform in New York City, 1890–1917.* Pittsburgh: University of Pittsburgh Press, 1962.

Marcuse, Peter. "A Useful Installment of Socialist Work: Housing in Red Vienna in the 1920's." In *Critical Perspectives on Housing,* edited by Rachel Bratt, Chester Hartman, and Anne Meyerson. Philadelphia: Temple University Press, 1986.

Marston, Sallie, and George Towers. "Private Spaces and the Politics of Places: Spatioeconomic Restructuring and Community Organizing in Tucson and El Paso." In *Mobilizing the Community: Local Politics in the Era of the Global City,* edited by Robert Fisher and Joseph M. Kling. Newbury Park, Calif.: Sage, 1993.

Marx, Karl. *The Eighteenth Brumaire of Louis Bonaparte.* In Karl Marx and Friedrich Engels, *Selected Works in One Volume.* London: Lawrence & Wishart, 1968.

———. *Grundrisse.* Translated by Martin Nicolaus. London: Penguin Books, in association with *New Left Review,* 1973.

———. *Capital.* Vol. 3. London: International, 1974.

———. "Economic and Philosophical Manuscripts." In *Early Writings*. Translated by Rodney Livingstone and Gregor Benton. London: Penguin Books, in association with *New Left Review;* first Vintage Books edition, 1975.

Massey, Doreen. "Flexible Sexism." *Environment and Planning: D, Society and Space* 9 (1991).

———. *Space, Place, and Gender.* Minneapolis: University of Minnesota Press, 1994.

May, Martha. "Bread before Roses: American Workingmen, Labor Unions, and the Family." In *Women, Work and Protest: A Century of U.S. Women's Labor History,* edited by Ruth Milkman. Boston: Routledge & Kegan Paul, 1985.

McCarthy, Thomas A. *The Critical Theory of Jürgen Habermas.* Cambridge: Polity, 1984.

McCreesh, Carolyn Daniel. *Women in the Campaign to Organize Garment Workers, 1880–1917.* New York: Garland, 1985.

Metcalf, Barbara, ed. *Making Muslim Space in Europe and North America.* Berkeley: University of California Press, 1996.

Moody, Kim. *An Injury to All: The Decline of American Unionism.* New York: Verso, 1988.

Moscovici, Serge, and Willem Doise. *Conflict and Consensus: A General Theory of Collective Decisions.* Translated by W. D. Halls. London: Sage, 1994.

Mouffe, Chantal. *The Return of the Political.* London, Verso, 1993.

Munch, Richard. *Theory of Action: Towards a Synthesis Going Beyond Parsons.* London: Routledge & Kegan Paul, 1987.

New York Times. "Feminists Design a New Type Home." April 5, 1914.

———. "Feminists Debate Plans for a House." April 22, 1914.

Offe, Claus. "New Social Movements: Challenging the Boundaries of Institutional Politics." *Social Research* 52, no, 4 (winter 1985).

———. *Disorganized Capitalism: Contemporary Transformations of Work and Politics.* Cambridge, Mass.: MIT Press, 1985.

Offe, Claus, and Ulrich Preuss. "Democratic Institutions and Moral Resources." In *Political Theory Today,* edited by David Held. Stanford, Calif.: Stanford University Press, 1991.

Ostrom, Elinor. "The Social Stratification–Government Inequality Thesis Explored. *Urban Affairs Review* 19 (1983).

Park, Robert. *Race and Culture.* Glencoe, Ill.: Free Press, 1950.

———. "The City: Suggestions for the Investigation of Human Behavior in the Urban Environment." In Robert E. Park and Ernest W. Burgess, *The City: Suggestions for the Investigation of Human Behavior in the Urban Environment.* 1925; Chicago: University of Chicago Press, 1967.

Pateman, Carol. *The Sexual Contract.* Stanford, Calif.: Stanford University Press, 1988.

Payne, Elizabeth Anne. *Reform, Labor, and Feminism: Margaret Drier Robins and the Women's Trade Union League.* Urbana: University of Illinois Press, 1988.

Peterson, Paul. *City Limits.* Chicago: University of Chicago Press, 1981.

Pickvance, Chris G. "The Structuralist Critique in Urban Studies." In *Cities in Transformation,* edited by Michael Peter Smith. Beverly Hills, Calif.: Sage, 1978.

———. "Marxist Theories of Urban Politics." In *Theories of Urban Politics,* edited by David Judge, Gerry Stoker, and Harold Wollman. London: Sage, 1997.

Piore, Michael. *Beyond Individualism.* Cambridge, Mass.: Harvard University Press, 1995.

Plotkin, Sydney. "Enclave Consciousness and Neighborhood Activism." In *Dilemmas of Activism: Class, Community, and the Politics of Local Mobilization,* edited by Joseph M. Kling and Prudence S. Posner. Philadelphia: Temple University Press, 1990.

Polanyi, Karl, Conrad Arensberg, and Harry Pearson, eds. *Trade and Market in the Early Empires.* Glencoe, Ill.: Free Press, 1957.

Pope, Jesse. *The Clothing Industry in New York.* 1905; New York: B. Franklin, 1970.

Przeworski, Adam. *Capitalism and Social Democracy.* Cambridge: Cambridge University Press, 1985.

Raban, Jonathan. *Soft City.* London: Harvill Press, 1998.

Radford, Gail Eileen. "Modern Community Housing: New Responses to the Shelter Problem in the 1920s and 1930s." Ph.D. diss., Columbia University, 1989.

Rawls, John. *Political Liberalism.* New York: Columbia University Press, 1993.

Rivera, Margo. "Linking the Psychological and the Social: Feminism, Poststructuralism, and Multiple Personality." *Dissociations* 2, no. 1 (March 1989).

Robertson, David, and Dennis Judd. *The Development of American Public Policy: The Structure of Policy Restraint.* Glenview, Ill.: Scott, Foresman, 1989.

Roediger, David. *Wages of Whiteness.* New York: Verso, 1991.

Rorty, Richard. *Objectivity, Relativism, Truth.* Philosophical Papers, vol. 1. Cambridge: Cambridge University Press, 1991.

———. "A Spectre Haunting the Intellectuals." Review of *Spectres of Marx,* by Jacques Derrida. *European Journal of Philosophy* 3, no. 3 (December 1995).

———. *Achieving Our Country: Leftist Thought in Twentieth-Century America.* Cambridge, Mass.: Harvard University Press, 1998.

Rosaldo, Renato. *Culture and Truth.* 2d ed. Boston: Beacon Press, 1993.

Sanders, H., and C. Stone. "Reexamining a Classic Case of Development Politics: New Haven, Connecticut." In *The Politics of Urban Development,* edited by C. Stone and H. Sanders. Lawrence: University of Kansas Press, 1987.

Sassen, Saskia. *The Global City.* Princeton, N.J.: Princeton University Press, 1991.

Sarup, Madan. *Identity, Culture, and the Postmodern World.* Athens: University of Georgia Press, 1996.

Saunders, Peter. *Social Theory and the Urban Question.* 2d ed. New York: Holmes & Meier, 1986.

Savage, Mike. Review of *Marxism and The City,* by Ira Katznelson. *International Journal of Urban and Regional Research* 17, no. 1 (1993).

Savage, Mike, and Allen Warde. *Urban Sociology, Capitalism, and Modernity.* New York: Continuum, 1993.

Schnore, Leo. "The City as a Social Organism." *Urban Affairs Quarterly* 1 (1966).

Schwartz, Alex, and Kian Tajbakhsh. "The Feasibility of Mixed-Income Housing." *Cityscape: A Journal of Policy Development and Research* 3, no. 2 (1997).

Scott, Allen J., and Edward W. Soja. *The City: Los Angeles and Urban Theory at the End of the Twentieth Century.* Berkeley: University of California Press, 1996.

Scott, Joan Wallach. *Gender and the Politics of History.* New York: Columbia University Press, 1988.

Sennett, Richard. *The Uses of Disorder: Personal Identity and City Life.* New York: Norton, 1970.

———. *The Fall of Public Man.* New York: Norton, 1976.

Silverman, Kaja. *The Subject of Semiotics.* New York: Oxford University Press, 1983.

———. *Threshold of the Visible World.* New York: Routledge, 1996.

Simmel, Georg. *The Philosophy of Money.* Translated by Tom Bottomore and David Frisby. London: Routledge & Kegan Paul, 1978.

Simons, May Wood. "Cooperation and Housewives." *The Masses: Women's Issue,* no.1 (December 1911).

Singer, Daniel. *Prelude to Revolution: France in May 1968.* New York: Hill & Wang, 1970.

Skocpol, Theda. *States and Serial Revolutions.* Cambridge: Cambridge University Press, 1979.

Skowronek, Stephen. *Building a New American State: The Expansion of National Administrative Capacities, 1877–1920.* Cambridge: Cambridge University Press, 1982.

Smith, Michael Peter. "Postmodernism, Urban Ethnography, and the New Social Space of Ethnic Identity." *Theory and Society* 21 (1992).

Smith, Michael Peter, and Joe R. Feagin, eds. *The Bubbling Cauldron: Race, Ethnicity, and the Urban Crisis.* Minneapolis: University of Minnesota Press, 1995.

Smith, Neil. *The New Urban Frontier: Gentrification and the Revanchist City.* London: Routledge, 1996.

Soja, Edward W. *Postmodern Geographies: The Reassertion of Space in Critical Social Theory.* London: Verso, 1988.

———. "Los Angeles, 1965–1992." In *The City: Los Angeles and Urban Theory at the End of the Twentieth Century,* edited by Allen J. Scott and Edward W. Soja. Berkeley: University of California Press, 1996.

———. *Thirdspace: Journeys to Los Angeles and Other Real and Imagined Places.* Cambridge, Mass.: Blackwell, 1996.

———. "Margin/Alia: Social Justice and the New Cultural Politics." In *The Urbanization of Injustice,* edited by Andy Merrifield and Erik Swyngedouw. New York: New York University Press, 1997.

Soja, Edward W., and Allen J. Scott. "Introduction to Los Angeles: City and Region." In *The City: Los Angeles and Urban Theory at the End of the Twentieth Century,* ed. Allen J. Scott and Edward W. Soja. Berkeley: University of California Press, 1996.

Spivak, Gayatri C. *The Post-Colonial City: Interviews, Strategies, Dialogues.* Edited by Sarah Harasym. New York: Routledge, 1990.

Stansell, Christine. "The Origins of the Sweatshop: Women and Early Industrialization in New York City." In *Working Class America,* edited by Michael Frisch and Daniel Walkowitz. Urbana: University of Illinois Press, 1983.

Stephenson, Charles, and Robert Asher. "Dimensions of American Working-Class History." In *Life and Labor: Dimensions of American Working-Class History,* edited by Charles Stephenson and Robert Asher. Albany: State University of New York Press, 1986.

Stone, Clarence. "The Study of Politics in Urban Development." In *The Politics of Urban Development,* edited by Clarence Stone and Heywood Sanders. Lawrence: University of Kansas Press, 1987.

Swanson, Gillian. "Drunk with the Glitter: Consuming Spaces and Sexual Geographies." In *Postmodern Cities and Spaces,* edited by Sophie Watson and Katherine Gibson. Cambridge, Mass.: Blackwell Press, 1995.

Szelenyi, Ivan. *Urban Inequalities under Socialism.* New York: Oxford University Press, 1983.

Tajbakhsh, Kian. "Postmodernism, Postmarxism, and the Question of Class." *Social Scientist* 19, nos. 3–4 (March–April 1991).

Thrift, Nigel. "An Urban Impasse?" *Theory, Culture, and Society* 10 (1993).

Tilly, Charles. *Big Structures, Large Processes, Huge Comparisons.* New York: The Russell Sage Foundation, 1984.

———. *The Contentious French.* Cambridge, Mass.: Belknap Press, 1986.

———. *Coercion, Capital, and European States, A.D. 990–1990.* Cambridge, Mass.: Blackwell, 1990.

Thompson, E. P. *The Making of the English Working Class.* Harmondsworth: Penguin, 1968.

Touraine, Alain. *The May Movement, Revolt and Reform: May 1968—The Student Rebellion and Workers' Strikes—The Birth of a Social Movement.* Translated by Leonard F. X. Mayhew. New York: Random House, 1971.

United Garment Workers. *Proceedings of the Founding Convention.* New York, 1891.

Vance, James. "Housing the Worker: The Employment Linkage in Urban Structure." *Economic Geography* 42 (October 1966).

Walden Kerr, M. *Socialism and the Home.* Chicago: Charles H. Kerr & Co, 1901.

Waldinger, Roger. "Another Look at the International Ladies' Garment Workers' Union: Women, Industry Structure, and Collective Action." In *Women, Work, and Protest: A Century of U.S. Women's Labor History,* edited by Ruth Milkman. Boston: Routledge & Kegan Paul, 1985.

Walker, R. "Regulation and Flexible Specialization as Theories of Capitalist Development: Challenges to Marx and Schumpeter?" In *Spatial Practices,* edited by Helen Ligget and David Perry. Thousand Oaks, Calif.: Sage, 1990.

Walzer, Michael. *Thick and Thin: Moral Argument at Home and Abroad.* Notre Dame, Ind.: University of Notre Dame Press, 1994.

Ward, Lester F. *Pure Sociology.* New York: Macmillan, 1921.

Weber, Max. "Basic Sociological Terms." In *Understanding and Social Inquiry,* edited by Fred Dallmayr and Thomas McCarthy. Notre Dame, Ind.: University of Notre Dame Press, 1977.

Weiher, Gregory. *The Fractured Metropolis: Political Fragmentation and Metropolitan Segregation.* Albany: State University of New York Press, 1991.

Wellman, Barry. "The Community Question." *American Journal of Sociology* 84 (March 1979).

Williamson, Judith. *Decoding Advertisements: Ideology and Meaning in Advertising.* London: Marion Boyers, 1978.

Wolff, J. "The Real City, the Discursive City, the Disappearing City: Postmodernism and Urban Sociology." *Theory and Society* 21 (1992).

Wright, Erik Olin, et al. *The Debate on Classes.* New York: Verso, 1989.

Young, Iris Marion. *Justice and the Politics of Difference.* Princeton, N.J.: Princeton University Press, 1990.

Zaretsky, Eli. *Capitalism, the Family, and Personal Life.* New York: Harper & Row, 1973.

———. "Identity Theory, Identity Politics: Psychoanalysis, Marxism, Poststructuralism." In *Social Theory and the Politics of Identity,* edited by Craig Calhoun. Oxford: Blackwell, 1994.

Zolberg, Aristide. "How Many Exceptionalisms?" In *Working-Class Formation: Nineteenth-Century Patterns in Western Europe and the United States,* edited by Ira Katznelson and Aristide Zolberg. Princeton, N.J.: Princeton University Press, 1986.

Zolberg, Aristide, and Long Litt Woon. "Why Islam Is Like Spanish: Cultural Incorporation in Europe and the United States." Negotiating Difference Series. ICMEC Working Papers. International Center for Migration, Ethnicity, and Citizenship at the New School for Social Research. June 1997.

Zukin, Sharon. *The Culture of Cities.* Cambridge, Mass.: Blackwell, 1995.

Index

agency, 23. *See also* identity
Alexander, Sally, 139
Althusser, Louis, 42–43
Amalgamated Clothing Workers of America (ACW), 145, 146–49, 150–51

Bell, Daniel, 161
Benjamin, Walter, 24
Berman, Marshall, 36, 174–75
Blackmar, Elizabeth, 142–43
Boydston, Jeanne, 141–42
Buhle, Mary Jo, 150

capitalist society, reproduction of, 79–80
Castells, Manuel, 35–36; on autonomy of urban agency, 46–47; *The City and the Grassroots*, 61–70, 194n43, 195n57, 195–96n59, 196n61; *City, Class, and Power*, 55–61; on class, 53–55; on class struggle, 16–17, 62; compared with Harvey, 72–73; compared with Katznelson, 114, 116, 122; on consumption, 56–57; on Marxist urban analysis, 15; model of multiple identities of, 68–69; on network society, 38–41, 186–87n15; on overdetermination, 51–52; *The Urban Question*, 41–42, 43–44, 46–55, 58, 60, 72, 194n36; on urban social movements, 58, 59
cities, 14; new views of, 21–22
class: Castells on, 53–55; four-tier model of, 122–24, 132–35; identity, 3, 45, 46; limitation to workplace in U. S.,

126; Marx's notion of, 44, 45. *See also* "gated communities"; Marxian class concept/theory; working class
class struggle, 57; Castells on, 16–17, 49, 62; displaced, 78, 81
collective action, 108–9
community, 180–81; local, 8–9
community-based organizations, xi–xii, 74
complexity, urban, 171–72
consumption, 56–57
critical urban theory, 11–12; emerging themes of, 20–22: limitations of, 22–28

Dagger, Richard, 181
de Lauretis, Teresa, on essentialism, 37
Derrida, Jacques, 156–57
Downs, Anthony, 178–79

Eagleton, Terry, 32
eclecticism, 165
economy/economic system, 10–11; as dominant system of social structure, 49; Marx on capitalist, 9–10, 121; underestimating influence of, 167
Edel, Mathew, 152
essentialism, 37–38

feminism, 149–50
Fischer, Claude, 174
Fraser, Steven, 147, 150
functionalism: critique of, 83–88; in Harvey's work, 75, 85–88, 93–95, 101–4
Fuss, Diana, on essentialism, 37

Text: 10/13 Sabon
Display: Sabon
Composition: Impressions Book and Journal Services, Inc.
Printing and binding: Thomson-Shore